T0305028

# Everyday
# Shakespeare

# Everyday Shakespeare

## LINES FOR LIFE

BEN CRYSTAL & DAVID CRYSTAL

Chambers

First published in Great Britain by Chambers in 2023
An imprint of John Murray Press
A division of Hodder & Stoughton Ltd,
An Hachette UK company

4

Text design by Craig Burgess

Internal artwork © Antonia Weir

A CIP catalogue record for this title is available from the British Library

Hardback ISBN 978 1 399 80933 7
eBook ISBN 978 1 399 80935 1

Typeset by KnowledgeWorks Global Ltd.

Printed and bound in Great Britain by Clays Ltd, Elcograf S.p.A.

John Murray Press policy is to use papers that are natural, renewable and
recyclable products and made from wood grown in sustainable forests.
The logging and manufacturing processes are expected to conform to the
environmental regulations of the country of origin.

John Murray Press
Carmelite House
50 Victoria Embankment
London EC4Y 0DZ

www.johnmurraypress.co.uk

# CONTENTS

JANUARY

FEBRUARY

MARCH

APRIL

MAY

JUNE

JULY

AUGUST

SEPTEMBER

OCTOBER

NOVEMBER

DECEMBER

# ABOUT THE AUTHORS

Ben is an actor, author, creative producer, patron of Shakespeare Week, Associate Artist with the new Shakespeare North Playhouse, and curator of the ShakespeareEnsemble.com. His solo writing includes *Lockdown Shakespeare* (Bloomsbury, 2022), *Shakespeare on Toast* (Icon, 2008; nominated for the Educational Book of the Year Award 2010) and the four titles of the Arden Springboard Shakespeare series: *Hamlet*, *Macbeth*, *A Midsummer Night's Dream* and *King Lear*.

David is Honorary Professor of Linguistics at Bangor University. His previous work on Shakespeare includes *Pronouncing Shakespeare* and *Think on My Words: Exploring Shakespeare's Language*. He has written or edited many books and articles for scholarly, professional, and general readerships on the history and development of English, including *The Stories of English*, *How Language Works*, and *Evolving English*.

Ben and David have collaborated on several books: *Shakespeare's Words* (Penguin, 2002), *The Shakespeare Miscellany* (Penguin, 2005) and *The Oxford Illustrated Shakespeare* Dictionary (Oxford University Press, 2015; shortlisted for the Educational Book of the Year Award 2016).

# INTRODUCTION

**Welcome to this book.** Whether you read it all in one go, daily over the course of a year, front-to-back or back-to-front, we hope you find the following pages inspiring. They contain a selection of lines from Shakespeare's works that we further hope you might feel excited to use, as you go about your everyday life.

These quotes are probably not the lines of Shakespeare that you may have already heard, such as *All the world's a stage*, or *To be, or not to be...*, or *A horse, a horse, my kingdom for a horse!* Many of the quotes in this book are to be found in the less studied and produced corners of Shakespeare's canon. We've chosen them because they sound so commonplace, so 'everyday'. In drawing them out, we found ourselves surprised by their apparent plainness or 'everyday-ness', each bringing an immediate, easy resonance with modern day-to-day living. Many carry a deeper level of meaning that makes returning to a quote equally valuable, as it continues to reveal further layers over the weeks and years.

Our intention, with this collection of writing gems, is that each day will be enjoyable in and of itself; that each daily offering isn't too long to remember, so that it can be dropped into conversation as occasion arises; and that each might also act as a springboard to jump into a play or a poem you haven't explored before.

These jewels make a treasure-chest of language, love and longing. They hold up a mirror for us to peer into, to see if any part of ourselves, familiar or strange, is visible. They provide the space for us to step back from taking part in life, and instead to simply reflect for a while on how we live. You won't necessarily see yourself every day, but as Shakespeare holds this mirror up to us, and the light refracts, you might get glimpses of loves you've known, jealousies you've felt, relationships you've entered into and situations you've encountered that bring a smile – or a wince – of familiarity.

Shakespeare had an ear and a hand that were somehow able to capture gossamer-thin butterflies of thought and pin them to a page, expressing them so well it can make us feel stunned to be seen.

It's nourishing (not to mention unusual) to experience eloquence on a daily basis, and to engage with well-expressed big – and simple – thoughts that question our morals and ethics.

To take ten minutes a day to be still, to disengage, to mull over whether there might be something beyond this corporeal realm (or to wrangle with the idea that there might not be). That is the question, as Hamlet attempts to explain, that each of us is welcome to contemplate, if we choose.

So, you're welcome to read this book day-by-day, all at once, or flip back and forth around the weeks and months until you find a quote that strikes a chord in you. Each has been chosen in part to be accessible and tangible, so that no selection is too unmanageable to reflect on, to chew on, to say out loud, to offer to a friend, to remember, to memorise or to dare to drop into daily conversation.

These quotes won't necessarily help you make friends and influence people, though at the least, if you start using them every day, a courage to speak Shakespeare's words may grow.

## A YEAR IN THEMES

Rather than presenting a jumble of emotions, ideas and reflections, we've gently curated the passing of the year, nudging each month towards a loose collection of themes, inviting a series of thoughts to flow together over a week.

January sees a grouping of some of the best quotes we could find; February a swing through love and laughter; March, a deep dive into grief, sorrow, hope and peace.

April brings a month of the 'everyday-ness' that can be found in Shakespeare. This is the month that collects the quotes which most frequently made us nod and say to each other, 'I felt this the other day', or 'This would be fun to say', or 'This is what I wanted to say in response to my co-author in the middle of that argument the other day'.

May invites a touch of nature, and June offers a useful selection in case you find yourself needing to insult or argue. July explores politics and tyranny, while August leans into lines of profound-yet-accessible wisdom.

September brings a month of work, honesty, secrets and money. October takes us through life, with quotes about birth, love, marriage, having children and grounded outlooks on death.

November brings a celebration of close friendship, as well as a few useful quotes for when friends have to leave each other. And December takes us home, with lines of arrival, celebration and kindly spirits, before we twinkle away across the year's end.

Shakespeare was broad in his subject reach, deep in his emotional intuition and bold in his philosophical outlook – and we have sought to mirror this breadth, depth and courage in our selection.

## DISCOVERY ON EVERY PAGE

Every day has a page, every page has a quote, and every quote has a few lines about its place in the play or poem from which it came.

We believe the quotes within these pages can speak for themselves. Others become clearer with a little help. We used www.ShakespearesWords.com to source our quotations, and also to define words that have changed their meaning or dropped out of use over the last four centuries. We often give multiple definitions for a single word, using a technique called 'lexical triangulation' that invites the meaning to be found 'in the middle' of multiple alternatives.

Many of the following pages have a commentary, either to explain what particular words mean, or to reflect on the 'everyday-ness' of the thought the quote is reaching towards. These commentaries are our interpretations and readings of these quotes. Having removed them from their original context, sometimes we draw on their original meaning, but often their isolation inspired a particular interpretation. In several cases, we allow the quotation to stand alone, with little we felt necessary to add.

Rather than exclude your interpretation, we hope our commentaries will inspire your own understanding of the lines you feel drawn to. And we hope from time to time you will disagree with our explanations, and find yourself saying, 'Well, the line means something completely different to me...'

Most of the quotes inspired us to bring in similar lines from elsewhere in Shakespeare's works, because they carry a kindred idea, or resonance, or offer a fun juxtaposition. A few have been selected to chime with a particular day or date, but most have not.

Each quote will, we believe, make every bit of sense caught here in isolation, separated from its play-full or poetic origin. Still, for those interested to pursue the quote further, we have 'stamped' every page with the quote's source, and with each play's stamp there are a few lines of context, describing the action that leads up to (or follows on from) the day's lead quote.

The exact location of each is listed in the index at the back of the book. There, the locations for a quote are listed as line references, e.g. *KL 1.1.92*: the abbreviated name of the play, then the number of the act and scene, followed by line number. These line references follow the numbering at www.ShakespearesWords.com.

We also include an index of the opening words of our lead quotes and an index of themes. The thematic index is the one to use if, for example, you're giving a speech and want to find a relevant quote to add to it. The opening words index will be useful if you can't remember where a particular quote was.

You'll notice that the words are sometimes laid out like this:

**Things without all remedy**
**Should be without regard: what's done is done.**

The first line has some blank space after it, and the following line(s) begin with a capital letter.

These are signs that the words were written in a poetic style. The blank space is an indication that there's a half line of poetry that we've intentionally left out, to allow the quote to stand more clearly on its own.

When speaking one of these lines out loud, there's an invitation to vocally indicate that, while you've reached the end of the line of poetry, you still have more to say. So when you reach the word *remedy* in *Things without all remedy*... the line ending leaves the thought hanging in the air, a moment of suspension, as if you haven't quite decided what to say next.

Poetry is a heightened form of expressing how we feel or what we think about things. The heart that needs to express itself in poetry beats faster, or perhaps, more fervently. Sometimes the lines rhyme – think of these quotes as having an especially impassioned heart beating behind them, your words needing to match your feelings, so that you just have to rhyme! There are also several quotes in prose, which don't show these poetic features.

And two general points about language, which you'll see on many pages. Some quotes use *thou* or *thee* or *thine*, which was a more informal and intimate way of saying 'you' or 'yours' in Shakespeare's time. Many modern languages, such as French, Spanish, and German, still make this distinction.

Throughout, Shakespeare will refer to *man* in a general sense, as was normal in his time. We encourage everyone to understand this usage as missing its first two letters, and to read in its stead, *human*, or to make what they feel is an appropriate gender substitution.

## WITNESS OUR CHOICES

If Shakespeare has a constant, it's that he poses a challenge to us. He held a mirror up to our species and its fantastic, furious, peculiar, passionate, curiously emotional ways of living and interrelating – he also invited us to look at all the bits we don't like about our natures.

It's true that Shakespeare gave his characters sentiments to express that might now come across as misogynistic, xenophobic or racist; these thoughts are now often taken to be his opinion, rather than deeper, darker observations of humanity.

This is the point: the full works are a playground to better understand all aspects of the human condition – the parts we want to celebrate, as well as the parts we might rather hide away. They were written for someone's friends, their family, the society around them, and the world to come after them. And they have become a sandbox for every generation to play in, and safely explore powerful thoughts and feelings.

As we read and re-read, we beheld an artist grappling with the slippery slope of the human condition, and not always saying things we enjoyed or agreed with. And while, when it came to our selection process, we did not seek to curate one type of ethics or moral code, as we went through his writings, our guiding light was to reach for inclusivity.

These quotes can resonate no matter who you are, or where you're from: the only demographic necessary for access here is 'human'. Whilst they are the writings of a white man living at the turn of the seventeenth century, that figure is barely visible. So full and wide-reaching are the ideas being explored that the personality of the author becomes indistinct, fading into the background. This allows the thoughts themselves, and how we relate to them, to stay firmly in the foreground.

This book, then, invites us to shift our focus away from whoever the writer was, who he was writing for, or what he believed in when he wasn't writing, and sharpen our attention to the view being offered, the complicated thoughts being eloquently verbalised, the desirable or hateful qualities of our kind being reflected back at us.

We don't explore Shakespeare's agenda and interests, his religion or faith, his private preferences or passions, because we'll never know them. But we do recognise and elevate the humanistic strains that run throughout: the importance of love, the dangers of indecision, the value of life, and the understanding that our time is brief and we must not waste it.

We witnessed an inquiry into the human condition, the handling of joy and suffering, and a brilliantly sharp wit. We found a canon rich in characters expressing, discussing, and arguing a vastly complex gamut of thought, emotion and relationships.

Time and time again we encountered a string of words that made us gasp as we recognised a universal truth of being; or we felt a shiver and the sudden desire to share a new-found revelation to someone, hoping that it would make them similarly inhale, and reflect. We hope that many of these pages will make you reach for the 'share' button, too.

This book is filled with lines we have frequently said to each other, every day, and we've taken great joy from borrowing and lending such eloquence from Will Shakespeare. There are lines here that somehow keep perfectly fitting moments in life. And there are lines we have never had the chance to say – but we remain ever hopeful that one day the opportunity will arise.

Ben Crystal & David Crystal
Wales, 2023

# Remembering Shakespeare Every Day

Some can look at a line of poetry once and never forget it, but not all of us have memories like sponges. So here are some tips if you find yourself drawn to a quote and want to carry it with you.

- Read the quote out loud, looking away from the page after every line, and repeat the words you've just spoken; repeat until you don't need to look at the page.

- Writing out the quote in your own hand is a terrific 'aide memoire'. Hold a line (or a few words at a time) in your head while you write the words out fresh in a notebook. Don't be tempted to look back and forth as you copy the quote – get used to keeping fragments in your short-term memory.

- Don't worry if the quote is here today, gone tomorrow. Give it another day to settle before you refresh your memory.

- Your memory is like a muscle, so practise exercising it. Give it time and patience. It'll soon grow stronger.

# ACKNOWLEDGEMENTS

Our book was inspired by the podcast *No Holds Bard*; Brian Browne Walker's edition of the *Tao Te Ching*; and Allie Esiri's *A Poem for Every Day of the Year*.

We would like to thank Hilary Crystal, Helen Foan, Edie, Antonia Weir, LionHeart, Andrew Codispoti, Cathryn Summerhayes, Sarah Cole, Jenny Campbell and everyone at Chambers for their kind support, sound advice, and their positivity and warmth throughout.

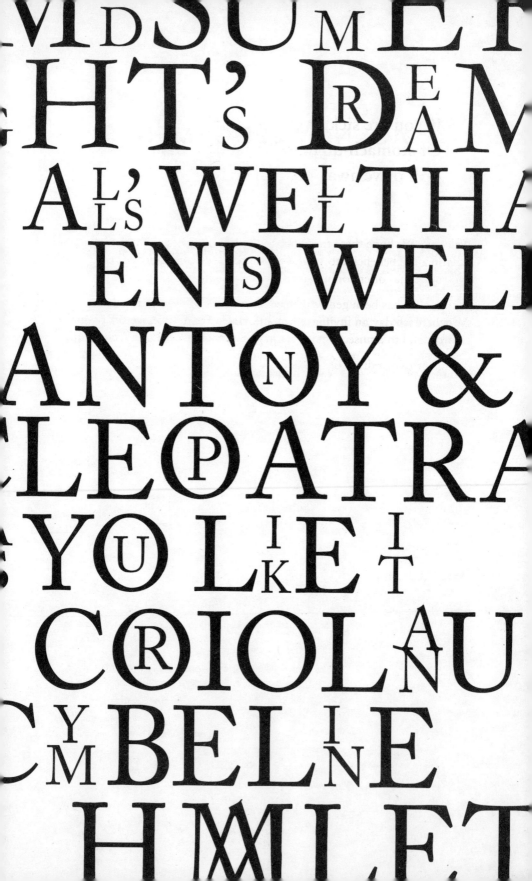

If you are sick at sea,
Or stomach-qualmed at land, a dram of this
Will drive away distemper.

— ⤰ —

Welcome. We hope these thoughts and reflections, these quotations in isolation, are beneficial to you. We'll share the circumstances of each one, and sometimes offer commentary too.

Each month has been gently themed, each week offers a journey of thought, each day an invitation to reflect, to learn, to use, to inspire, to comfort and to amuse.

A page or two, a dram of this book, will cure what ails you.

Here, Princess Innogen is about to leave the royal court of her father King Cymbeline, to find her love, Posthumus. The court physician gives her a potion, with these words. She will later discover the draught will do more than just cure *distemper* ('illness')...

CYMBELINE

## The air bites shrewdly. It is very cold.

—— ∞ ——

A slightly more flamboyant way to observe the temperature, followed by a more straightforward way. Shakespeare often gets his characters to explain themselves when they speak poetically (*shrewdly* means 'sharply' or 'severely').

Late at night, Prince Hamlet is brought to the walls of Elsinore, his family's castle, by his friend Horatio and the night-watch guard Marcellus. Hamlet has been told he will see the ghost of his father, and the scene begins with Hamlet saying this line. Perhaps Hamlet is nervous, or excited, or both …

HAMLET

# And I have heard it said, unbidden guests
# Are often welcomest when they are gone.

— ❧ —

A line for when someone unexpectedly turns up and you don't want their company. *Welcomest* meant 'the most welcome', just as *happiest* means 'the most happy'.

The English are at war with France. The French Countess of Auvergne invites the great English general Talbot, infamous throughout France, to visit her at her home. Talbot suggests that his colleagues the Dukes of Bedford and Burgundy go with him, but Bedford says no, as they haven't been invited. So, Talbot leaves to visit the Countess alone – but what if it's a trap …?

H E N RY VI : I

## Better three hours too soon than a minute too late.

— ❦ —

Everyone will relate to a line of Shakespeare differently.

There are those (e.g. David) who arrive at a station to catch a train so early that they're able to take the previous departure. And then there are those (e.g. Ben) who arrive at the last minute, and almost miss their train (but always catch it).

The speaker of this line is evidently of David's mind.

*Betimes* was a common way of saying 'soon' in Shakespeare's day. In *Richard 3*, Richard invites the Duke of Buckingham to dinner, and says *let us sup betimes* – 'let's eat soon', in other words.

*Betimes* can also convey great urgency, meaning 'right now'. To express less urgency, *by and by* was available. When the Duke of Exeter speaks about the conspirators in *Henry 5*, he says, *They shall be apprehended by and by* – meaning 'they'll be arrested in due course'.

Both authors of this book, arriving to catch a train, could say, 'The train's leaving betimes.'

(But only David would be able to say, 'The train's leaving by and by.')

The drunken knight Sir John Falstaff says he plans to have an affair with Master Ford's wife at eleven o'clock in the morning. Ford is determined to catch them together, and heads off straight away, saying this line; he really doesn't want to be late.

MERRY WIVES OF WINDSOR

## You come most carefully upon your hour.

— ∞ —

This quote is good to greet someone being punctual (especially if they're normally late).

*Carefully* here means 'considerately' or 'attentively' – in other words, 'You're right on time!'

It's the opening scene of the play, and Francisco is on night watch, guarding the walls of Castle Elsinore, and waiting for his colleague Barnardo to take over his shift. Francisco is *bitter cold*, and *sick of heart* – he's been guarding where a ghost has been seen – and is perhaps surprised or gladdened, and certainly relieved, to see Barnardo arrive on time.

HAMLET

## It gives me wonder, great as my content,
## To see you here before me.

— ∞ —

Say this to someone you love, when you haven't seen them for a long time. You're really delighted to see them again, and you want to say that they look beautiful.

*Wonder* meant 'astonishment', or 'amazement'. *Content* meant 'pleasure', 'satisfaction', 'happiness'.

Once you start using this line, 'Lovely to see you' won't ever quite be the same again.

Othello and Desdemona have travelled to Cyprus on different ships, which were separated by a ferocious storm. Desdemona is the first to arrive safely, and Othello arrives soon after. When Othello sees his wife, he speaks these words. This is the first time they've seen each other since they were married a few days earlier.

# Men's evil manners live in brass; their virtues We write in water.

— ∞ —

*Brass* in Shakespeare's day was thought of as one of the hardest materials, along with stone, steel and flint, and so was often used as a symbol of 'hardness', 'permanence', or 'steadiness' of mind or body.

As we'll see throughout this book, Shakespeare often takes an idea, holds it up to the light, and gifts it to multiple characters across the plays, so we can hear a similar thought expressed in different ways.

In Antony's famous *Friends, Romans, countrymen ...* speech in *Julius Caesar*, he comments:

> The evil that men do lives after them,
> The good is oft interred with their bones.

Whether in a grave, or in water, the message is clear: evil is often remembered long after good is forgotten.

Queen Katherine's servant is telling the story of how Cardinal Wolsey died. Katherine lists all Wolsey's faults, but her servant asks her permission to paint an alternative picture of the Cardinal. When the servant is finished, Katherine expresses her hope that when she dies, she will have such an honest chronicler ...

HENRY VIII

## Live a little, comfort a little, cheer thyself a little.

— ∞ —

Shakespeare offers advice to hold close to your chest.

*Comfort* means 'take comfort, console yourself'.

Orlando and his old servant Adam have gone into the Forest of Arden to escape dangers at home. Adam says he can go no further, he's so hungry. Orlando tries to cheer him up with these words, and then leaves to find food for them both – though his search delivers him far more than just food …

AS YOU LIKE IT

## Love all, trust a few,
## Do wrong to none.

———— ∞ ————

Fine words to offer someone about to travel, who you won't see again for a long while.

Bertram has been commanded to join the French King's court, so must leave home. He asks for his mother's *blessing* (a combination of 'permission' and a 'prayer of protection') to leave, and she gives it to him with these words of advice.

ALL'S WELL THAT
END WELL

# Enjoy the honey-heavy dew of slumber.

———— ⌘ ————

We might say, 'Sleep well!' This speaker is being more poetic: to apply honey to sleeping is both to wish someone 'sweet dreams' and 'deep sleep'.

It's unusual for Shakespeare to use honey in this way: the substance normally suggests ideas of sweetness, rather than heaviness, although it clearly does have a weight, as it slows itself off a spoon.

There's a hint of this meaning when the golden colour of honey is mentioned by Anne in *Richard 3*:

> For never yet one hour in his bed
> Did I enjoy the golden dew of sleep,
> But with his timorous dreams was still awaked.

Here, *timorous* means 'terrifying' and *still* means 'always'.

Titus brings together honey and the morning dew when describing the tears of his daughter Lavinia, in *Titus Andronicus*, sparking the image of a near-dead flower, with droplets on its petals:

> ... fresh tears
> Stood on her cheeks, as doth the honey-dew
> Upon a gathered lily almost withered.

Several characters in the plays relate heaviness and sleep, as we might do today. In *King Lear* a doctor tells Cordelia how they're looking after her father, the maddened King:

> ... in the heaviness of sleep
> We put fresh garments on him.

Brutus has had a late-night meeting with the conspirators plotting Caesar's assassination. When they've left, Brutus calls for his young servant Lucius – but finds him sound asleep. Deciding to leave him be, Brutus offers these lines to the sleeping youth.

## Infected minds
## To their deaf pillows will discharge their secrets.

—— ∞ ——

An image of the worst thoughts and stresses you might have pouring into your pillow, flooding your dreams. Or perhaps it's an image of being kept awake by your thoughts.

Or, it's a warning to anyone who talks in their sleep (and, if you're Lady Macbeth, anyone sleep-walking) – that your darkest deeds may be revealed while you slumber.

*Cymbeline* reminds us that after a hard day's work, it's easy to sleep on *flint* ('hard stone') – while those experiencing a lazier day might find even a soft pillow uncomfortable:

> **Weariness**
> **Can snore upon the flint, when resty sloth**
> **Finds the down-pillow hard.**

And yet, we hear (in the same play) that sleep can also be a blissful respite from life's woes, with this truth:

> **He that sleeps feels not the toothache.**

A doctor has been listening to what Lady Macbeth says while she sleepwalks around the castle. As she sleep-talks about her past actions, the doctor is taken aback by the revelations …

# The nature of bad news infects the teller.

——— ∞ ———

A truth that's easy to relate to, if you ever had to give someone bad news. Here's another from *King Lear*, which has a resonance with the proverb 'Many a true word is spoken in jest':

> Jesters do oft prove prophets.

In Shakespeare's time a *jester* was a professional role, an entertainer employed by a monarch or an aristocratic household. They're usually called 'Fools' by their employers, and in some plays, especially *Twelfth Night*, *King Lear* and *As You Like It*, they play an important part in the story.

Fools had licence to say whatever they wanted, and their jests often turned into truths, so *jesters* ('jokers') did frequently turn out to be *prophets*. Indeed, to be a professional Fool didn't just mean to provide superficial foolishness. Perhaps, though, the chief accolade for Fools comes from a disguised Viola in *Twelfth Night*, who says of Feste:

> This fellow is wise enough to play the fool;
> And to do that well craves a kind of wit.
> He must observe their mood on whom he jests,
> The quality of persons, and the time,
> And, like the haggard, check at every feather
> That comes before his eye. This is a practice
> As full of labour as a wise man's art.

A *haggard* was a 'wild hawk'; *man* – 'human'. These lines bring the image of a comedian, carefully choosing their words, their timing, and their targets.

ANTONY &
CLEOPATRA

A messenger has brought Antony reports of foreign affairs. He has told Antony one piece of bad news – and is about to give him another message – but finds it difficult to express himself. Antony tells the messenger not to be a coward, and to speak the facts. (It does indeed turn out to be *more* bad news ...)

> For I have neither wit, nor words, nor worth,
> Action, nor utterance, nor the power of speech
> To stir men's blood; I only speak right on.

— ∞ —

*Wit* was an everyday word in Shakespeare's time, and meant 'mental sharpness'. *Men* stands for 'people'.

Speaking 'plainly' is often seen as a positive personality trait in Shakespeare's plays. Indeed, a few lines later the speaker reinforces his claim, calling himself *a plain blunt man*.

In the day-to-day life of London in the 1600s, speaking meant more than just communication. Speaking was a craft, an opportunity to play, to demonstrate your understanding of the art of 'rhetoric': the skill of being able to articulate thought into spoken word, clearly or poetically, but passionately, often in order to persuade.

And these lines from today's lead quote offer a clever rhetorical trick: to deny you have any rhetorical skills, while doing it simply, efficiently, economically.

Even the great speech-maker King Harry likes plainness in speech, telling Princess Katherine in *Henry 5* that he won't use rhetoric to woo her:

> I speak to thee plain soldier.

JULIUS CAESAR

Antony speaks to the Roman citizens after the assassination of Caesar, just after Brutus gives a speech defending the action of his fellow conspirators. Antony claims he cannot compete with Brutus' speech-making – *I am no orator, as Brutus is* – but his words nonetheless turn the tide, and the people rise up against the murderers ...

# When a world of men
# Could not prevail with all their oratory,
# Yet hath a woman's kindness overruled.

— ✺ —

*Oratory* meant 'eloquence', or 'persuasiveness', and *kindness* had a broad meaning in the 16th century – not only the sense we have today, but also notions of 'courtesy' and 'goodwill'.

Women, this quote is suggesting, have a kind and powerful nature which can help calm any negotiation, and cut past the red tape of the world of men.

Shakespeare makes the point more than once. In another history play the sentiment is reprised: the French Queen, Isabel, offers to help thrash out the articles of a peace treaty in *Henry 5*. She comments:

> **Haply a woman's voice may do some good,**
> **When articles too nicely urged be stood on.**

*Haply* meant 'perhaps', or 'with luck'; *nicely* meant 'fastidious', or 'too carefully'; *to stand upon something* meant to 'make an issue of'.

This broader sentiment of kindness isn't restricted to women. The sailor Antonio offers to be servant to the shipwrecked Sebastian in *Twelfth Night*; Sebastian responds that his heart is *full of kindness* – full of 'affection' and 'friendship'.

> The English general Talbot, having recently won a battle with the French army, has been invited to the castle of the Countess of Auvergne, who wants to meet the *warlike Talbot*. He responds with these lines, perhaps hoping there might be peace negotiations ahead. But the Countess has other plans …

HENRY VI : I

## Fortune brings in some boats
## that are not steered.

—— ∞ ——

*Brings in* meant 'bring safely in to harbour', which would normally require careful piloting. A safe mooring of an uncontrolled vessel could take place by chance, although in Shakespeare's time such an event was only thought to happen if Fortune smiled upon it.

The goddess Fortune is known to be fickle – we never know whether we'll next be rising in fortune or falling. She is often portrayed as blind, and turning a wheel (or a boat's rudder). With this line from *Cymbeline*, there's an invitation to cultivate a peaceable, patient, and healthy respect for the blind mercurial mistress of destiny.

Characters frequently call on Fortune in the plays: Pistol in *Henry 5* complains about his friend Bardolph's fate, thanks to the turning of *Fortune's furious fickle wheel*. In *Romeo and Juliet*, Juliet prays *Be fickle, Fortune* – Romeo has been taken from her, and she hopes Fortune will soon send him back.

And the Duke of Kent in *King Lear*, down on his luck and imprisoned in the stocks, bids Fortune good night with the words, *smile once more; turn thy wheel.*

Pisanio has been helping Posthumus and Innogen, but is no longer in a position to 'steer' them to safety. He hopes the goddess Fortune will bring them home safely. (At the end of the play we see the gods in action, doing just that …)

CYMBELINE

## Look, he's winding up the watch of his wit. By and by it will strike.

— ∞ —

Sometimes, there's a pause in conversation. Someone clearly has something important to say, and from the look on their face it's probably going to be funny. The pause indicates they're still working out the best way to express their thought – and this is when you could mutter this quote to a nearby friend.

Comparing 'waiting' to 'winding a watch' was a really new image for the audience in Shakespeare's day. Portable timepieces were just coming into use towards the end of the 16th century, and quickly became a fashionable novelty.

They were at first fastened to clothing, or worn on a chain around the neck, and later placed in pockets (and some were able to strike the hours, as this speaker acknowledges). They had to be regularly wound by hand, as the servant Malvolio imagines doing in *Twelfth Night*, once he's gone up in the world and finds himself bored:

I frown the while, and perchance wind up my watch.

The priest in the same play has a watch too, as he's able to eloquently tell how long it's been since he married Olivia and Sebastian:

Since when, my watch hath told me, toward my grave
I have travelled but two hours.

THE TEMPEST

The old royal counsellor Gonzalo has been trying to cheer up King Alonso, but is told to be quiet. Anticipating (correctly) that the request for silence won't stop Gonzalo's verbosity, Sebastian says these words to Antonio, as they watch the old man preparing to speak again …

# His wit's as thick as Tewkesbury mustard. There's no more conceit in him than is in a mallet.

———— ✧ ————

*Wit* here means 'mental ability', and *conceit* means 'intelligence' or 'understanding'.

In Shakespearean times, *Tewkesbury mustard* was known all over the country, with some writers saying it was the best in England. It was sold in the form of mustard balls – hence the allusion to thickness – which the purchaser soaked to make pliable.

Its manufacture died out at the beginning of the 19th century, though there's still a thriving local cottage industry preserving the traditional recipe. This is the only time Shakespeare refers to it – and the image of a mallet is also a solitary usage in the plays.

The combination makes for a really strong insult – which can, of course, be used to someone of any gender. Just replace *his* and *him* with *her* or *their*.

Prince Hal and his friend Poins disguise themselves as staff of a tavern, so they can overhear Falstaff insulting them. These lines are Falstaff's response to *They say Poins has a good wit*.

HENRY IV:II

# 'Tis not for gravity to play at cherry-pit with Satan.

—— ⚬∞⚬ ——

*Cherry-pit* was a popular game: a small hole is dug, and players aim their stones, standing at various distances. The goal is to get your stone closest to the centre – both David and Ben used to play a similar game with marbles when they were young.

*Gravity* meant 'authority', or 'someone in a dignified position'. So there's a sense here of 'Don't play games when you should be serious'.

And there's another sense: when playing a game based on the laws of gravity with the Devil (who can cheat all laws), then even Gravity (personified) would suffer defeat.

In other words, 'Don't play a game you know you're going to lose.'

The drunken Sir Toby and his friends are teasing the servant Malvolio, suggesting he's mad and in league with the devil, Satan. Toby pretends to treat Malvolio as a child, and offers him these words of advice …

# TWELFTH NIGHT

# Life is as tedious as a twice-told tale,
# Vexing the dull ear of a drowsy man.

— ∞ —

These lines are for anyone who's feeling beaten down by life.

Feeling even gloomier? Try Macbeth, after he hears of the death of his wife:

> Life's but a walking shadow, a poor player
> That struts and frets his hour upon the stage
> And then is heard no more.

We'll look at these lines in more detail on August 13th.

Lewis the Dauphin (the heir to the French throne) is distraught at France having lost a battle, and Prince Arthur having been taken prisoner by the English. But Cardinal Pandulph is about to give the Dauphin grounds for optimism to renew the fight …

# KING JOHN

O, that a man might know
The end of this day's business ere it come!
But it sufficeth that the day will end,
And then the end is known.

———— ✂ ————

We might often wish to know the future, or how a plan, a project, or a gamble might turn out – but, in a very pragmatic way, this quote reminds us that patience is the best companion to that wish.

*O* is the word Shakespeare uses to represent an emotional sound, voiced by a character, driven by the context they find themselves in. It's the sound of a gasp, or intake of breath, or realisation, or surprise, or … that expresses a character's feelings about what they're saying.

*Suffice* means 'serve', or 'satisfy'; the *-eth* ending is an old form. We'd now write *suffices*.

Brutus and Cassius are talking before the final Battle of Philippi, and reflecting on what they will do if they lose. The friends and comrades bid farewell, thinking it may be the last time they see each other, and Brutus ends the scene with these words.

JULIUS CAESAR

# It easeth some, though none it ever cured,
# To think their dolour others have endured.

— ∞ —

This is a pull towards empathy, in the midst of despair. *Easeth* means 'eases'; *dolour* isn't common in English any more, but is familiar in modern French and Spanish, to mean 'pain'.

The line has special force during a time of widespread distress, such as the plague, rife in England when Shakespeare wrote these lines. And it still resonates after the global pandemic. *The Rape of Lucrece* has another similar thought:

> Sad souls are slain in merry company;
> Grief best is pleased with grief's society.
> True sorrow then is feelingly sufficed
> When with like semblance it is sympathized.

Essentially, both point to the modern 'misery loves company'. *Sad* could mean both 'serious' or 'sorrowful' in Shakespeare's time – a sorrow or seriousness that can only be *sufficed* ('satisfied') with the company of others having *like* ('similar') griefs. *Sympathy* today usually suggests a sorrowful setting, but in earlier times it simply meant having 'affinity' – a *like semblance* – with someone.

In Shakespeare's day *dolour* was pronounced like 'dollar', allowing for a pun. In *The Tempest*, Sebastian rudely interrupts Gonzalo by saying his thoughts on grief are only worth a *dollar* – the English name for a German silver coin. Gonzalo replies by saying *Dolour comes to him indeed*.

The German coin was nicknamed *Thaler*. At a 17th-century rate of five thalers to the pound, one dollar would be very little in today's money, making Sebastian's comment very dismissive indeed.

Tarquin has raped Lucrece. Alone and distraught, she sees a painting of the sacking of Troy, and looks for a face where distress is portrayed. She finds it in Hecuba, looking at her dead husband. She cries for the sad scene depicted there, calling her own situation her *Troy*.

## Make not your thoughts your prisons.

— ∞ —

It's easy to overthink so much that we feel imprisoned. Whether lost in thought, caught in a spiral of worry, or struggling to be led by our heart, the advice here is not to let beliefs, fears, or expectations constrain our life.

A worthy alternative to the corporate world's call to think 'outside the box'.

The victorious Caesar is displaying generosity and magnanimity towards Cleopatra, and tells her in these words not to let her fears dominate her mind. But she doesn't trust him, and after he leaves she turns to her maids and says, *He words me, girls, he words me.*

ANTONY & CLEOPATRA

For there is nothing either good or bad
but thinking makes it so.

— ∞ —

Hamlet, in conversation with his fellow university
students Rosencrantz and Guildenstern, has
described Denmark as a prison. Rosencrantz demurs:
*We think not so, my lord.* Hamlet accepts this:
*Why, then 'tis none to you* and says these words.

HAMLET

> 'Tis with my mind
> As with the tide swelled up unto his height,
> That makes a still-stand, running neither way.

———— ∞ ————

This quote is for anyone in a quandary. The sea's tide is at its highest point, having just risen, and is now in a place of relative stasis (*a still-stand*) flowing in neither direction, before beginning to fall.

A perfect image of uncertainty, of not going one way nor t'other, recalls a familiar dilemma: that feeling we face when we can't decide between two courses of action.

Shakespeare's characters often reflect on the nature of choice, and the problems it can pose. In *The Merchant of Venice*, Portia's father has arranged that the suitors wishing to marry her have to choose between three caskets to find her portrait and win her hand – a situation that Portia herself finds difficult to accept:

   Is it not hard … that I cannot choose one, nor refuse none?

And Hamlet begins his most famous speech with the simple words, *To be, or not to be …*, a reflection that we all carry a greater choice with us every day – a decision to make – between life and death, action or inaction, agency or passivity.

The Earl of Northumberland is of two minds about what to do. He wants to travel to be with the rebel forces, as a matter of honour, but his wife is strongly opposed to it. He finally decides to stay away: *many thousand reasons hold me back*.

HENRY IV:II

# Be that thou know'st thou art, and then thou art As great as that thou fear'st.

———⚮———

Be yourself. As fully as you possibly can. And then you'll be bigger than anything you fear.

The final scene of the play. Everyone is confused, not knowing that Viola and Sebastian are twins and have been mistaken for each other. Olivia has married Sebastian, and now finds Viola denying knowledge of the union ... It takes the arrival of Sebastian alongside Viola to resolve matters.

TWELFTH
NIGHT

# To mourn a mischief that is past and gone
# Is the next way to draw new mischief on.

— ∞ —

*Mischief* today has a mild force, usually referring to prankish behaviour that might be troublesome, but isn't especially evil or malicious.

But in Shakespeare's time the meaning was much stronger, referring to 'an evil deed' or, as here, 'a calamity or serious misfortune'.

This quote reveals a Stoic attitude: things break, we can't undo a tragedy, regret is futile. And a deeper lesson within: come to peace with the past, and don't let it destroy the present, or harm the future.

Lady Macbeth says exactly this, trying to connect with her husband, and expands on the idea:

> Things without all remedy
> Should be without regard; what's done is done.

Joan la Pucelle in *Henry 6 Part 1* makes the same point:

> Care is no cure, but rather corrosive,
> For things that are not to be remedied.

*Corrosive* means 'destructive', and the sound of the word works well with 'care' and 'cure'. La Pucelle later vehemently wishes just such a catastrophe on her enemies:

> ... mischief and despair
> Drive you to break your necks or hang yourselves!

The Duke of Venice hopes to appease the anger of Desdemona's father, Brabantio. Desdemona has married Othello without Brabantio's knowledge. The Duke offers a series of pithy statements all expressing the same thought – the past can't be changed – and begins with these words.

# Cease to lament for that thou canst not help, And study help for that which thou lamentest. Time is the nurse and breeder of all good.

— ∞ —

A modern saying might be 'Don't cry over spilt milk'. *Lamenting* ('getting upset') is not going to fix things. Rather, we need to *study* ('reflect on') ways in which we can remedy the situation in the future. It will take time, but things will work out well in the end – or so the hope goes.

Several Shakespearean characters, faced with an apparently impossible situation, think like this. Proteus in *The Two Gentlemen of Verona* assures the Duke with these words in relation to his daughter Silvia's sadness:

**A little time, my lord, will kill that grief.**

Perhaps Viola, in *Twelfth Night*, sums up the healthiest approach:

**O time, thou must untangle this, not I!**
**It is too hard a knot for me t' untie.**

Here, Viola has found herself in the middle of a complicated set of relationships. Her master, the Duke Orsino, is in love with the Countess Olivia. Viola has fallen in love with Orsino. And Olivia has just become infatuated with Orsino's new 'male' servant (Viola, disguised as a man). All Viola can do is hope that time will sort everything out – which it does …

Valentine is in anguish; he's been banished by the Duke, and so has to leave his love, Silvia. Proteus counsels his friend with these words – hypocritically, as he has secretly fallen in love with Silvia too …

TO GENTLEMEN OF VERONA

# The apparel oft proclaims the man.

When you see *man* or *men* in these works, it usually means a 'human (or humans) of any gender'.

*Apparel* and *clothes* are both used by Shakespeare, and are almost identical in meaning, although there is a nuance in *apparel* of 'display' and 'ornament'.

Modern-day mentalists might say that what someone wears gives an indication of their character, but not all agreed that this was so in Shakespeare's time. In *Pericles*, a character advises that

> Opinion's but a fool, that makes us scan
> The outward habit by the inward man.

In other words, it's foolish to *scan* ('judge') somebody's *habit* ('clothing') to divine their personality.

Several proverbs express the sentiment behind these lines: 'Don't judge a book by its cover', 'Appearances can be deceiving', and the Scottish saying, 'A rich heart may be under a poor coat'.

And yet, while a person may be *ill-favoured* ('unattractive') in looks or behaviour, this next speaker from *The Merry Wives of Windsor* believes that the prospect of marrying someone wealthy can hide all deficiencies:

> O, what a world of vile ill-favoured faults
> Looks handsome in three hundred pounds a year!

An annual income of £300 would make someone very well-off indeed (according to the National Archives, £1 in 1600 was roughly equivalent to £100 today).

Polonius is advising his son Laertes what clothes to wear when away from home – and he adds that this would be especially noted in France, where the nobles paid particular attention to the way one dressed.

# There's no art
# To find the mind's construction in the face.

—— ∞ ——

Proverbs give the 'face' mixed reviews: some allow that it's possible to 'read a face like a book', others tell us that 'the face is no index to the heart'.

This speaker has been totally let down by someone they trusted, and refuses to accept that there's any *art* ('skill') that can determine the *construction* ('right interpretation') in a face.

Nonetheless, several characters believe in the face as a guide to personality. Hastings in *Richard 3* is in no doubt about Richard:

> For by his face straight shall you know his heart.

And in *The Two Noble Kinsmen*, someone is described:

> ... by his face, a prince.
> His very looks so say him.

And the speaker of *Sonnet 93* certainly believes it:

> But heaven in thy creation did decree
> That in thy face sweet love should ever dwell.

But it takes the teenage wisdom of Juliet to recognise that looks can be deceiving, when she thinks Romeo a motiveless murderer:

> O serpent heart, hid with a flowering face!

King Duncan has been brought news of the Thane of Cawdor's death; he has been executed for treason. Duncan reflects on how he was misled: Cawdor was someone in whom he had *built an absolute* ('complete') *trust.*

# Make not impossible
# That which but seems unlike.

— ∞ —

*Unlike* here means 'unlikely, difficult to believe'.

The power of positive framing runs through Shakespeare's works, as does the power – or, indeed, the weakness – of the mind, and the way we can sometimes find ourselves thinking negatively:

> Our doubts are traitors
> And make us lose the good we oft might win,
> By fearing to attempt.

Along with today's lead quote, these lines are from Shakespeare's subversive play *Measure for Measure*. Each carries a warning against groundless self-doubt, which can lead to lost opportunities. Shakespeare's characters, who often seem prone to doubt, have to find inner resolve to achieve their aims.

The Duke of York, aiming for the crown in *Henry 6 Part 2*, finds himself in a 'now or never' frame of mind:

> ... steel thy fearful thoughts,
> And change misdoubt to resolution.

Changing *misdoubt* ('disbelief') into surety is easier said than done, but this very human mental task manifests throughout Shakespeare's writings.

It is the final scene of the play, and Isabella is trying to convince the Duke of the wickedness of his subordinate, Angelo. She has called Angelo a hypocrite and an adulterous thief. The Duke (who actually knows what has been going on) pretends not to believe her, which leads Isabella to cry out these words.

# He that will have a cake out of the wheat must needs tarry the grinding.

— ∞ —

Much like a parent to a hungry child, this quote argues for patience.

The proverb 'Good things come to those who wait' echoes here; replace *wait* for *tarry* in Shakespeare's day.

The usual meaning of *tarry* was 'stay' or 'remain', as in *The Two Gentlemen of Verona*, when Panthino tells the clownish servant Launce: *you'll lose the tide, if you tarry any longer.*

Troilus is talking with Cressida's uncle Pandarus. Troilus is in love with Cressida, and Pandarus advises the young man to be patient in pursuit of his niece. Pandarus uses a series of images about the several stages of baking a cake to make his point. He goes on to say that after the grinding there are many other steps – sifting, leavening, kneading, then the actual making of the cake, heating the oven, and baking it.

# TROILUS & CRESSIDA

# Your worship was the last man in our mouths.

———— ∞ ————

'We've just been talking about you!', we'd say today, when someone arrives unexpectedly.

*Your worship* was used as a respectful form of address – to any adult, not just religious men – and is still used formally in that way when addressing mayors and magistrates.

In *Henry 4 Part 2*, Shallow calls to his servant, who replies:

**Your worship! I'll be with you straight.**

which basically means 'I'm paying attention, I'll be with you immediately'.

Bassanio has been trying to persuade Shylock to lend Antonio three thousand ducats. Then Antonio arrives, to be greeted by Shylock with these words.

Abide the change of time,
Quake in the present winter's state, and wish
That warmer days would come.

— ⚬ —

Posthumus is in love with King Cymbeline's
daughter, Innogen, but is out of favour with the
King. Posthumus has yet to make any approaches
to heal the rift with Cymbeline. All he feels he can
do is wait, and wish for happier days ahead. Both
he and Innogen will go through many trials before
those better times arrive.

CYMBELINE

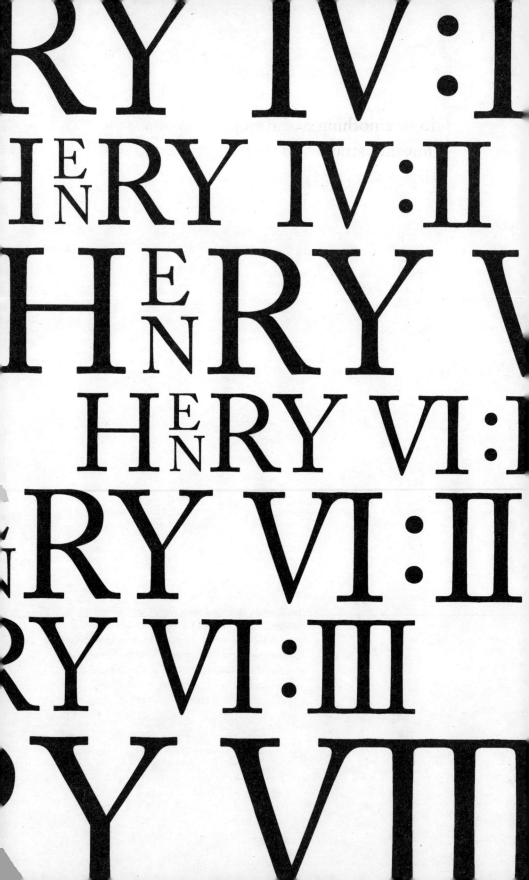

**I do love nothing in the world so well as you. Is not that strange?**

— ∞ —

Beatrice and Benedick are finally alone together. We have seen them bicker, and then fall in love with each other. Benedick is the first to admit his love with these words, and Beatrice will soon after acknowledge her love for him too. But Beatrice's love comes with a catch …

MUCH ADO ABOUT
NOTHING

# The sea hath bounds, but deep desire hath none.

—— ∞ ——

Anyone newly in love – or lust – might know this feeling. The sea, deeper than our tallest mountains, powerful and relentless, restorative and destructive. And yet, it is restricted, held back by cliffs, lands, and human interventions.

Desire, on the other hand, whether for someone or something, can make us feel like there's no obstacle in the world that can stand in our way.

And when it comes to love, there are no limits. Juliet compares her love for Romeo to the sea, dismissing any limitation:

> My bounty is as boundless as the sea,
> My love as deep. The more I give to thee,
> The more I have, for both are infinite.

This notion of boundless desire isn't restricted to love: any deeply held emotion can be viewed in the same way. After the murder of his father Polonius, Laertes' desire for revenge is reinforced by King Claudius in *Hamlet*:

> Revenge should have no bounds.

The goddess Venus makes her first advances towards the beautiful young man Adonis, who just wants to be left alone. His only worry is that he's lost his horse, which has met a mare, and run off with her. Venus defends the horse's instinct – *Affection is a coal that must be cooled* – and then hints at her own desires with these words.

## All days are nights to see till I see thee, And nights bright days when dreams do show thee me.

———— ∞ ————

A quote for missing someone you love: it sets up the idea that every day feels dark, and must be endured; but at night, I see you in my dreams!

The more proverbial expression 'Absence makes the heart grow fonder' may ring true, but might sound a little trite by comparison.

(And the use of the informal *thee* makes it clear that these lines are for someone you know intimately.)

Shakespeare's *Sonnets* is a treasure-trove collection, with many of the poems rich in ways to express your feelings when you're apart from a loved one.

These are the last lines of a poem in which the writer has been praising the brightness and beauty of his love. He says life is best when he's asleep, as then he can dream of the one he loves …

THE SONNETS

FEBRUARY 3RD

**As plays the sun upon the glassy streams,**
**Twinkling another counterfeited beam,**
**So seems this gorgeous beauty to mine eyes.**

If you lack words to describe the sight of the one you love, Shakespeare can provide them.

Here, the beauty of sunlight plays on *glassy* ('smooth') water. But the sunbeams aren't just twinkling, in the modern sense of 'flickering'. More than that, they 'twinkle another beam'.

The sense is of 'reflecting' that first beam of sunshine, and this second reflected beam is a mirror or copy of the original: it's *counterfeited*. *Counterfeit* could mean a 'false imitation', but here it means an 'exact, duplicate image' of that first beauty.

It brings to the mind's eye an idealistic, shimmering reflection of simple, sun-kissed, natural beauty.

The *Sonnets* offer plenty of lines to celebrate someone you love. Here's another:

> **For well thou know'st to my dear doting heart**
> **Thou art the fairest and most precious jewel.**

The Duke of Suffolk has been sent to France to woo Margaret, daughter of the King of Naples, on behalf of King Henry 6. But when Suffolk sees Margaret, he immediately falls in love with her, and these lines form part of his admiration of her beauty. She will become King Henry's Queen, but Suffolk plans to become her lover, and the two of them to rule over Henry ...

HENRY VI:I

Love is not love
Which alters when it alteration finds,
Or bends with the remover to remove.
O no, it is an ever-fixed mark
That looks on tempests and is never shaken.

— ∞ —

Perhaps these lines attempt to express what real, true love is like –
unshakeable. Or perhaps they try to articulate the epitome of constant
love. Either way, it is a love that doesn't *bend* ('waver') when it encounters
changed circumstances.

The *Sonnets* often refer to *constancy*: at one point, the poet writes that
his love is *Still constant in a wondrous excellence*. *Still* meant 'always'.
Another line, from *Romeo and Juliet*, captures the way people approach
love with great eagerness – and leave love with equally great reluctance:

> Love goes toward love as schoolboys from their books;
> But love from love, toward school with heavy looks.

Shakespeare may not have enjoyed his schooldays much.

The sonnet that begins this day continues with the following lines, and
makes it clear that true love stands the test of time:

> Love alters not with his brief hours and weeks,
> But bears it out even to the edge of doom.

*Bears it out* means 'endures'; *edge of doom* means 'until the end of eternity'.

T͟H͟E SONNETS

This is one of Shakespeare's most
famous sonnets and is often read
at weddings, in part because of its
opening:

> *Let me not to the marriage of true
> minds
> Admit impediments.*

## Love looks not with the eyes, but with the mind, And therefore is winged Cupid painted blind.

— ◯◯ —

The Roman god of love was traditionally depicted as a young boy. He is winged and so can fly; he also is armed with a bow and arrow, and the shafts when shot wound the victim with love at first sight.

Perhaps most importantly, the mischievous young imp is blind, and so not always clear or precise with his targets. This means that his arrows fall and bestow love without caring who they hit, or – as Titania experiences for Bottom in *A Midsummer Night's Dream* – how anyone may look on the outside.

It's Cupid's blindness that provokes the modern phrase 'Love is blind', an idea that echoes through Shakespeare's writing.

A line from *The Merchant of Venice* captures the consequences that come with Cupid's arrow when we're madly in love – even though we're unaware of it:

> But love is blind, and lovers cannot see
> The pretty follies that themselves commit.

Here, *pretty* means 'clever' or 'ingenious'; *follies* could mean 'foolishness', and even 'lewdness'. Some characters, including Rosalind from *As You Like It*, are more critical of Cupid:

> That blind rascally boy that abuses everyone's eyes because
> his own are out, let him be judge how deep I am in love.

The lovers Lysander and Hermia have decided to leave Athens secretly. Helena decides to tell her love Demetrius (who currently loves Hermia) of the lovers' escape – and so, the plot of the play begins to unfold …

**Thou art a summer bird,**
**Which ever in the haunch of winter sings**
**The lifting up of day.**

— ∞ —

Gift this line to someone who brings you good news, and lifts you out of dull spirits. Or pass it to someone you love who surprises you with a visit, and turns the darkness of the day bright with their presence.

Westmorland has lifted up the spirits of the dying King Henry with news of the defeat of the rebels and the restoration of peace. The King responds with these words.

HENRY IV:II

If I could write the beauty of your eyes,
And in fresh numbers number all your graces,
The age to come would say this poet lies:
Such heavenly touches ne'er touched
   earthly faces.

— ∞ —

Shakespeare usually talks about 'lines' of poetry, as we do today. But in this quotation he uses a different word, *numbers* – a reference to the number of rhythmical beats in a line of poetry.

We hear it in Hamlet's love letter to Ophelia, which contains a poem, but he doesn't think it's any good: *I am ill at these numbers*, he writes.

There are plenty of powerful testaments to love throughout Shakespeare's works. Here's another good one from *The Two Gentlemen of Verona*, gifting someone great praise (you can replace *His* with *Her* or *Their*):

His words are bonds, his oaths are oracles,
His love sincere, his thoughts immaculate,
His tears pure messengers sent from his heart,
His heart as far from fraud as heaven from earth.

A *bond* was a 'contract'; an *oath* was a 'promise, sworn on your honour'; and an *oracle* was a 'source of wisdom, that could peer into the future'.

The poet attempts to capture his love's excellence in words. But he feels if he were ever to manage it, nobody in the future would believe him …

T^H_E SONNETS

His tend'rer cheek receives her soft hand's print
As apt as new-fall'n snow takes any dint.

— ∞ —

Venus, the goddess of love, approaches the young man Adonis for the first time. She kneels before him and puts her hand to his cheek, where it fits, perfectly. Her touch is compared to the way a new fall of snow is so *apt* ('susceptible') to any mark or *dint* ('impression') made in it. A gentle image, soft and tender.

VENUS
& ADONIS

# A lover's eyes will gaze an eagle blind,
# A lover's ear will hear the lowest sound.

— ❦ —

The heat of love, fully felt, is often described by Shakespeare as being incredibly powerful.

Remember falling in love for the first time? Remember being entranced with their eyes? Or noticing the slightest sound that falls from their lips, or hearing their laughter across a crowded and noisy room?

Love, though, can sometimes provoke a kind of 'love-sickness'. In *As You Like It*, Orlando has met the disguised Rosalind in the Forest of Arden. She's seen her name carved on trees and wonders who was responsible. Orlando admits:

> I am he that is so love-shaked.

Love often has an unusual effect on the perception of time, too. In *Much Ado About Nothing*, Claudio (newly engaged to Hero) wishes their wedding could be the next day. But this doesn't impress Hero's father, who says they need to wait a week. To which Claudio replies:

> Time goes on crutches till love have all his rites.

The King of Navarre and his friends have finally admitted to each other their love for the newly-arrived French ladies, but have vowed to do nothing but study. Berowne provides them with a persuasive set of arguments for breaking their vows, and uses several analogies, including the two in today's lead quote.

LOVE's LABOR's LOST

## The true love 'tween maid and maid may be More than in sex dividual.

— ✠ —

*Dividual* means 'separate' or 'different'.

These lines are spoken by Emilia, as she reflects on the nature of the mutual affection with a girl friend she remembers having in childhood, and on the similar bond that links Theseus and Pirithous. She concludes that love between man and man, or man and woman, bears no comparison to the love felt between *maid and maid* – a wildly provocative idea for Shakespeare's audience.

Emilia describes the close bond she had with a playmate when they were both eleven years old. She thinks she will never love a man – but her encounter with the two friends Arcite and Palamon will soon change her mind ...

## I had rather hear my dog bark at a crow than a man swear he loves me.

———— ✺ ————

There's little to add; romance isn't for everyone.

Beatrice is engaged in a slanging match with Benedick, who's just declared that he loves no lady. She replies that at least they are agreed on one thing – their attitude towards love – and offers this line back.

MUCH ADO ABOUT NOTHING

# It is as easy to count atomies as to resolve the propositions of a lover.

— ∞ —

A friend, newly in love, can be tiresome.

So: this is a quote for when someone keeps asking *propositions* ('questions') about the person they've just fallen in love with, but you know it's impossible to satisfy their need, no matter how you *resolve* ('respond').

*Atomy* is first recorded in English during Shakespeare's lifetime. It meant the 'smallest conceivable part of something' visible to the naked eye, such as a mote, or speck of dust.

Celia is bombarded with questions about Orlando, the man Rosalind loves, and with these words she admits finding them impossible to answer …

AS YOU LIKE IT

# Alas, 'tis true, I have gone here and there,
# And made myself a motley to the view.

—— ∞ ——

*Alas* is an emotional word, used to express grief. In medieval times *motley* was 'cloth woven from threads of different colours'; during the 16th century it came to describe the multicoloured costume of a jester – and then people used it to describe the jester himself.

The jesting thoughts of a professional Fool aren't always stupid. This point is made by Feste, the Fool in *Twelfth Night*, who assures Olivia that there's more to him than his outward appearance:

I wear not motley in my brain.

He then proceeds to outdo her in a jesting exchange.

Back to today's quote, which can be read as an acknowledgement of infidelity in love. In misbehaving here and there, we can become amusing fools for others.

The line can also apply to anyone who's failed to keep a promise, or searched all over town for a lost wallet.

It's easy to feel shame for your actions, and so it's important to fully own and take responsibility for them, no matter what judgement they might attract. To luxuriate in the view of others, as the mercurial Mercutio, from *Romeo and Juliet*, feels:

Men's eyes were made to look, and let them gaze.

The poet hasn't been faithful to his love, and the sonnet ends with the speaker asking for a second chance.

T^H_E SONNETS

# We that are true lovers run into strange capers.

— ∞ —

We find ourselves doing odd and unusual things when we're in love. *Caper* could mean to 'dance with joy'; and rather than the modern meaning of 'bizarre', *strange* could mean 'remarkable', 'special', or 'not previously experienced'.

In the same play, the disguised Rosalind goes further, talking with her love Orlando:

> Love is merely a madness and, I tell you, deserves as well
> a dark house and a whip as madmen do; and the reason why
> they are not so punished and cured is that the lunacy is so ordinary
> that the whippers are in love too.

Many of us find ourselves doing a strange caper, sooner or later, in the name of love. And we can find ourselves saying unusual things, too, as this quote from *Measure for Measure* captures:

> It oft falls out
> To have what we would have, we speak not what we mean.

Touchstone tells Rosalind of a series of unusual events that took place when he was in love and wooing, and sums it all up with this line.

Even as one heat another heat expels,
Or as one nail by strength drives out another,
So the remembrance of my former love
Is by a newer object quite forgotten.

— ⁓ —

*Remembrance* here means more than just 'memory', it's an active 'bringing to mind', a conscious recollection.

It happens: love is found, and is felt to be deep, and profound. And then, by carelessness, or by life simply taking its natural course, that love can find itself being immediately replaced, forcefully knocked out of the heart.

Today's lead quote might have been spoken by Romeo when he sees Juliet for the first time and forgets his former crush, Rosaline. It can be used in any situation where an enthusiasm or obsession (for an object, a place, a hobby, a pastime …) is replaced by another.

And yet, two loves can be held in the heart at once. Emilia from *The Two Noble Kinsmen* has this problem, needing to choose between two equally appealing lovers:

What a mere child is fancy,
That having two fair gauds of equal sweetness,
Cannot distinguish, but must cry for both!

*Mere* means 'utter'; *gauds* means 'trinkets'.

Today's quotes can also be useful if you're presented with a box of assorted chocolates.

To begin with, Proteus – one of the 'two gentlemen' – is in love with Julia, but then he sees Silvia (his best friend Valentine's love), and he speaks these words as he realises what's happened to his heart. Proteus shortly comes up with a plan that he hopes will get him Silvia's love, displacing it from Valentine …

## Is it not strange that desire should so many years outlive performance?

— ∞ —

A simple (and unfortunate) truth of life.

It sits hand-in-hand with this next quote from *Troilus and Cressida*: the two lovers have been left alone by Pandarus, and are tentatively expressing their feelings for each other. Troilus has just made a speech about the extraordinary nature of love, and this is Cressida's reply:

> All lovers swear more performance than they are able, and yet
> reserve an ability that they never perform; vowing more than
> the perfection of ten, and discharging less than the tenth part of one.

Poins and Prince Henry secretly observe the drunken Falstaff making loving advances to Doll Tearsheet. Poins is amazed that at his age Falstaff still has such desires (while being unable to do anything about them).

I had rather hear a brazen canstick turned,
Or a dry wheel grate on the axle-tree,
And that would set my teeth nothing on edge,
Nothing so much as mincing poetry.

---

Poetry does seem to elicit rather strong reactions, both for and against.

This speaker clearly can't stand it, as it reminds him of the scraping of a brass *canstick* ('candlestick') holder against a hard surface, or the sound of an unoiled wheel grinding against its axle. Think nails on a chalkboard.

For anything that grates, especially if you've been asked to do something you really don't want to do, here's a line from *The Merry Wives of Windsor*:

I had rather be set quick i'th' earth,
And bowled to death with turnips.

This is the only time Shakespeare uses the word *turnip*. *Quick* has a range of senses that have at their heart the notion of 'being alive'. Hamlet uses it to one of the gravediggers about the grave the man is standing in:

'Tis for the dead, not for the quick.

It's natural to complain when we don't like something, or when we're unhappy, and this line from *Much Ado About Nothing* argues that no amount of Zen-like philosophy can solve all of life's difficulties:

For there was never yet philosopher
That could endure the toothache patiently.

Hotspur is having a political argument with the Welsh Glendower. He tells him to make his point in Welsh, but Glendower says he can speak English very well, and is even able to write poetry. But poetry evidently isn't something Hotspur appreciates …

## Beauty is a witch
## Against whose charms faith melteth into blood.

— ∞ —

This quote would be useful if you believed your friend has fallen in love with someone you love, and is trying to steal them away from you. The *faith* ('constancy') of their friendship is gone, because of their *blood* ('passion') – the heat of their feelings. *Against* meant 'in the face of'.

*Witch* has lost its force these days for most people, and is rarely used as a compliment. It's more commonly used as an insult, or is echoed in words like *bewitching*. But in a period when people profoundly believed in the power of witches, and were intensely afraid of being accused of witchcraft, *witch* was a daring metaphor for a writer to use. Henry tells Katherine in *Henry 5*:

> You have witchcraft in your lips.

So *witch* could be used to describe anyone who generates an impelling attraction; Henry feels spellbound, in other words.

In *Othello*, there's a quote that pushes back against jealous thoughts rising from within. Othello places his feelings safely in the hands of his love:

> Nor from mine own weak merits will I draw
> The smallest fear or doubt of her revolt,
> For she had eyes and chose me.

Another's faithfulness can be simply and strongly expressed by their agency to choose who to be with, and this should be enough to banish fear or *doubt* ('suspicion') of their *revolt* ('faithlessness').

MUCH ADO ABT NOTHING

Claudio has been fed the misleading impression that his friend Don Pedro is going to court the beautiful Hero for himself. He believes the rumour, and reflects how an infatuation can cause a faithful friendship to be quickly forgotten.

But jealous souls will not be answered so;
They are not ever jealous for the cause,
But jealous for they're jealous. It is a monster
Begot upon itself, born on itself.

— ∞ —

Desdemona and her maid Emilia are discussing
Othello's strange behaviour. Emilia hopes there is
no jealous fancy in him. Desdemona replies that
she never gave him cause to be jealous. This is
Emilia's reply – that jealousy isn't rational, and acts
like a virus …

O, how this spring of love resembleth
The uncertain glory of an April day,
Which now shows all the beauty of the sun,
And by and by a cloud takes all away.

— ∞ —

These lines can apply to a new job, new house, or any situation where things might suddenly go wrong.

And the lines work especially well around the uncertainties that can accompany the early stages of falling in love. Passion for something new can change suddenly, like the weather in April (at least in the British climate).

*By and by* could mean both 'immediately', or 'soon' – and both meanings work well here.

Shakespeare often associates springtime and love. In *Antony and Cleopatra*, Antony sees Octavia weeping as her brother prepares to leave, and says:

The April's in her eyes; it is love's spring,
And these the showers to bring it on.

Proteus is being sent to the Emperor's court in Milan, to learn something of the world. But he's in the early stages of love with Julia, and has just received his first encouraging letter from her. His father tells him he must leave the next day, and Proteus mourns how quickly his new love is being taken from him.

## Our wooing doth not end like an old play; Jack hath not Jill.

— ✿ —

Not all love stories end well, and these lines call on the proverbial names for a pair of lovers to make the point.

Indeed, this next quote from *Richard 2* recognises how quickly love can sour:

> Sweet love, I see, changing his property,
> Turns to the sourest and most deadly hate.

And for anyone who loves another when the feelings aren't returned, who has reached a point of desperation, and is willing to survive on morsels of kindness, here's a simple, tragic line from *As You Like It*:

> Loose now and then
> A scattered smile, and that I'll live upon.

It's almost the end of the play, and Berowne is reflecting on all that has taken place between the lords and ladies. He and his companions had hoped to woo the French ladies, but all merry plans have been postponed because of the news that the Princess' father has died. So there is no happy ending … yet.

LOVE'S LABOUR'S LOST

# What passion hangs these weights upon my tongue?

— ∞ —

This line is for when you find yourself overpowered by emotion, lost for words, tongue-tied – but can't work out what *passion* ('powerful feeling') is causing it. Is it love, lust, or misery?

For Joan la Pucelle in *Henry 6 Part 1* the cause is fear:

> Of all base passions fear is most accursed.

Resistance to speaking your feelings can cause even more trouble, as these lines from *Venus and Adonis* suggest:

> For lovers say, the heart hath treble wrong
> When it is barred the aidance of the tongue.

*Treble* is one of those intensifying numerals that isn't to be taken literally, in much the same way as today we might say 'I'll be with you in a couple of minutes', where we don't mean 'exactly two'.

When the heart is *barred* ('denied') the *aidance* ('help') of speech, then it's (at least) three times more difficult to gain someone's affection.

And it can simply mean, 'Give your heart words, or you'll cause yourself more pain.'

Orlando has just beaten the Duke's wrestler, and Rosalind and Celia come to congratulate him. Orlando and Rosalind seem to fall in love with each other immediately. She gives him a chain of hers as she leaves, but he can't bring himself to say 'thank you'. She returns to ask if he had called her, but again he's unable to speak, and he wonders why, with these lines.

AS YOU LIKE IT

# Why, what's the matter,
# That you have such a February face,
# So full of frost, of storm and cloudiness?

— ∽ —

A lot is taken from the faces of characters in Shakespeare's plays. These lines might make less sense in the southern hemisphere, as they reference the wintry February weather of the northern latitudes, intended to be a description of someone looking gloomy.

Characters are quick to notice the mood of people bringing them news. In *Cymbeline*, Pisanio has unwelcome news in a letter for Innogen, and is showing it in his *countenance* ('face'); but Innogen cannot interpret Pisanio's expression – is it *summer* ('pleasant') or *winter* ('unpleasant') news?

> If't be summer news,
> Smile to't before: if winterly, thou need'st
> But keep that count'nance still.

And yet other characters are quick to complain at their fellows' frowning *frontlet* ('forehead'). Here King Lear has arrived to stay at his daughter Goneril's castle, accompanied by his Fool and a hundred of his knights. She's understandably angry at the disruption this has brought, while Lear can't understand why she's so disturbed.

> What makes that frontlet on?
> You are too much of late i'the frown.

*Of late*, or *lately*, meant 'recently'. It's a nice play on being 'too much in the sun', to be 'too much in the frown'.

Benedick has just asked the Friar to marry him and Beatrice, and he's evidently still wondering whether he's doing the right thing. Don Pedro greets Benedick, and is surprised to find him looking so serious …

# This man's brow, like to a title-leaf,
# Foretells the nature of a tragic volume.

A great quote for anyone you see who looks gloomy, like the cover of a book that gives you a hint of the tone of the story. *Leaf* was a word for 'page', and *volume* a word for 'book'. This book image is still with us: 'I can read you like a book', we might say.

The *brow* is frequently used to show how Shakespeare's characters are feeling. It can mean either the 'eyebrows' or the 'entire forehead'.

We hear the 'eyebrow' sense in *All's Well That Ends Well* when Helena describes Bertram's *arched brows*, and in *Pericles* when Thaisa and Marina are both said to have *square brows*. We hear the 'forehead' sense whenever anyone talks about headgear, especially crowns and victory wreaths, as when Macbeth sees a vision of a future king who

> wears upon his baby brow the round
> And top of sovereignty.

And Hamlet refers his mother to a portrait of his dead father, saying *See what a grace was seated on this brow*, while Juliet defends Romeo with the words *Upon his brow shame is ashamed to sit.*

The Earl of Northumberland is waiting for news about the result of the Battle of Shrewsbury. Morton arrives, and Northumberland can tell from his face that the news is going to be bad.

HENRY IV:II

# 'Tis a cruelty
# To load a falling man.

—∽—

Sometimes Shakespeare's lines are simple enough to create a sharp image that can quickly bring a laugh, like the Roadrunner dropping a boulder onto an already falling Wile E. Coyote in the Warner Bros. cartoons.

'Don't kick someone while they're already down,' we might say.

But too often, we do overload ourselves and each other, especially when we're already feeling blue. It can help to adopt a positive mindset, and modern media is full of advice for people in adversity to be resilient. Shakespeare was there first, with *Cymbeline* reminding us why we fall:

**Some falls are means the happier to arise.**

Still, it can be difficult to see the bright side. This is Romeo's state of mind, having just learned of his banishment from Verona. He talks of killing himself, but Friar Lawrence gives him some perspective: Juliet is alive, Romeo has survived Tybalt's assault, and he's avoided execution.

After each piece of positivity, the Friar repeats the words *There art thou happy* – and Romeo rises up again.

Archbishop Cranmer has been summoned to appear before the Council. They are determined to overthrow him, and his doom seems set. The Bishop of Winchester is so sharply critical that he prompts Cromwell, the meeting secretary, to speak these words.

HENRY VIII

# I think the devil will not have me damned, lest the oil that's in me should set hell on fire.

———— ∞ ————

This line is from the drunken, overweight character Falstaff: he wonders why the devil should stymie his plans to commit adultery, and concludes it must be that Satan wants to keep Falstaff out of hell, because all the fat in his body would be too dangerous there.

Here's another good one from Falstaff, this time in *Henry 4 Part 1*. Giving his word that he'll be on time, he says:

> I am as vigilant as a cat to steal cream.

We don't know if Shakespeare had pets, but cats and dogs (and weasels and whales) abound in Shakespeare's writings. There's a doggish line in *Twelfth Night*, when Fabian meets Feste the Fool, and asks to see a letter Feste is carrying. Feste answers affably, telling Fabian to grant him a request. *Anything*, Fabian declares, to which Feste replies: *Do not desire to see this letter*. Fabian responds with the words:

> This is to give a dog, and in recompense desire my dog again.

And a line from *Henry 8* can bring both a smile and a grimace – it's used as an angry curse when someone interferes in public affairs:

> No man's pie is freed
> From his ambitious finger.

It could equally be used if a hungry someone comes to steal food from the kitchen before everything is ready.

As ever with these quotes, substitute *woman* for *man*, *drink* for *pie*, and *her* for *his*, and perhaps *lips* for *finger*, depending on the situation you find yourself in …

The drunken Falstaff has been lured into the woods at night, supposedly for an illicit liaison with Mistress Ford. Mistress Page turns up as well. It's a trap to teach him a lesson, and they run off, leaving him alone.

## I can suck melancholy out of a song, as a weasel sucks eggs.

— ∞ —

Some words can bring a smile, without knowing exactly why they do. And some people are drawn to moody, thoughtful pieces of music, often in an attempt to feel even moodier.

*Melancholy* was thought to be the result of too much black bile in the blood, and the source of bad temper, sullenness, gloominess and sadness. Kaleidoscopic emotions are the core of Shakespeare's characters. And, in case you didn't know, weasels love eggs.

Weasels are a good source of comedy in Shakespeare's writing. Hamlet tries to convince Polonius that a cloud is shaped like a weasel; and here's a line from *Henry 4 Part 1*, for anyone you know who can be really moody:

> **A weasel hath not such a deal of spleen**
> **As you are tossed with.**

The *spleen* was thought to be the source of both gloomy and mirthful feelings; *tossed*, as you might be in churning seas; and, well, the weasel returns, evidently thought to be a creature of varying emotions. In *Cymbeline*, Pisanio advises Innogen how to disguise herself as a man, telling her to be *as quarrelous as the weasel*.

*Quarrelous* meant 'quarrelsome'. And from *Julius Caesar*, an instruction to swallow bad temper even if it splits someone in two (*disgest* meant 'digest'):

> **...disgest the venom of your spleen,**
> **Though it do split you.**

Either line will put a forceful end to an argument.

Amiens has been singing to the group of nobles in the Forest of Arden. The melancholy Jacques asks him to sing again, but Amiens worries that if he does so, it will make him even more melancholy – a feeling Jacques appears to welcome and seek.

# Though I am not naturally honest, I am so sometimes by chance.

— ∞ —

An honest line, about lying. It's a lovely idea, that liars can sometimes find themselves being honest, but unintentionally.

Characters are quick to be evasive and equivocate in Shakespeare, slipping away from the truth of the matter like mercury.

In *All's Well That Ends Well*, the Countess chides her Clown for his dismissive attitude. The Clown offers in defence that he has an answer that will serve everyone:

> Countess: That's a bountiful answer that fits all questions.
> Clown: It is like a barber's chair that fits all buttocks.

This exchange is useful for anyone quick with a reply that avoids answering a question. Try it out with someone.

The rogue Autolycus is disguised as a pedlar, and has overheard the Shepherd and his son talking. He's about to trick them, as he has done before. But he sees instead an opportunity to help them – and (of course) in so doing, to further his own interests …

THE WINTER'S TALE

# I was adored once, too.

———∞———

A line for anyone finding themselves lonely for love.

(Or only celebrated once every few years.)

Maria the maid has just bid Sir Toby and Sir Andrew 'good night'. Andrew comments that *she's a good wench* – an affectionate term, meaning 'girl' or 'lass'. Toby agrees, adding that she adores him. This prompts Andrew's sweetly nostalgic reflection.

TWELFTH
NIGHT

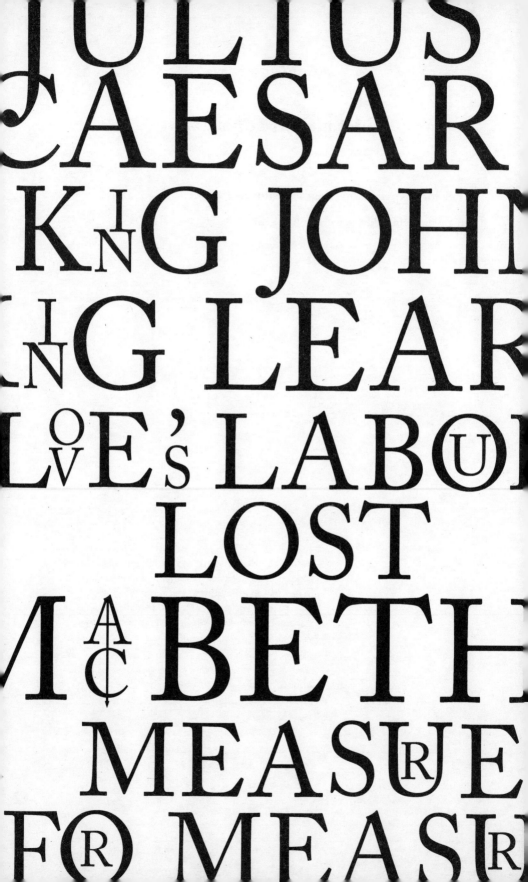

## Grief makes one hour ten.

—— ∞ ——

King Richard has banished Henry Bolingbroke for
six years. His father, John of Gaunt, tries to comfort
him with the thought that *six winters … are quickly
gone. That may be*, replies his son, *if men are
joyful; but not if they are in grief.*

RI<sub>C</sub><sub>H</sub>ARD II

**In sooth I know not why I am so sad.**
**It wearies me, you say it wearies you;**
**But how I caught it, found it, or came by it,**
**What stuff 'tis made of, whereof it is born,**
**I am to learn.**

— ⁂ —

Someone asks how you're feeling, and you recognise you're feeling *sad*, which means 'unhappy' to modern ears, but could also mean 'serious', or 'solemn', in Shakespeare's time.

Either way, your mood is starting to bother them, and it's starting to bother you, too. You've no idea why you've started to feel *sad*, whether it's something that happened, or that hasn't happened yet. Or perhaps it's something that's been done to you, or that you've done to someone else. *In sooth* ('truly'), you can't explain why you feel this way.

If you find yourself feeling similarly dejected, you are keeping company with the prince in *Pericles*, who describes himself as having acquired

   The sad companion, dull-eyed melancholy.

*Melancholy* was thought to be the source of gloominess.

Antonio, the speaker of today's lead quote, is pressed further about his mood by his friend Gratiano. But all Antonio can say is that he thinks the world is like a stage, in which he has been given a sad part to play:

   I hold the world but as the world, Gratiano,
   A stage where every man must play a part
   And mine a sad one.

Later events in the play will prove him right ...

Antonio, 'the merchant of Venice', is acknowledging his recent mood with his friends Solanio and Solerio, and tries to unpack it ...

# I am amazed, methinks, and lose my way
# Among the thorns and dangers of this world.

This speaker finds so many worries growing up around him, he's having difficulty coping.

A modern equivalent might be 'I'm having trouble keeping my head above water', when feeling overwhelmed.

To see the meaning clearly, it's important to appreciate that *amazed* doesn't have its present-day sense of 'astounded' or 'surprised', which was a new development in the 16th century. Rather, *amazed* could mean 'stunned', 'confused', or 'bewildered'. This is how Hermia uses the word in *A Midsummer Night's Dream*, after her quarrel with Helena:

> I am amazed, and know not what to say!

'Problems' echo as thorns or briars in Shakespeare. In *As You Like It*, Rosalind bemoans our *working-day* ('everyday') world, filled with so many things that can snag or hold us up:

> O, how full of briars is this working-day world!

And Richard, in *Henry 6 Part 3*, describes how much he's tormenting himself, thinking of the difficulties that lie in his way, in his pursuit of the crown, as

> ... one lost in a thorny wood,
> That rents the thorns and is rent with the thorns,
> Seeking a way and straying from the way.

Philip the Bastard doesn't often sound confused, but the news of the death of the young Prince Arthur has left him bewildered. He reflects on the mess that England is going to be in, adding *heaven itself doth frown upon the land.*

**An hour before the worshipped sun
Peered forth the golden window of the East,
A troubled mind drive me to walk abroad.**

— ∞ —

Today, we have a few quotes for when you want to be left alone: just me, myself and I.

Here's one from *Cymbeline*:

**Society is no comfort
To one not sociable.**

And another, from *Henry 8* (perhaps this one is a little stronger than the other two):

**Leave me alone,
For I must think of that which company
Would not be friendly to.**

And this last from Orsino, in *Twelfth Night*, who perhaps puts it most simply:

**I myself am best
When least in company.**

Lord and Lady Montague arrive at the scene of a fight between their family members and the Capulets. Lady Montague admits she's glad that her son Romeo wasn't at the fight; Benvolio says he saw Romeo walking alone, not wanting company.

**What is it that takes from thee**
**Thy stomach, pleasure, and thy golden sleep?**
**Why dost thou bend thine eyes upon the earth,**
**And start so often when thou sittest alone?**

— ∞ —

Grief, depression, sadness. They do terrible things to the appetite, to the joy taken from daily life, and especially to sleep (*golden* = the most restorative of all). They can incite a staring into space, or a feeling of being lost in thought and unaware of those around; sometimes such feelings can provoke an anxious *start* ('twitch').

Shakespeare evidently liked to give his characters natural human reactions, and this often happens after they've been through a heightened experience. Macbeth, having just killed King Duncan, comes downstairs (hearing voices, and still holding the blood-stained daggers). He suddenly hears someone knocking at his castle door, which makes him *start*, and he notices how jumpy he is:

How is't with me when every noise appals me?

Or this line from *Henry 4 Part 2*:

Oft have I heard that grief softens the mind,
And makes it fearful and degenerate.

The words capture a premodern scientific idea; psychology and neuroscience now acknowledge that people who are grieving feel more anxious than normal. *Fearful* can have opposing meanings: it can mean to 'cause fear', and it can mean to feel 'timid', 'frightened'. *Degenerate* is an unusual word, meaning 'declined in character or qualities'. Shakespeare uses it to suggest falling from a higher to a lower state.

HENRY IV:I

Hotspur is part of a conspiracy planning the overthrow of King Henry. His wife asks him why he spends so much time alone and is neglecting her. She gets no satisfactory answer from him in this scene, but she'll learn the truth later.

## It argues a distempered head
## So soon to bid good morrow to thy bed.

———∞———

If a friend (or child) gets up abnormally early in the morning, you can use this line to joke that there must be a medical reason for such a premature rise …

A *distempered head* is one that's disturbed in some way, physically or mentally – though not seriously so. *Temper* relates to 'temperament', which in Shakespeare's day was thought to be the result of an excess or deficiency of some element within the body.

So, to be *dis-tempered* was to be 'disordered, diseased', and could even mean 'insane'. Here, though, it's probably closer to the modern meaning of 'troubled'.

Romeo has arrived to visit Friar Lawrence early in the morning. The Friar thinks his friend must either be ill, or he hasn't yet been to bed. That last is true, says the young lover, for Romeo has come straight from his first encounter with Juliet, and has a request for the Friar …

> When to the sessions of sweet silent thought
> I summon up remembrance of things past,
> I sigh the lack of many a thing I sought,
> And with old woes new wail
>     my dear times' waste.

— ∞ —

How do we avoid the repeated calling to mind of past failures when we're alone with our thoughts, and putting ourselves in *session* ('trial')? Mindfulness books advise not to dwell on the past, but to live in the moment.

Finding himself in silence, the poet calls up memories to be witnesses in an imagined court of law. Remembering the many things he failed to get in life, he bewails the time he wasted. (*Waste* used to rhyme with *past*.) But in the final lines of the same poem the poet finds a solution. Thoughts of friendship can cure all:

> But if the while I think on thee, dear friend,
> All losses are restored, and sorrows end.

Further grounded advice comes from *Romeo and Juliet* – that bad times and unhappiness will, in the future, serve as things to laugh about:

> All these woes shall serve
> For sweet discourses in our times to come.

And Edgar in *King Lear*, living as a beggar, thinks he is in the worst possible state. But then he sees his estranged father, who has had his eyes plucked out. Edgar acknowledges there's always room for things to get worse:

> The worst is not,
> So long as we can say 'This is the worst'.

THE SONNETS

This sonnet has the speaker remembering all the negative things about his past. He goes on to talk about friends who have died, and the hurts of old love affairs, and cries all over again for things lost … But this all disappears when he thinks about his present love.

# All strange and terrible events are welcome,
# But comforts we despise.

———— ∞ ————

And then there are the days when you just want to wallow, to stand in the rain and welcome someone to drive through a muddy puddle, to soak you further.

This line from *The Rape of Lucrece* acknowledges how we feel when we know comfort is out of our reach:

> 'Tis double death to drown in ken of shore;
> He ten times pines that pines beholding food;
> To see the salve doth make the wound ache more;
> Great grief grieves most at that would do it good.

*Ken* today means 'know', but used to mean 'see'; *salve* means 'ointment'.

As is often the case with Shakespeare, pragmatism provides a brighter way through sorrow back to comfort. The Thane of Ross presents this view to the warrior Macduff's wife, in *Macbeth*:

> Things at the worst will cease or else climb upward
> To what they were before.

'When you're down, the only way is up' would be a modern take on these lines.

Cleopatra and her maids are awaiting the arrival of the Guard carrying the dying Antony. Cleopatra refuses to be comforted, acknowledging her great sorrow, and says these words.

ANTONY &
CLEOPATRA

# Melancholy is the nurse of frenzy.

———∽———

One way of preventing *frenzy* ('distraction, agitation, delirium'), it seems, is to avoid its *nurse* ('nourisher'), *melancholy*.

*Frenzy* today usually means 'a state of wild agitation'. This can be positive, as in a 'frenzy of delight', or negative, 'a frenzy of despair'.

In older uses, there were much stronger associations too: being in a state of delirium, or approaching madness. In *Titus Andronicus*, Young Lucius is scared of Lavinia's strange behaviour, and worries that *some fit or frenzy do possess her*. *Frenzy* can even be fatal, as we hear in *King John*, where Lady Constance *in a frenzy died*.

We think of *melancholy* today as 'a state of pensive gloom or sadness' – and a symptom of depression. In Shakespeare's day, though, it was thought to be the result of one of the four major *humours* ('fluids') that control the state of mind and body.

In the case of *melancholy*, an excess of black bile would make someone serious, brooding and gloomy. More extreme instances of melancholy brought seemingly causeless bad temper and sullenness, and provoked people to be generally unsociable. Perhaps the most famous case in Shakespeare's writing is the melancholy Jacques, in *As You Like It*.

One of the Lords persuades Christopher Sly to hear a play, to help him recover from a supposed illness. He tells Sly that *too much sadness hath congealed your blood*, and warns him of a likely outcome with this line. Sly is persuaded, but soon wishes the play were over.

THE TAMING OF THE SHREW

My grief lies all within,
And these external manners of laments
Are merely shadows to the unseen grief
That swells with silence in the tortured soul.

———— ✿ ————

Sometimes it can feel impossible to express emotion. Grief can feel unspeakable, and the visible elements of it merely shadows, soft echoes of the mass felt growing silently within.

Modern psychology acknowledges the five stages of grief – denial, anger, bargaining, depression, and acceptance – and the importance of going through each, and allowing each its time.

A first step is noticing that something's not right, as this quote from *Troilus and Cressida* suggests:

O heart, heavy heart,
Why sigh'st thou without breaking?

This line is spoken when the two lovers embrace for the last time. Note the invitation of the emotional word *O* for the speaker to let out an emotional sound, relevant to the situation they find themselves in.

And here's a truth about grief from *Much Ado About Nothing*:

**Everyone can master a grief but he that has it.**

(As ever, replace *he* with *she, they…*) In other words, any problem or unhappy feeling is easy to solve and give advice about – unless you're going through it yourself …

King Richard, about to be deposed by Henry Bolingbroke, has asked for a mirror. After looking in it, he shatters the mirror, seeing its pieces as a parallel to his own misfortunes. Bolingbroke points out that he has destroyed only the *shadow* ('imitation, copy') of his face, and Richard agrees: his grief lies not in the fragments of his fortunes, but within the fragments of himself.

# O, full of scorpions is my mind.

— ∞ —

This image of poisonous insects inside your head that try to sting when jostled might understandably make your skin crawl. It is, perhaps, a reach towards encapsulating the feeling of being overwhelmed. The 'O' is an invitation to make an emotional sound of some kind.

Shakespeare often captures moments of great grief. Here, in *King John*, Constance expresses the grief she feels at the absence of her son Arthur:

> My grief's so great
> That no supporter but the huge firm earth
> Can hold it up.

And grief can do unusual things to our normal behaviours and habits. In *Much Ado About Nothing*, Leonato is so upset that he says even the smallest thing could persuade him – even the weakest of *twine* ('string') could pull him in one direction or another:

> Being that I flow in grief,
> The smallest twine may lead me.

Macbeth and his wife are preparing to host a royal banquet; but Macbeth feels disturbed. He attempts to explain what it feels like to be him …

M<small>A</small><small>C</small>BETH

If that thou couldst see me without eyes,
Hear me without thine ears, and make reply
Without a tongue, using conceit alone,
Without eyes, ears, and harmful sound
   of words;
Then, in despite of brooded watchful day,
I would into thy bosom pour my thoughts.

———— ∞ ————

Here, *conceit* means 'imagination'; *brooded* means 'being full of brooding, of morbidly dwelling on a subject'. *Bosom* means 'heart, inner person'. *Bringing someone into thy bosom* means taking someone 'into your confidence', or 'entrusting someone with your secrets'.

It can be a kind of torture, to want to let someone know how you feel, but not to have the words. If only we could sometimes do this without words.

*The Rape of Lucrece*, a narrative poem with a terrible story, captures this feeling – *power* here means 'ability':

And that deep torture may be called a hell,
When more is felt than one hath power to tell.

The problem is that a sorrowful way of thinking can build up momentum:

For sorrow, like a heavy-hanging bell
Once set on ringing, with his own weight goes.

And, to end this trio from *Lucrece*, an acknowledgement that when in grief or sorrow, night-time and day-time can feel equally wearying; both seem to pass slowly and only make sadness more sharply felt:

Though woe be heavy, yet it seldom sleeps,
And they that watch see time how slow it creeps.

## KING JOHN

King John tries to persuade Hubert to kill the young prince Arthur. He wishes Hubert could understand what he wants, without forcing him to put his desire into words …

## Sorrow breaks seasons and reposing hours, Makes the night morning and the noontide night.

— ∞ —

Mood and behaviour interfere with our relationship to time, and our sleep patterns. The root cause might be stress, having too much on our minds, or – as with today's lead quote – *sorrow* ('sadness').

The *seasons* (the 'normal times of the day') turn upside-down, especially our *reposing hours* ('the time when we should be sleeping'). In other words, the night becomes our morning, and midday becomes our midnight. It's a good description of jetlag.

And Demetrius in *A Midsummer Night's Dream* knows tiredness doesn't help when we're feeling down:

So sorrow's heaviness doth heavier grow
For debt that bankrupt sleep doth sorrow owe.

If we re-order the second line, and gloss the words, the meaning becomes clearer:

*Bankrupt sleep owes sorrow debt* = 'Sleeplessness will make sorrow richer'

The 'weight' of sorrow feels *heavier* ('weightier') when we're tired. The notion of bankruptcy is often used in highly emotional situations. When Juliet thinks Romeo has died, she calls to her heart, *Poor bankrupt, break at once.*

In short: a lack of sleep makes everything seem worse. You don't need to read a Shakespeare play to know this truth, but now you have a fancy way of saying how exhausted you feel.

RICHARD III

The imprisoned Clarence tells his Keeper that he passed a miserable night, and then recounts his bad dreams. He eventually falls asleep again, but Clarence will soon be woken by unwelcome visitors …

# When sorrows come, they come not single spies,
# But in battalions.

—ꝏ—

When you're down it's easy to feel surrounded by woes, as Claudius does here in *Hamlet*.

Sorrows, problems, woes … whatever we call them, this speaker is in no doubt that, as the idiom goes, 'one thing leads to another'. Queen Gertrude (also in *Hamlet*) breaks the news to Laertes that his sister is drowned, and echoes the sentiment:

> One woe doth tread upon another's heel,
> So fast they follow.

*So fast they follow* means they're 'almost chasing in pursuit'. Cleon, the Governor of the lands of Tarsus, makes a similar point in *Pericles*. He's seen ships approaching his famine-stricken country and assumes the visitors have come to take advantage of their weakened state:

> One sorrow never comes but brings an heir
> That may succeed as his inheritor.

(With the arrival of the goodly Pericles, Cleon's melancholic assumption will prove to be wrong.)

King Claudius laments to his wife Gertrude about the troubles they have experienced: the death of Polonius, Hamlet's departure to England, the Danish people stirred up to rebellion, Ophelia's madness, and the impending return of Laertes. He sums up his feelings in these words.

HAMLET

> Give sorrow words: the grief that
>     does not speak
> Whispers the o'erfraught heart
>     and bids it break.

———— ∞ ————

The burning need to speak to one's sorrow is frequently and vividly encountered in the plays. A powerful instance is in *Titus Andronicus* when Marcus meets his mutilated niece Lavinia, and wishes he could rage at whoever caused her such harm, because:

> Sorrow concealed, like an oven stopped,
> Doth burn the heart to cinders where it is.

Some are more reticent at expressing how they feel, like Iago, in *Othello*:

> It were not for your quiet nor your good,
> Nor for my manhood, honesty, and wisdom,
> To let you know my thoughts.

And some find it impossible to speak to their feelings. Cordelia in *King Lear* has found herself unable to obey her father's command. He publicly asks her to speak to how much she loves him, and when she doesn't, Lear gives her a second chance to speak. She still finds it impossible, and says,

> Unhappy that I am, I cannot heave
> My heart into my mouth.

And then there's Kate in *The Taming of the Shrew*, who offers a line for those whose feelings just can't be suppressed:

> My tongue will tell the anger of my heart,
> Or else my heart concealing it will break.

Macduff has just learned of the murder of his wife and family, and has fallen silent; Malcolm urges him to express his feelings with these words …

# Grief fills the room up of my absent child.

— ⁓ —

The quote for March 14th talked of giving sorrow words, and perhaps one of the most heart-breaking thoughts is expressed here, by Lady Constance. A line for anyone unfortunate enough to know the private, personal, unspeakable pain of having lost a child.

Shakespeare reminds us, though, that there needs to be a limit to grief. Lafew and the Countess in *All's Well That Ends Well* have been remembering Helena's dead father, which makes Helena burst into tears. The Countess offers Helena some advice, nudging her towards acceptance:

> Moderate lamentation is the right of the dead, excessive grief
> the enemy to the living.

Lady Capulet agrees in *Romeo and Juliet*. She sees Juliet crying – she believes the tears are for the death of Juliet's cousin Tybalt – and tells her:

> Some grief shows much of love;
> But much of grief shows still some want of wit.

The idea of judging the appropriate amount of time for grieving is a notion we'll explore again on October 27th. (*Want of wit* means 'a lack of common sense'.)

And, if you find yourself with someone who's in grief, there's wise advice from *Love's Labour's Lost*. Berowne reinforces the power of speaking plainly, simply and directly in such encounters:

> Honest plain words best pierce the ear of grief.

KING JOHN

Arthur, the young son of Lady Constance, has been taken prisoner by the English. The French King Philip tells her, *You are as fond of grief as of your child,* and she replies with this devastating line.

# Venus smiles not in a house of tears.

———∞———

*Venus* here is the Roman goddess of beauty and love, and *a house* is one of the twelve divisions of the astrological zodiac. In other words, 'Love doesn't come to a house of grief', or, 'Love isn't welcome during a period of mourning'.

What is your relationship to tears? Some see crying as a weakness, or profess that they rarely cry. The great warrior Coriolanus, moved to pity, spares the city of Rome from destruction with the words

> It is no little thing to make
> Mine eyes to sweat compassion.

Sometimes emotional upset is too great to allow tears, as with Richard in *Henry 6 Part 3*, vowing revenge after hearing of the killing of his father:

> I cannot weep, for all my body's moisture
> Scarce serves to quench my furnace-burning heart.

And arguing with Brutus in *Julius Caesar*, Cassius believes he could cry so hard his soul would come out through his eyes:

> O, I could weep
> My spirit from mine eyes!

In Shakespeare's time, the eyes were understood to be the windows to the *spirit*, or soul (and the place where love would strike). *Spirit* is also used in the plays to refer to 'a person's temperament or frame of mind', and especially to 'a mind that's courageous and determined'. At the beginning of *As You Like It*, Orlando refuses to accept the servile state imposed on him by his brother:

> The spirit of my father, which I think is within me, begins to mutiny
> against this servitude. I will no longer endure it.

He's possessed – but by his father's courage, not his ghost.

Juliet is still in tears. Her suitor Paris thinks she's upset over the death of Tybalt – as the Capulet household is in mourning – rather than the banishment of Romeo. Paris is wise enough to know it isn't possible to woo someone in such a situation.

## Mine eyes smell onions, I shall weep anon.

— ⚮ —

Actors aren't supposed to eat onions before they perform (because their breath would be unpleasant for their fellow players), but they equally know that an onion is a great tool that can help you cry.

These quotes will be useful when you find yourself welling up, or see someone else in tears. The warrior Enobarbus finds himself moved towards the end of *Antony and Cleopatra*:

> I, an ass, am onion-eyed.

Some can find themselves overcome by their emotions; here's a description of Cranmer, having broken down in gratitude, in *Henry 8*:

> **He has strangled**
> **His language in his tears.**

And yet others, like King Alonso in *The Tempest*, find themselves so emotionally exhausted, they wish that sleep would come to stop all tears, and every other thought:

> **I wish mine eyes**
> **Would, with themselves, shut up my thoughts.**

Lafew finds the end of *All's Well That Ends Well* too much …

## 'Tis pity …
## That wishing well had not a body in't
## Which might be felt.

— ∞ —

Having hope that things will change is different from wishing things would change. Wishes can't be felt. In fact, while they can be well intentioned, they're empty. And yet, we send wishes to each other all the time, as do Shakespeare's characters.

Lysander in *A Midsummer Night's Dream* wishes to Hermia, as they lie down for the night: *sleep give thee all his rest*, and she responds: *With half that wish the wisher's eyes be pressed.*

And Jessica in *The Merchant of Venice* bids farewell to Portia: *I wish your ladyship all heart's content*. Portia replies elegantly:

> I thank you for your wish, and am well pleased
> To wish it back on you.

It's hard not to read a touch of scepticism in the usefulness of wishes, so elegant is Portia's reply. The Egyptian Queen agrees, in *Antony and Cleopatra*:

> Wishers were ever fools.

Helena is upset at the departure of Bertram. She loves him, but says simply, *he is one that I wish well*. She adds *it is a pity* … and Parolles asks her what she means by *pity*. She replies with these words …

ALL'S WELL THAT ENDS WELL

## Diseases desperate grown
## By desperate appliance are relieved,
## Or not at all.

———— ∞ ————

*Desperate* could mean 'reckless', 'bold', or 'risky', as well as 'hopeless'.

When things are truly desperate, there is perhaps nothing as audacious and pernicious as the human spirit and its capacity for hope. *Measure for Measure* reinforces this powerful inner strength:

> The miserable have no other medicine
> But only hope.

So does *The Two Gentlemen of Verona* – especially in love:

> Hope is a lover's staff; walk hence with that,
> And manage it against despairing thoughts.

A character in *Richard 3* reflects on the true nature of hope:

> True hope is swift and flies with swallow's wings;
> Kings it makes gods, and meaner creatures kings.

And *Julius Caesar* suggests that nothing can *be retentive to* ('imprison or confine') someone who is strongly resolved to follow a course of action:

> Nor stony tower, nor walls of beaten brass,
> Nor airless dungeon, nor strong links of iron,
> Can be retentive to the strength of spirit.

Hamlet has just killed Polonius, and King Claudius thinks his nephew is now so dangerous that he needs to be sent away as quickly as possible. So he plans to send Hamlet to England (where he is to be executed ...)

MARCH 20TH

# In Nature, there's no blemish but the mind; None can be called deformed, but the unkind.

———— ∞ ————

Perhaps the only *blemish* ('fault') in life is the way we think, or the way we treat each other. Be kind. (Especially to yourself.)

The sea captain Antonio has been arrested for setting foot in Illyria. He asks the disguised Viola for help, supposing her to be his friend Sebastian (who turns out to be Viola's lost twin brother) … When he/she refuses, Antonio is distraught, and harangues him/her for being so shameful.

TWELFTH NIGHT

# Those wounds heal ill that men do give themselves.

———— ∞ ————

*Wound* can mean the literal 'mark of physical injury'. It can also take on a more abstract meaning: 'an emotional or mental injury inflicted on another'. *Men* stands for 'humans'.

Some, like Coriolanus, don't like to speak of their injuries. He says he'd rather go through the experience of being hurt and having to heal again, than retell the story of his pain:

> I had rather have my wounds to heal again
> Than hear say how I got them.

*Wounds* can also be used to allude to injuries – or grievances and upsets – in relationships. If a wound is healing, it's unwise to *gall* ('chafe') it, as the soreness will return. Here's the Lord Chief Justice in *Henry 4 Part 2*:

> I am loath to gall a new-healed wound.

Shakespeare advising us all not to pick at the scab.

*Gall* was a bodily fluid reputed for its bitterness, so it was a common image to use in situations of severe mental distress. It's often contrasted with sweetness. Romeo uses the image in his conflicting thoughts about the nature of love:

> A choking gall and a preserving sweet.

TROILUS & CRESSIDA

A challenge has been sent to the Greeks: will one of them fight with the Trojan Hector? The Greeks think their champion Achilles won't do it, and that Ajax will take up the challenge. Patroclus advises Achilles to rouse himself, if his reputation isn't to suffer.

And if Achilles won't fight, it's his own fault (says Patroclus, in an attempt to persuade the famed Greek warrior), and he'll regret it in times to come …

# I am that I am, and they that level
## At my abuses reckon up their own.

— ∞ —

A testament from Shakespeare in his sonnets, that whoever you are, whatever you feel yourself to be, own it and never feel bad if others *level at* ('make a target of') what they see as your *abuses* ('weaknesses').

Instead they should *reckon up* ('list') their own faults. In effect, 'Take me as I am, warts and all, and go take a look in the mirror.'

If you'd like a more subtle version, along these lines of 'the pot calling the kettle black', then try this one, from *Troilus and Cressida*:

**The raven chides blackness.**

The best comeback for any cowardly bullies who try to strike at their own faults in others.

The poet is condemning those who think ill of him (even though they're no better or worse than he is). He thinks their criticisms only serve to make their own failings clear.

THE SONNETS

# 'Tis in ourselves that we are thus, or thus. Our bodies are our gardens, to the which our wills are gardeners.

— ∞ —

There's long been a practice of comparing a country, a person, the world, or even your mind, to a garden. Here, a point is being made about personal responsibility: we're in charge of our own thoughts, feelings and deeds.

The Gardener in *Richard 2* talks about Britain in this way, although his comparison indicates he's not very happy about the political situation:

> Our sea-walled garden, the whole land,
> Is full of weeds, her fairest flowers choked up,
> Her fruit trees all unpruned, her hedges ruined.

And Hamlet uses the metaphor for the whole world:

> ...'tis an unweeded garden
> That grows to seed. Things rank and gross in nature
> Possess it merely.

*Rank* had multiple meanings, including 'lewd', 'violent' and 'diseased'; *merely* means 'totally'. Meanwhile *All's Well That Ends Well* offers a pragmatic, secular approach to life's problems:

> Our remedies oft in ourselves do lie,
> Which we ascribe to heaven.

In other words: you can solve anything yourself, if you put your mind and heart to it.

Roderigo hopes to win Desdemona, even though she's just married Othello. Roderigo knows he's infatuated, and doesn't feel able to do anything about it. Iago offers him some grounding advice with these lines, and eventually persuades him to continue pursuing Desdemona ...

# Good counsellors lack no clients.

— ∞ —

We might say, 'a problem shared is a problem halved'. However you cut it, talking out your problems is good for you, and those who are good at listening will never find themselves short of people wanting to share their woes.

*The Comedy of Errors* reminds us that it's not always easy to hear people complain, and sometimes we might wish them to be quiet (even though we know that when we suffer, we'll likely be as vocal, if not more so):

> **A wretched soul, bruised with adversity,**
> **We bid be quiet when we hear it cry.**
> **But were we burdened with like weight of pain,**
> **As much or more we should ourselves complain.**

Listening is different from giving advice, and some, like Leonato in *Much Ado About Nothing*, have no patience for counsel when they're upset, no matter how well-intentioned (*profitless* means 'useless'):

> **I pray thee, cease thy counsel,**
> **Which falls into mine ears as profitless**
> **As water in a sieve.**

And others can be quick to give advice, even though they're the ones who need the counsellor, as Agamemnon notes in *Troilus and Cressida*:

> **He will be the physician that should be the patient.**

MEASURE FOR MEASURE

Pompey the servant has just brought news to Mistress Overdone about a new Viennese law, that all brothel houses (like hers) are to be pulled down. She wonders what she will do, and Pompey tries to reassure her with these words – 'if you're selling valuable goods you'll always have buyers' ...

# Let us not burden our remembrances with A heaviness that's gone.

———— ∞ ————

The Stoics teach that the past is only a story we tell ourselves. Still, it can be easy to dwell in that story for a mistake long since made.

This speaker is untypically generous in his recommendation that we shouldn't *burden our remembrances* ('weigh down our memories') with a *heaviness* ('sadness') from long ago.

*Heaviness* in Shakespeare's time could literally mean 'weightiness', but also 'drowsiness'. Most often it meant 'sorrow' or 'grief' – the Duke of Clarence in *Henry 4 Part 2* says he's *full of heaviness* at the sight of his seriously ill father.

In *The Winter's Tale*, Paulina acknowledges this idea of not holding on to old griefs:

> What's gone and what's past help
> Should be past grief.

And Antony makes it clear he's a man of pragmatism and stoicism in *Antony and Cleopatra*, when a messenger brings him bad news relating to events that have already taken place. But as far as Antony is concerned, that's over and done with:

> Things that are past are done, with me.

The Duke in *Othello* says it more poetically:

> When remedies are past the griefs are ended
> By seeing the worst which late on hopes depended.

When we're met with the worst, when it's too late to do anything, and even hope has failed – acceptance must come, and grief will, eventually, go.

Alonso starts to ask forgiveness of Miranda for his former treatment of her and her father; but Prospero stops him with these words.

## For gnarling sorrow hath less power to bite
## The man that mocks at it and sets it light.

— ∞ —

The true scourge of the things that seriously weigh us down is laughter. If we (of any gender) can find the balance in the heaviness, find the funny in the foolish, then perhaps we can regain peace and happiness – though few characters in Shakespeare take this speaker's advice and *set* ('value') sorrow lightly.

*Gnarling* – an evocative combination of growling and snarling – appears to be a Shakespearean invention, as this instance is the first recorded usage in English (though the verb *gnar* is much older).

A more optimistic gloss is put on sorrow in *Henry 4 Part 2*:

> **Therefore be merry ... since sudden sorrow**
> **Serves to say thus, 'Some good thing comes tomorrow'.**

In *Love's Labour's Lost*, Costard the Fool is taken into custody for breaking the King's law against consorting with women – in his case, with his love Jaquenetta, and says:

> **Affliction may one day smile again, and till then sit thee down, sorrow!**

And in *Henry 8*, Anne Bullen is talking with a companion about Queen Katherine's fall from grace. Anne thinks it's better to be lowly born than to be a queen, as that is where contentment lies. Her companion agrees, with these truthful, brilliantly simple words:

> **Our content**
> **Is our best having.**

John of Gaunt is saying farewell to his son, Bolingbroke, who's been banished by King Richard. With these words, Gaunt advises his son to see his banishment as a fresh opportunity, and to laugh at his misfortune ...

## Your present kindness
## Makes my past miseries sports.

—— ❧ ——

A moment of kindness can turn an unhappy memory into *sports* – 'something pleasurable'.

*King John* offers a line for when you don't know how to thank someone for such a compassionate gift:

> I have a kind soul that would give thanks,
> And knows not how to do it but with tears.

Kindness and compassion are the salves to grief and sorrow, and the offer of either from a stranger can bring us to tears. 'I'm fine, as long as no one is kind to me', some might say.

Several characters in the plays seem at a loss to put their gratitude into words, and fall back on the simplest of statements (or by bursting into tears). Sebastian in *Twelfth Night* responds to Antonio's offer to keep him company:

> I can no other answer make but thanks,
> And thanks.

Some even apologise for the poverty of their thanks, as Hamlet does, in thanking Rosencrantz and Guildenstern for their visit to Castle Elsinore:

> Beggar that I am, I am even poor in thanks. But I thank you.

In the last scene of the play, Pericles is finally reunited with his wife Thaisa and daughter Marina. He addresses the gods with these words.

PERICLES

## Self-love ... is not so vile a sin
## As self-neglecting.

— ∞ —

*Self-love* ('narcissism') is a quality thought to be *vile* ('despicable'). But self-neglect is worse.

Perhaps this is Shakespeare pushing for self-care, effectively suggesting both to 'look after yourself', and to 'love yourself'.

The French nobles are preparing to discuss the forthcoming war with England. The Dauphin tells the King (perhaps sensing a lack of resolve) that he must be firm, and not neglect to let the English ambassadors see his power.

HENRY V

**Thou seest we are not all alone unhappy.**
**This wide and universal theatre**
**Presents more woeful pageants than the scene**
**Wherein we play in.**

— ∞ —

It's helpful to remember when you can't see past your own problems that you're not alone in unhappiness, that there are others with you in the pits of despair.

And if that isn't help enough, *All's Well That Ends Well* reminds us that there are always ups and downs in life:

The web of our life is of a mingled yarn, good and ill together.

Orlando stumbles across the camp of the banished Duke, in the Forest of Arden. The Duke invites him to join them. But Orlando says he won't eat anything until he finds and fetches his old servant Adam. After he leaves, the Duke comments to the nobles that they are evidently not alone in their unhappy state.

AS YOU LIKE IT

## For this relief much thanks.

— ∞ —

*Relief* here is intended in its military sense, of one soldier taking the place of another. But it's most often used by Shakespeare in its modern sense of 'alleviation of distress, anxiety or physical pain'.

When Stephano first encounters Caliban, in *The Tempest*, he thinks he's a monster with a fever, so decides to give him some relief – this time in the form of a drink from his bottle of wine.

So, today's lead quote can be used when you're busy, or in a stressful or difficult situation, or doing something you really don't want to be doing – and, wonderfully, someone comes along and offers to help!

It's the opening scene of the play, and Barnardo has come to relieve his fellow sentry Francisco on the battlements of Castle Elsinore. Francisco is glad to see his colleague, not only because he's *bitter cold*; he's also *sick at heart*, even though the night has, so far, been quiet. But soon the ghost of Hamlet's father appears …

This above all: to thine own self be true,
And it must follow, as the night the day,
Thou canst not then be false to any man.

— ∞ —

These are the parting words of Polonius to his
son Laertes, who is about to leave on a journey to
France. Polonius has given a few precepts to
follow, and this one is the last, though by no
means the least. (*False* here means 'disloyal,
unfaithful', or 'unfair, double-crossing'. For *man*
read 'human'.)

HAMLET

MERY WIVE
OF WINDS
MUCH ADO ABOU
NOTHING
OTHELLO
PERICLES
RICHARDI
RICHARD III
ROMEO
& JULIET

## Wisely and slow. They stumble that run fast.

—— ∞ ——

Friar Lawrence has been persuaded to marry Romeo and Juliet; Romeo is in a hurry, and ends the scene with the plea *O, let us hence! I stand on sudden haste*. The Friar has the last word with this line for anyone in a rush (*haste* would have rhymed with *fast* 400 years ago).

A jest's prosperity lies in the ear
Of him that hears it, never in the tongue
Of him that makes it.

— ✧ —

Rosaline has told Berowne that if he wants to win her love, he must spend a year in hospitals using his wit to help seriously ill people smile. Berowne says it can't be done, that *Mirth cannot move a soul in agony*. But Rosaline reminds him of a comedic truth with these words …

LOVE'S LABOR'S LOST

# A surfeit of the sweetest things
# The deepest loathing to the stomach brings.

———— ∞ ————

Today's lead quote acknowledges the predictable effects on the stomach of any *surfeit* ('excess') in eating and drinking sweet things. Perhaps the modern equivalent of this might be something you heard as a child, 'You'll make yourself sick if you eat more sweets.'

The sickness theme is extended in *Timon of Athens*, when Apemantus asks Timon:

> Will the cold brook,
> Candied with ice, caudle thy morning taste,
> To cure thy o'ernight's surfeit?

In other words, the cold river, *candied* ('sweetened') with ice, will *caudle* ('provide a medicinal drink') for the morning taste in your mouth, and rebalance you after drinking too much the night before.

Over-indulgence will sometimes have a physical outcome: in *Henry 4 Part 2*, the newly crowned King Henry 5 offers a phrase for anyone who's overweight like Falstaff, calling his old friend *surfeit-swelled*.

Indeed, too much of something we know is bad for us can even push us to hatred. In which case, use this line from *Antony and Cleopatra*:

> In time we hate that which we often fear.

The notion in today's lead quote can of course be extended beyond food and drink: an excess of anything – love, care, attention, travel, children's TV shows – can quickly turn the stomach …

The love-juice of the fairies has made Lysander fall in love with Helena. When he sees his former love, Hermia, asleep, he wonders how he could ever have been so devoted to her. Having had an excessive amount of sweetness from her, he now feels only the greatest possible hatred. It will take more fairy-work to resolve the situation.

# A man loves the meat in his youth that he cannot endure in his age.

———— ∞ ————

Ben used to hate peas when he was a kid, and now loves them. David used to feel lucky to have lumps of coal for his meals, and now hates them (and isn't too fond of broccoli, either). Tastes alter with time.

Today's quote doesn't exclude vegetarians or vegans, of any gender (*man* stands for 'human' here), as the original meaning of the word *meat* used to be much wider, to mean 'food' generally, and over the centuries has narrowed to the 'animal flesh' sense it has today. Both meanings are used by Shakespeare, the sense changing even as he was writing.

We still use *meat* in the more general sense of 'sustenance', but there are only hints of it – in 'sweetmeat', or proverbs such as 'one man's meat is another man's poison'. There are also Shakespearean idioms that have stayed with us, like Slender's in *The Merry Wives of Windsor*, when he tells Anne that he's not worried when he sees bears loose in the streets, and says (perhaps attempting to sound courageous), *That's meat and drink to me, now* – 'That's everyday to me.'

So when the Fool in *King Lear* says he has *cut the egg i'the middle and eat up the meat*, or Katherina in *The Taming of the Shrew* says she's *starved for meat*, or Cade in *Henry 6 Part 2* says he's *eat no meat these five days*, they're just talking about 'nourishment'.

Go on. Give peas a chance.

Don Pedro and Claudio have been describing Beatrice's love for Benedick, knowing Benedick can hear them. As a result, Benedick changes his opinion about marriage: he admits that he's spoken strong words against it in the past, but asks: *doth not the appetite alter?*

# For never anything can be amiss
# When simpleness and duty tender it.

— ∞ —

*Simpleness* here means 'unassuming simplicity', 'unpretentiousness'. *Duty* needs to be thought of as more than just 'respect due to a superior'. It meant any feeling of 'obligation', such as you might feel when returning a favour.

This speaker believes that anything done with good intentions will be appreciated for its sincerity, and people will allow for mistakes, and perhaps even enjoy them. Think: parents watching a children's Christmas play.

The notion of 'unpretentiousness' is heard again in *All's Well That Ends Well*, when the Countess describes Helena's virtues:

**In her they are the better for their simpleness.**

Simpleness, gentleness, and innocence are admired qualities in the plays. In *As You Like It*, Orlando comes across Duke Senior's camp in the Forest of Arden, and angrily demands food. The Duke welcomes Orlando to join them, adding that a gentle approach is going to be more successful than an angry one:

**Your gentleness shall force,**
**More than your force move us to gentleness.**

Although when Cleopatra beats her messenger and even threatens to kill him – just for bringing her bad news – she says:

**Some innocents 'scape not the thunderbolt.**

Philostrate tells Duke Theseus which plays have been put forward to provide the court with entertainment. Theseus chooses the one that the Athenian mechanicals have prepared, and when Philostrate tries to dissuade him, on the grounds that the play is terrible, the Duke disagrees, giving this reason.

# 'Tis an ill cook that cannot lick his own fingers.

———— ❦ ————

Whatever you like to eat, remember this absolute truth. (*Ill* means 'bad, poor'.)

Capulet needs twenty skilful cooks to prepare the wedding banquet for Juliet and Paris. His servant says he will prove they are good cooks by asking them to lick their fingers. As far as he's concerned, that is the ultimate test for fine food.

## What need the bridge much broader than the flood?

—— ⚬⚭ ——

This is *flood* in the sense of 'river' or 'stream'.

In other words: a bridge only needs to be wide enough to cross the water.

Or: you don't need to say more than is necessary, or do more than is needed, to get a job done.

Claudio has told Don Pedro that he loves Hero, and is worried that he hasn't said enough, but Don Pedro says anything extra isn't necessary: that Claudio loves Hero is all he needs to know …

MUᴄH AᴅO ABᴼᵁT
NOTHING

# Now is the woodcock near the gin.

— ✇ —

Not *gin* as in 'the alcoholic drink'. A *gin* or *springe* is an old word for a 'snare' or 'trap'; it's related to 'engine'.

The *woodcock* is a type of game bird, thought to be easily tricked or snared, and so was a common expression for someone considered to be 'simple' of mind. In *The Taming of the Shrew*, the wealthy old man Gremio is called one: *O this woodcock, what an ass it is.* And one of the lords in *All's Well That Ends Well* uses it when they catch Parolles lying: *We have caught the woodcock.*

The word even appears at a moment of high tragedy. Laertes, fatally wounded by his own poisoned sword, is asked how he is, and replies:

> **Why, as a woodcock to mine own springe, Osrick.**
> **I am justly killed with mine own treachery.**

Maria has set a trap to fool Malvolio: she's written him a love letter that appears to be from Olivia, and leaves it in a place where she knows he will walk. Malvolio sees the letter and picks it up, leading Fabian (who's hiding and watching with Toby and Andrew) to say these words.

TWELFTH
NIGHT

# I can swim like a duck.

If someone asks if you can swim, you never have to say a simple 'yes' ever again. And, when they ask what you mean, just as you jump in, tell them you're quoting Shakespeare.

Stephano meets Trinculo, after both have escaped from a shipwreck. Asked how he managed it, Trinculo says that he simply swam ashore, like a duck.

T<sub>H</sub><sub>E</sub> TEMP<sup>E</sup><sub>S</sub>T

# There is that in this fardel will make him scratch his beard.

— ∞ —

Instead of saying 'a package' has arrived, use the more mysterious, exciting word, *fardel*. It is an Old French word meaning 'little burden'.

The Shepherd and his son have gathered the evidence of Perdita's origins, and are on their way to show it to the King, certain that he will be impressed.

THE WINTER'S TALE

> Coward dogs
> Most spend their mouths
>    when what they seem to threaten
> Runs far before them.

— ∞ —

When dogs hunt, they *spend their mouths* ('bark most loudly') when there's no chance of the prey threatening them. Arguably, we humans can be much the same.

Indeed, in *A Midsummer Night's Dream* we see the thought acted out: Lysander and Demetrius have gone into the forest to fight, but Puck is confusing the love-drugged, quarrelling lovers by keeping them apart, and adopting their voices. So when Lysander hears Puck taunting him using Demetrius' voice, he declares *He goes before me, and still dares me on.*

The quality of someone's voice is often under a microscope in the plays. The disguised Rosalind in *As You Like It* almost gives herself away: Orlando is puzzled to meet a forest-dweller with *an accent something finer than you could purchase in so removed a dwelling.* She quickly thinks up a plausible reason, telling him that *an old religious uncle of mine taught me to speak, who was in his youth, an inland man.*

The English ambassadors have arrived in the French court, and the Dauphin describes the invading foreigners with these words …

HENRY V

## Suspicion always haunts the guilty mind;
## The thief doth fear each bush an officer.

— ∞ —

*Suspicion* here means 'anxiety, trepidation, apprehension'. *Officer* is exactly as you might guess, carrying the familiar sense of someone who holds a position of authority in law enforcement – as in, 'officer of the law'. The *bush* represents the innocent remarks or actions of other people, wrongly interpreted as awareness of guilt.

So these lines describe the mental and emotional state of guilty people who wonder if they'll be caught, and see every innocent flinch and eyebrow raise as judgement: to the guilty or fearful mind, each bush has the shape of an accusing officer. Our brain may be the seat of our thinking, but it can still play tricks on us.

Meanwhile, we set great value on our 'gut instinct', or the 'feeling in the heart'. When Martius falls into a deep pit in *Titus Andronicus*, he asks his brother Quintus to help him out. Quintus has a very bad feeling about what is going on:

> I am surprised with an uncouth fear:
> A chilling sweat o'erruns my trembling joints;
> My heart suspects more than mine eye can see.

– and it's a feeling that will shortly be proved right, when they discover that the pit contains the body of murdered Bassianus ...

The imprisoned Henry 6 thinks he's in danger, and compares himself to a harmless sheep whose throat is about to be cut. His feeling is correct, for Richard will shortly kill him; his murderer, hypocritically, reassures Henry with these words.

HENRY VI : III

# My thoughts are whirled like a potter's wheel; I know not where I am nor what I do.

— ∞ —

Today brings a couple of quotes for when you feel the world spinning around you.

The lead quote is for when you're feeling confused and unsure of what to do. Given the ancient history of pottery, you may be surprised to know that this is the earliest recorded use in English of the expression 'potter's wheel'.

Next, a line about a feeling of antici-\*, from *Troilus and Cressida*. Troilus is meeting Cressida for the first time, and is evidently so excited it's making him feel dizzy:

I am giddy; expectation whirls me round.

And here's another useful one, this time from *Cymbeline*. Have it ready for the occasions when you're so surprised you can't quite believe the world is actually turning – and then quick, ask someone to pinch you to check you're awake:

Does the world go round?

---

\*-pation

Talbot thinks Joan la Pucelle is a witch, instilling fear into his soldiers' hearts so that they all run away from her. Although he speaks these lines, he will soon regain his composure to fight again …

H<sub>E</sub><sub>N</sub>RY VI:I

**The time and my intents are savage-wild,**
**More fierce and more inexorable far**
**Than empty tigers or the roaring sea.**

— ∽ —

*Inexorable* means 'unstoppable' This is a great quote for when you're feeling fierce. Here are three more, for when you're feeling 1) pragmatic, 2) flexible, or 3) keen to remind others not to make assumptions about you.

The first, from *Troilus and Cressida*, suggests, 'Time will decide':

**Time must friend or end.**

The second is from *The Winter's Tale*, when Leontes refuses to believe that Hermione's new-born baby is his. He orders that it should be killed, but all the nobles in his court kneel to beg for the baby's life. Leontes says these words and reluctantly changes his mind:

**I am a feather for each wind that blows.**

(While the jealous tyrant declares himself persuadable with this line, he will shortly order that the child be left in a remote place, in a far and distant country.)

And lastly, a terrific quote if someone makes an assumption about you. In *Henry 4 Part 2*, Prince Hal has been crowned king as Henry 5, and is in procession through the streets of London. Falstaff has travelled to greet him, but Henry says he has changed. He then disowns his old drinking companion with the words, *I know thee not, old man*:

**Presume not that I am the thing I was.**

Romeo is about to break into Juliet's tomb, and warns his servant Balthasar not to follow him …

**The robbed that smiles steals something
from the thief;
He robs himself that spends a bootless grief.**

— ∞ —

*Bootless* means 'useless', 'worthless'.

The only person you're hurting when you get upset over *a bootless grief* ('something you can't do anything about') is yourself.

Smile in the face of adversity.

Unhappy at their wedlock, Brabantio has demanded that his daughter Desdemona and Othello be brought before the Duke of Venice. The Duke says that, as their marriage is now a fact, it's pointless for Brabantio to keep mourning a situation that cannot be changed …

# My heart is ready to crack with impatience.

— ∞ —

The sound of a heart bursting, in Shakespeare, is represented by the word O. To find your O, take a breath, and as you exhale, make a sound relevant to how you feel.

Here are a few from the plays – the first, from *King Lear*, when the King recognises his current line of thinking could drive him mad:

O, that way madness lies.

The next, from *Coriolanus*:

O world, thy slippery turns!

By *slippery turns* Coriolanus means the 'treacherous changes of fortune' that have placed him in his current situation.

If you're ever late for something, take this line from Innogen in *Cymbeline*, for someone to bring you a Pegasus:

O, for a horse with wings!

If you're feeling especially upset (and perhaps a little frumpy and wanting attention, like Cleopatra) you can always tell a friend exactly what you want them to do:

Pity me, Charmian,
But do not speak to me.

The jealous husband, Ford, discovers that the adulterous Falstaff has already been invited to meet his wife, and he can't wait to catch them.

# I have not that alacrity of spirit
# Nor cheer of mind that I was wont to have.

— ∞ —

... said the elder co-author, one morning. There are occasions when even the bounciest of us lack the energy we were *wont* ('used') to have.

*Alacrity* is one of those words that hasn't changed its meaning in centuries: it means 'liveliness' or 'briskness', usually with a cheerfulness of spirit. The fat Falstaff, having been thrown into the Thames in *The Merry Wives of Windsor*, is relieved to have got out safely, *for I have a kind of alacrity in sinking.*

Coriolanus offers a simple way to express that feeling when you're so tired your brain hurts:

**I am weary; yea, my memory is tired.**

*Here's the pang that pinches* (*Henry 8*): fatigue and poor memory come to us all. Dogberry, in *Much Ado About Nothing*, reminds us that the older we get, the less *wit* ('mental ability') we have:

**When the age is in, the wit is out.**

And yet, in *As You Like It*, Adam reminds Orlando:

**Though I look old, yet I am strong and lusty.**

Indeed, age often receives praise in the plays. The character of aged Nestor in *Troilus and Cressida* is a symbol of wisdom, experience and oratory – which explains why Richard 3 (reflecting on his dreams for the crown) says *I'll play the orator as well as Nestor.*

It is towards the end of the play, and the eve of the Battle of Bosworth. King Richard is in his tent, evidently feeling tired. He hasn't eaten. He's also about to have a series of very bad dreams, and some ghostly guests from his past ...

RICHARD III

## Then join they all together,
## Like many clouds consulting for foul weather.

———⸎———

The goddess Venus is full of emotions, each competing to be the chief cause of her sadness. She finds none of them stands out, rather that they all combine like a group of clouds, meeting to discuss a day of bad weather.

Shakespeare had a knack for describing feelings, and often compared a strong emotional reaction inside us to something out there in the real world:

> To climb steep hills
> Requires slow pace at first. Anger is like
> A full hot horse, who being allowed his way
> Self-mettle tires him.

These lines from *Henry 8* describe a horse allowed to run *full hot* ('very fast') that will soon tire itself out with its own *self-mettle* ('vigorous activity'). In other words, treat a steep hill, life, negative emotions or anything challenging, like a marathon, not a sprint.

This is the only time Shakespeare uses the expression *self-mettle*, but *mettle* by itself turns up thirty times in the plays and poems; it has the sense of 'spirit' or 'vigour'. One of the apparitions advises Macbeth to be *lion-mettled*.

It's a torture that, when we do find our furies, we tend to blame the very thing (or person) that's trying to help, and end up fuelling the fire that burns us. So, next time you get angry at someone who's being nice to you, remember this line from *King Lear*:

> Kill thy physician and thy fee bestow
> Upon the foul disease.

The goddess of love is in a sorrowful state: Adonis isn't interested in her, and she feels a medley of emotions tumble through her ...

**Between the acting of a dreadful thing**
**And the first motion, all the interim is**
**Like a phantasma or a hideous dream.**

— ∞ —

*Motion* here means 'urging', 'imagining', 'inward prompting'.

A truth of life; and another example of Shakespeare using an unusual word (*phantasma*), and then telling us what it means ('hideous dream').

He's showing two types of generosity: empathy in offering a life-truth, and compassion in providing a definition of the unusual word.

Brutus is at his house reflecting on a message he's received asking him to *speak, strike, redress* the wrongs being done to Rome. He knows that this refers to Caesar, and the intended assassination.
    He hasn't slept, and today's quote points towards his state of mind.

JULIUS CAESAR

# What cannot be eschewed must be embraced.

———— ⚬∽⚬ ————

What to do, when faced with the inevitable? Whether it's a task or a life choice, Shakespeare offers that the best course of action (when something cannot be *eschewed* – 'avoided') is acceptance.

(This is the only time that Shakespeare uses the word *eschew*; he prefers *remedy*, when talking about solutions, as we saw in *Macbeth* on January 24th).

Queen Margaret expresses a similar sentiment in *Henry 6 Part 3*, as she attempts to bolster the spirits of the King's forces:

> **What cannot be avoided**
> **'Twere childish weakness to lament or fear.**

*The Two Gentlemen of Verona* offers that avoidance only leads to calamity:

> **Thus have I shunned the fire for fear of burning,**
> **And drenched me in the sea, where I am drowned.**

And sometimes you have to plunge in up to the elbows, and fully commit to the path you're on. Or as Lady Macbeth puts it, wash your hands of it:

> **A little water clears us of this deed.**

Macbeth and his wife's hands are covered in Duncan's blood, having just murdered him. They suddenly hear someone knocking at their castle door: they must quickly put on their night-clothes to give the impression that they've been sleeping. And they must also wash their hands …

Hopefully your tasks and life choices will be less heinous; Lady Macbeth's line is useful for when you've finished painting the house, too.

Fenton and Anne Page have been successful in their plan to marry. They appear before her father, who asks *What remedy?* He realises there's none, with these words …

## I know this is a joyful trouble to you,
## But yet 'tis one.

— ∞ —

You've just asked someone to help you move out. Or dry, while you wash the dishes. Or keep you company while you run a tedious errand. That's a perfect opportunity for this line: 'I know it's a happy pain, but it's still a pain'.

In the UK, if you agree to help someone like this, you may find *them* apologizing – 'Sorry to trouble you' or 'Sorry to be a trouble …' – even though you're willing to assist!

A conventional reply could be 'It's no trouble', or 'Not at all' – which is how we hear it used in the plays. Here's an interchange to learn, from *Troilus and Cressida*, as Hector apologises to Ajax:

> Hector: I trouble you.
> Ajax: No, not a whit.

*Not a whit* means 'not at all'. *Whit* has an uncertain origin: it could be from 'white', meaning 'a small white spot', so that *not a whit* means 'not the tiniest part'.

Macduff has arrived at Macbeth's castle early in the morning to rouse King Duncan, at the King's request. He apologises to Macbeth for the early arrival, with these words. *Joyful* is ironic, under the circumstances, as Macbeth knows, and we do too, that Duncan is already cold and dead …

MᴬCᵀBETH

# I cannot tell if to depart in silence
# Or bitterly to speak in your reproof
# Best fitteth my degree or your condition.

———— ∞ ————

Leave in silence, or give someone a piece of your mind? Can you leave with your dignity intact? Do you feel that it's worth speaking to how you feel when you're upset – will it do any good? And what to do when faced with a challenge to your beliefs? Today's quote will resonate with anyone who has these questions.

Perhaps, if you find yourself in a tense moment, some wise advice might be gleaned from the philosophical Jacques, in *As You Like It*, who offers:

'Tis good to be sad and say nothing

– although Jacques also says he prefers melancholy to laughing. (*Sad* here could mean 'sorrowful', though it more commonly meant 'serious'.)

*Degree* ('rank') and *condition* ('social position') were factors that would sway a decision in Shakespeare's day, as they were felt to be essential features in the fabric of society. *O, when degree is shaked*, says Ulysses in *Troilus and Cressida, Then enterprise is sick*. He later adds,

Take but degree away, untune that string,
And hark what discord follows!

And people needed to know who they were talking to. It's one of the first things the King asks Alexander Iden in *Henry 6 Part 2: What is thy degree?*

*Degree* also made it clear where you should sit at a banquet, as when the newly crowned King Macbeth greets the Scottish lords:

You know your own degrees, sit down.

RICHARD III

Richard wants the Mayor of London and the citizens to beg him to take the royal crown. Buckingham tries to persuade him too, and these lines are spoken by Richard in reply. He doesn't depart in silence, of course, but continues the charade before finally accepting the kingship.

I do not like 'But yet'; it does allay
The good precedence. Fie upon 'But yet'!
'But yet' is as a gaoler to bring forth
Some monstrous malefactor.

— ∞ —

Anyone being brought good news would suddenly feel on their guard if their news-bringer went on to say, 'However …'.

In Shakespeare's time, *but yet* was a way of saying 'however'. Olivia in *Twelfth Night* judges Orsino in the following way: she lists his good qualities, and then concludes, *But yet I cannot love him.*

The speaker of today's lead quote feels that words like this tend to *allay* ('spoil' or 'dilute') *the good precedence* (the 'nice previous utterance').

*Fie* is a great word. It's a sound that was generally understood to mean 'an exclamation of disgust'. *Fie upon it* might translate nowadays to 'darn it!' *Malefactor* means 'evil-doer', and the two *m*s make *monstrous malefactor* go very well together, especially when said out loud.

Competitive television programmes are especially prone to *but yet*. Having praised a contestant for a piece of dancing or cookery, judges often continue with an ominous 'however', before launching into a list of criticisms …

A messenger brings Cleopatra news of Antony, and starts with the good news, that Antony is well and friends with Caesar. When the messenger tries to tell her the bad news, he begins *But yet, madam* – and she interrupts him with these words …

ANTONY &
CLEOPATRA

**But words are words; I never yet did hear
That the bruised heart was pieced through
the ear.**

— ∞ —

Words get a mixed reception among Shakespeare's characters

*Words are but wind*, says Dromio in *The Comedy of Errors*, but those in love tend to believe in them – Ophelia recalls how Hamlet sent her love letters with

> Words of so sweet breath composed
> As made the things more rich.

Many consider words unnecessary, like Queen Isabel in *Richard 2*, who says it *boots not* ('it's of no use') to *complain* ('lament' rather than 'object to') about what she *wants* ('lacks'):

> For what I have I need not to repeat,
> And what I want it boots not to complain.

When Troilus and Cressida meet for the first time, he can't speak – he's dumbstruck at the sight of Cressida, and says rather sweetly,

> You have bereft me of all words, lady.

And Cressida's uncle Pandarus offers, perhaps rather lewdly:

> Words pay no debts, give her deeds.

As today's lead quote suggests, words can struggle to *piece* ('mend') a broken heart. Only deeds can do that.

A hug, a touch, a look, a pony or a diamond ring (especially on a birthday) can sometimes do the work of a thousand words.

The Duke of Venice has given Brabantio a set of maxims that he hopes will help him accept the marriage of his daughter, Desdemona, to Othello. Brabantio finds the advice ambiguous, and dismisses the maxims with these lines …

# I do not much dislike the matter, but
# The manner of his speech.

— ∞ —

'It's not what they said, but the way that they said it'. Very often the *matter* ('content') is acceptable, but the tone of voice, or an infelicitous choice of words, can be the pang that pinches.

Someone's choice of words can readily elicit praise: Don Armado in *Love's Labour's Lost* describes the 'afternoon' as *the posteriors of the day*, and this appeals to the schoolmaster Holofernes: *the word is well culled, choice, sweet, and apt.*

But not all words are favoured. Doll in *Henry 4 Part 2* comments that *occupy ... was an excellent good word before it was ill-sorted* – it fell into bad company (because *occupy* could also mean 'fornicate'). And Benedick in *Much Ado About Nothing* scorns Claudio, newly in love, for the way romantic words have replaced his military ones:

> His words are a very fantastical banquet, just so many strange dishes.

In *King John*, folk who engage in bombastic speech have a hard time:

> Here's a large mouth, indeed,
> That spits forth death and mountains, rocks and seas,
> Talks as familiarly of roaring lions
> As maids of thirteen do of puppy-dogs.

Puppies are mentioned eleven times in the plays; here's one from *Henry 8*, for when someone's nagging you (*presently* means 'immediately'):

> Servant: Do you hear, master porter?
> Porter: I shall be with you presently, good master puppy.

ANTONY &
CLEOPATRA

Octavius Caesar and Antony are arguing with each other. Enobarbus and Maecenas try to calm them down, and Caesar becomes calmer with these words – though he doubts that any friendship will last, as their temperaments are so different.

# Happy are they that hear their detractions and can put them to mending.

— ∞ —

Hearing of your *detractions* ('the worst things about you') can bring some people down, but if you can reframe these criticisms as opportunities for *mending* ('self-improvement') then that can bring great happiness.

In *Measure for Measure*, the Duke points out that living can be a complex business – that the mercurial quality of happiness is always just around the corner with That Next Thing we desire:

> **Happy thou art not,**
> **For what thou hast not, still thou striv'st to get,**
> **And what thou hast, forget'st.**

And if you need some advice, or aren't happy with someone, then perhaps the nicest way of asking them for a chat is by using this line, from *Coriolanus*:

> **I would crave a word or two,**
> **The which shall turn you to no further harm**
> **Than so much loss of time.**

If you don't like *crave* (which here means 'beg'), then you can use *beseech*, as Longaville does with Boyet in *Love's Labour's Lost*: *I beseech you a word.*

And if you want to be extra polite, especially to someone you need to pay respect to, then using *vouchsafe* (which means 'allow' or 'permit') will do the job, as Egeon does in *The Comedy of Errors*:

> **Most mighty Duke, vouchsafe me speak a word.**

Benedick has overheard Don Pedro and Claudio describing how Beatrice loves him, but in the process he's also heard what they really think of him, and says, *I hear how I am censured* – 'judged, criticised'. He especially notes their criticism that he's against marriage – and he's determined to change.

# How will this fadge?

*Fadge* is an unusual word, and a terrific one to speak out loud (try it now: it's a similar sort of sound to 'fudge').

It appears out of nowhere in the last decades of the 16th century, and etymologists, studying the origin of words, have absolutely no idea where it came from.

It seems to have been quite popular because of its punchy sound. It continued in use into the 19th century, and is probably still around in some dialects – perhaps you use it, or your grandparents did?

Shakespeare uses it just twice: here, it has the general sense 'turn out' or 'end up' – you could use today's quote if you're not sure whether your team is going to win a game.

The other time he uses it is in *Love's Labour's Lost*, when Don Armado asks Holofernes and Nathaniel to help organise a pageant for the King and the Princess of France. Holofernes has an idea, and here *fadge* carries a meaning of 'succeed', or 'be suitable':

> We will have, if this fadge not, an antic.

Here, an *antic* meant 'a fantastic spectacle'. It could also be 'a bizarre dance' or any kind of grotesque entertainment, as when the Gaoler's Daughter fantasises in *The Two Noble Kinsmen*, and says, *We'll dance an antic 'fore the Duke.*

TWELFTH
NIGHT

The disguised Viola is reflecting on the complicated set of relationships that has arisen after her visit to Olivia on Orsino's behalf. Orsino loves Olivia; Viola loves Orsino; and now Olivia has fallen in love with Viola, thinking her to be a man. She's no idea how all this will *fadge* – sort itself out.

# What's the new news at the new court?

— ∞ —

A Shakespearean equivalent of 'Hey, how's it going?', 'What's up?', 'What's new with you?', or 'What's going down in David-town?'.

In a world when most news was spread by word of mouth, characters are often keen to hear the latest: they ask each other *What news?* or *What's the news?*.

Also in *As You Like It*, Rosalind coins a new(s) turn of phrase when Monsieur Le Beau arrives, brimming with news:

> Celia: Here comes Monsieur the Beau.
> Rosalind: With his mouth full of news.
> Celia: Which he will put on us, as pigeons feed their young.
> Rosalind: Then shall we be news-crammed.

(Celia's *put* means 'force'.)

Oliver has a plan in mind to harm his brother Orlando, but before he unveils it he asks what's been happening in the new court of Duke Frederick, who has usurped the throne and banished his brother, Duke Senior.

AS YOU LIKE IT

# A night is but small breath and little pause
# To answer matters of this consequence.

— ∞ —

It can be easy to rush into decisions too quickly; modern life (and especially the internet) is filled with urgency, pressing us to act or buy before it's too late.

Faced with big decisions (or purchases), reach for this line. (Though it might be poorly said after a marriage proposal, and would not go down at all well in response to a waiter asking what you'd like to eat.)

One of our favourite 'night' quotes is from *King Lear*, useful when with a friend who insists on going out in torrential rain (*naughty* here means 'nasty' or 'horrible', while *swim* gives the impression of a lot of rain):

’Tis a naughty night to swim in.

And from *The Tempest*, a line for anyone who feels that words of a serious nature are not fit for night, or the first moment of meeting – and certainly not for the breakfast table:

No more yet of this,
For ’tis a chronicle of day by day,
Not a relation for a breakfast, nor
Befitting this first meeting.

The combination of breath and pause is also seen in *Henry 4 Part 1*, when Falstaff and Prince Hal trade insults. After a particularly rich and inventive stream of acrimonious vituperation from Falstaff, Hal says: *Well, breathe awhile, and then to it again* – 'Let's catch our breath, and then get into it once more'. A quote fit for the day or the night.

The French King has told the English ambassadors that he'll respond to their demands the following day. They point out that speed is essential, as the English army is already in France. The King replies with these words ...

# Our foster-nurse of nature is repose.

— ⁓ —

What can be done to restore our minds to health? Shakespeare is unequivocal: *repose* ('sleep') is the *foster-nurse* ('nanny') of *nature* ('mortal life').

Sleep can escape some, like the King in *Henry 4 Part 2*:

> O sleep, O gentle sleep,
> Nature's soft nurse, how have I frighted thee,
> That thou no more wilt weigh my eyelids down
> And steep my senses in forgetfulness?

And from *The Tempest* – sleep can elude us when we're upset:

> Do not omit the heavy offer of it.
> It seldom visits sorrow; when it doth,
> It is a comforter.

The poet in *The Rape of Lucrece* agrees:

> Now leaden slumber with life's strength doth fight,
> And every one to rest themselves betakes,
> Save thieves and cares and troubled minds that wakes.

And Macbeth reminds us that when we have strange thoughts in our head, we probably just *lack the season of all natures, sleep* (here, *season* is a 'preservative', something that keeps the mind whole). He describes our nocturnal rest as:

> Sleep that knits up the ravelled sleave of care,
> The death of each day's life, sore labour's bath,
> Balm of hurt minds, great nature's second course,
> Chief nourisher in life's feast.

*Sleave* here literally means 'threads', although the similar-sounding modern word 'sleeve' works here too. *Ravelled* means 'tangled'.

Every Shakespeare play contains a reference to sleep, or to dreams.

KING LEAR

Lear has been wandering around singing, with weeds about his head. Cordelia asks what can be done to restore his mind to health, and this is the doctor's reply.

# The day shall not be up so soon as I
# To try the fair adventure of tomorrow.

— ∞ —

To *try a fair adventure* ('accomplish a promising enterprise'), then get up before dawn. 'The early bird catches the worm', we might say. *Day … be up* might sound unusual, until we switch *day* for 'sun'; there's a similar expression in *Macbeth*, when Fleance observes: *The moon is down* ('The moon hasn't risen yet'). *Adventure* has a much less dramatic meaning than our modern sense of 'an exciting experience, often involving risk, peril or daring', so we have to forget any association with Indiana Jones (although there's no harm in saying today's lead quote this way, all heroic and bold).

*Antony and Cleopatra* offers a slightly more poetic alternative (*betime* means 'early in the morning'):

> To business that we love we rise betime
> And go to't with delight.

And for those running late, and wanting to hurry others along (especially if you feel they're wasting time, or if they're online and idly doom-scrolling), call out this line from *The Merry Wives of Windsor*:

> We burn daylight!

This line from *Henry 4 Part 1* is good for when a friend asks what time it is, but you know they're only interested in eating, drinking and sleeping:

> What a devil hast thou to do with the time of the day?

*What a devil …* was a way of saying 'What the devil …' – useful when you're surprised by a friend waking up late in the morning, demanding adventure. As is this, from *Twelfth Night*:

> More matter for a May morning!

KING JOHN

The Dauphin is tired after a long day's fighting against the English. As he wishes his followers a good night, he feels excited about what the next day will bring. (In fact, he will make an offer of peace – and it will be accepted.)

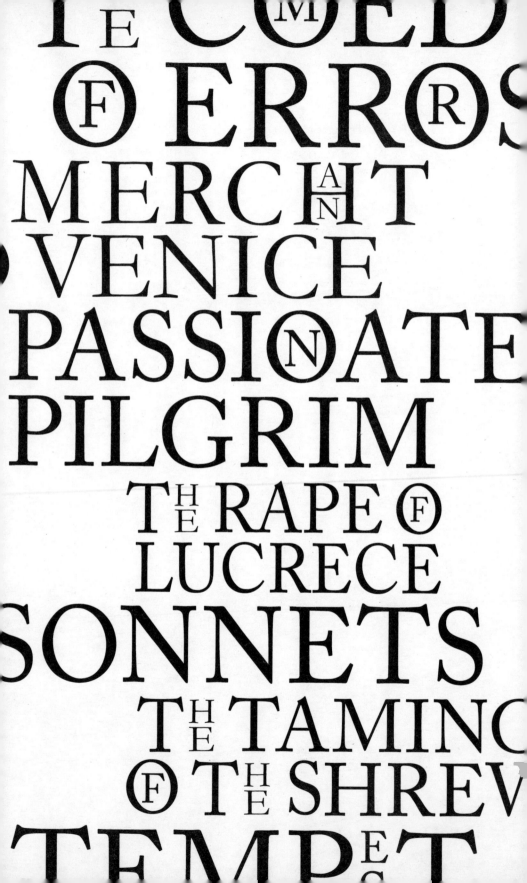

**In Nature's infinite book of secrecy
A little I can read.**

— ∞ —

A soothsayer is called to talk to Cleopatra's maids, Charmian and Iras. Charmian asks if the man 'knows things', and this is his reply. He then proceeds to tell their fortunes …

ANT🜨NY &
CLE🜨ATRA

O mickle is the powerful grace that lies
In plants, herbs, stones, and their true qualities.
For naught so vile that on the earth doth live
But to the earth some special good doth give.

———∞———

*Mickle* means 'great, much, large'. Today's quote is a strong statement of respect for the biodiversity of our planet, an assertion that everything in nature has its own *mickle grace* ('great qualities') and powers. O is the invitation for an emotional sound of some kind – perhaps here, a gasp of appreciation?

So, even though it might appear *vile* ('of little worth' rather than the modern 'disgusting') to the eye, everything has a special role to play in maintaining what we could describe as an ecological balance.

Friar Lawrence is pottering about in his garden early in the morning, and reflecting about the plants growing there. He will soon be interrupted by Romeo, with news of a new love ...

## Nature does require
## Her times of preservation.

— ∞ —

A line about the way the natural world works. Also fit to be used while making jam.

*Nature* means 'Mother Nature'.

And, if you talk about yourself in the third person, you can turn this line to your advantage. 'David does require his time of preservation', says Ben's co-author, sipping an evening glass of wine.

Also, if anyone calls you lazy lying there in the sun, then utter this quote, and don't even lift up your sunglasses.

King Henry has seen evidence that Cardinal Wolsey has been using the Church's money for himself. The King begins a leading conversation by asking how Wolsey balances his earthly and spiritual functions, and Wolsey replies that he devotes some time to spirituality, some to state business, and some to what he calls *preservation*, 'relaxation'. His explanations will not save him.

HENRY VIII

**Now would I give a thousand furlongs of sea for an acre of barren ground. Long heath, brown furze, anything.**

— ∞ —

One for the seasick. Or airsick, for that matter.

(Not that this was a problem in Shakespeare's time. *Horsesick*, on the other hand. Or *cartsick* …)

It's the opening scene of the play. The ship carrying King Alonso and his companions is about to be wrecked in a magical storm. The counsellor Gonzalo is convinced they will not drown, but nonetheless wishes he was on land, even a small, worthless piece of land, so long as it was dry …

THE TEMPEST

# This earthly world, where to do harm
# Is often laudable, to do good sometime
# Accounted dangerous folly.

— ⌘ —

The fight between good and evil drives the plot in many of Shakespeare's plays, and motivates the heart of many characters too. *Laudable* means 'deserving praise'; *folly* here means 'foolishness' or 'madness'.

It's a curious world, says this speaker, where people who do evil things are rewarded, and people reaching for good are *accounted* ('described') as dangerous, and *full of folly* ('foolish'). *Measure for Measure* echoes this:

> Some rise by sin, and some by virtue fall.

The contrary is affirmed in *All's Well That Ends Well* (*we must do good against evil*); and the entire premise is seen more optimistically in *Henry 5* on the morning of the Battle of Agincourt, as Henry encourages his army:

> There is some soul of goodness in things evil,
> Would men observingly distil it out.

There is always good to be found in the bad, and it's easy to see and untangle, with proper observation. (*Men* stands for 'humans'.) Henry concludes:

> Thus may we gather honey from the weed,
> And make a moral of the devil himself.

The moral of the day? We can take good from the bad, wisdom from the worst matters, and turn the dark side back against itself.

May the fourth be with you.

Lady Macduff has been left alone with her children. A messenger warns of impending danger and advises her to flee. She says she has done no harm – but then reflects on the nature of the world with these lines, shortly before murderers enter …

# There are more things in heaven and earth, Horatio, Than are dreamt of in your philosophy.

— ∞ —

Whatever you believe, whether you feel science has all the answers, or that there are things in the universe beyond our wildest dreams, this quote is for you.

*Philosophy* could mean 'way of thinking about things', as when people talk about their 'philosophy of life'. Horatio is Hamlet's friend and fellow student of philosophy, and he's pretty famous now – this is one of the more commonly-quoted lines in Shakespeare. It can be used if you encounter a belief differing from your own, and want to (respectfully) disagree.

In one of the first editions of *Hamlet*, today's lead quote runs like this:

> There are more things in heaven and earth, Horatio,
> Than are dreamt of in our philosophy.

This slight edit turns the quote into an agreement, the *our* perhaps in reference to humanity as a whole, suggesting that there are greater things out there than many of us can possibly imagine.

It's thought that Shakespeare tweaked his writing as he worked with his actors. If he often changed what he wrote, we can too. So there's room for you to make this quote your own: Horatio can be changed to Margaret, May, Mary, Frank, Freddie, Father, or …

Hamlet, Horatio and Marcellus have encountered a ghost. Hamlet asks them to be sworn to secrecy. They're reluctant, and the ghost calls on them three times to swear. Hamlet moves away from the voice, and each time the voice follows them. As they dart about, Horatio exclaims: *this is wondrous strange*, and these words of Hamlet's follow …

## In the night, imagining some fear,
## How easy is a bush supposed a bear?

— ∞ —

This line nicely echoes the quote on April 11th.

Perhaps you can remember lying awake at night as a child and imagining terrifying things born from the innocent shadows. According to this speaker, such fears never leave us.

One sense of *imagination* in Shakespeare's time was 'delusion' or 'fancy', and we hear this in *King Lear*, when the blinded Gloucester wishes he were mad. That way, he thinks, he would have *wrong imaginations* that would make him forget his griefs.

And in *The Merry Wives of Windsor*, Page criticises Ford for thinking that Falstaff is in his house. When they've searched everywhere and found nobody he says, *What devil suggests this imagination?*

Bears were relatively common creatures in London, used for the cruel sport of bear-baiting, and were probably best well-avoided. According to Prospero in *The Tempest*, bears are *ever-angry*. Dromio in *The Comedy of Errors* is in no doubt: *from a bear a man would run for life*. And Fabian in *Twelfth Night* describes Andrew, frightened to fight with the disguised and equally fearful Viola, as someone who *looks pale as if a bear were at his heels*.

They're right to be scared: in *The Winter's Tale*, we see Lord Antigonus *Exit, pursued by a bear* (which then literally makes a meal of the poor man).

Duke Theseus and Hippolyta discuss the strange story that the lovers have told them about the previous night. Theseus thinks their tale is due to the fevered imagination of people in love; but Hippolyta thinks there was more to the night than that ...

A MIDSUMMER NIGHT'S DREAM

## The night comes on and the bleak winds
## Do sorely ruffle.

—— ∞ ——

Words for when we're inside at night-time and hear a storm brewing – or, worse, when we have to go out in it. Here's more, from *King Lear*:

> Here's a night pities neither wise men nor fools.

– the type of night that will bring comfort to no one. Lear's servant Kent is also incisive in his comments:

> Things that love night
> Love not such nights as these.

And Lennox in *Macbeth* offers:

> The night has been unruly ...
> My young remembrance cannot parallel
> A fellow to it.

While Lord Cerimon, in *Pericles*, witnesses a storm the like of which he's never experienced before:

> Such a night as this
> Till now I ne'er endured.

Indeed the storm has been so severe that it has caused the sailors on Pericles' ship, passing nearby, to throw the coffin of his apparently dead wife overboard. It will arrive in due course on Cerimon's shore ...

Many of these quotes could also be companions for someone plagued by nightmares ...

KING LEAR

Furious at his children's words, Lear leaves his daughter Regan's castle. There's the sound of a storm, and night is falling. Gloucester goes out after him, but returns with these words of the worsening weather, as Cornwall has the castle doors closed against the old king ...

# I have been troubled in my sleep this night, But dawning day new comfort hath inspired.

— ∞ —

That comforting feeling, after a troubled night's sleep, of looking out and seeing the warm colours of dawn; the promise of a good day ahead.

*Good dawning* was an early-morning greeting in Shakespeare's time – *Good dawning to thee, friend*, says Oswald in *King Lear*. A little later in the day he would have said *Good day* or *Good morrow*. 'Good morning' didn't become popular until the 18th century.

Mornings are evocatively painted in words by Shakespeare. In *Hamlet*, Horatio gives a magnificently poetic description of the new day:

> The morn in russet mantle clad
> Walks o'er the dew of yon high eastward hill.

A *russet* ('reddish-brown') glow in the east seems to resemble a *mantle* (a 'loose sleeveless cloak'); *clad* means 'clothed': the sun flowing across the dew-laden grass of an eastern hill, like a rippling reddish-brown cloak …

*Julius Caesar* has a good description of the breaking dawn, too:

> Yon grey lines
> That fret the clouds, are messengers of day.

Nowhere else in his writings does Shakespeare use *messenger* to talk about something as ethereal as atmospheric phenomena. *Fret* is normally used to describe a repeating ornamental design, like you might find on a ceiling of a beautiful house. In one other place it's applied to the atmosphere, when Hamlet reflects on the air above the earth, describing it as *this majestical roof fretted with golden fire*.

You'll never need to say, 'Ooh, it looks like a nice day', ever again.

Titus is in an ebullient mood, unaware that soon disaster will strike him and his family. There will be no further comfort for him in the rest of the play.

The grey-eyed morn smiles
  on the frowning night,
Chequering the eastern clouds
  with streaks of light,
And darkness fleckled like a drunkard reels
From forth day's pathway made
  by Titan's wheels.

— ❧ —

A fine description of a sunrise. *Fleckled* is a lovely mixture of 'flecked', 'dappled', and 'speckled'. *Titan* was the sun god (also known as Helios), who pulls the sun across the sky in a horse-drawn chariot. Here, he erratically (like the way a drunkard walks or staggers) displaces darkness as he blazes a path across the sky.

We don't have to be living near mountains to appreciate the beauty of these lines from one of his *Sonnets*, though it seems Shakespeare must have done at some point:

Full many a glorious morning have I seen
Flatter the mountain-tops with sovereign eye,
Kissing with golden face the meadows green,
Gilding pale streams with heavenly alchemy.

*Sovereign eye* gifts the sense of an imperious but proud and warm greeting.

*Alchemy* was the medieval study of physical substances, especially exploring the possibility of changing base metal into gold. Here, the word suggests the idea of 'wondrous transformation', caused by the sun reflecting on the water, and the sonnet offers that the filter of love turns everything to perfection.

Romeo is leaving Juliet, after their first meeting, full of the joys of love. He describes the sunrise as he makes his way to Friar Lawrence to arrange his marriage. Some editors give these words to Lawrence, as he tends his garden.

# It is the bright day that brings forth the adder,
# And that craves wary walking.

These lines advise caution – but not just in relation to where to walk on a sunny day. As the temperature increases, so does the temperament; blood boils, and so the line invites us to be wary.

Heat was often used as a metaphor for anger, passion and desire, as it still is.

Benvolio (in *Romeo and Juliet*, worrying about meeting a gang of Capulets, and a fight brewing) agrees:

> For now, these hot days, is the mad blood stirring.

The heat of the day makes the Bastard in *King John* expect trouble:

> This day grows wondrous hot.
> Some airy devil hovers in the sky
> And pours down mischief.

Today, we know the adder's bite is rarely fatal. But in Shakespeare's time it was thought to be very deadly; indeed, the goddess in *Venus and Adonis* hears hounds barking, and it makes her jump:

> ... like one that spies an adder
> Wreathed up in fatal folds just in his way.

Brutus wonders what will happen if Caesar is crowned. He thinks such a *bright day* could change his nature, turning Caesar into a harmful tyrant. These thoughts motivate him to join the conspiracy, and kill Caesar ...

# Men judge by the complexion of the sky
# The state and inclination of the day.

— ∞ —

It's natural to look at the sky and comment on the weather. Today's lead quote reflects on the way people (not just *men*, of course) interpret the *complexion* ('appearance') of the sky as an indication of whether the day's events will be successful or not.

As we'll soon see (on May 15th), this idea of 'prophetic fallacy' is taken further in *King Lear*, where some suggest that the maddened King's mental and emotional state creates a terrible storm. It's there too in *Julius Caesar*, where the weather is very much a reflection of human events. Casca and Cicero meet on the streets of Rome during a great squall of thunder and lightning. Casca says he has never experienced a storm like it. There has to be a supernatural explanation, he thinks:

> Either there is a civil strife in heaven,
> Or else the world, too saucy with the gods,
> Incenses them to send destruction.

Edmund, in *King Lear*, hears his father worrying about the recent eclipses of the sun and moon – he's sure they *portend no good* (*portend* means 'signify'). He pours scorn on such thinking, and on the Zodiac too:

> This is the excellent foppery of the world, that when we are sick in fortune – often the surfeits of our own behaviour – we make guilty of our disasters the sun, the moon, and stars, as if we were villains on necessity.

Sir Stephen Scroop brings King Richard news about the state of the rebellion against him. Richard can see from his face that the news is bad, and with these lines Scroop confirms that *his dull and heavy eye warns of a sad tale …*

RI<sup>C</sup><sub>H</sub>ARD II

When clouds are seen, wise men
   put on their cloaks;
When great leaves fall, the winter is at hand;
When the sun sets, who doth not
   look for night?
Untimely storms make men expect a dearth.

— ∞ —

*Dearth* means 'a shortage', often of food.

These words are from a speaker warning about difficult times ahead, and thinking about inevitability. The first line suggests something can be done about the impending situation; the middle lines, and especially the third, imply that actually there's nothing anyone can do; and the last line offers the thought that an unexpected event is a bad omen. There's an air of superstition, which runs through Shakespeare's time, that's present here.

Clouds in Shakespeare, when used to describe moods and situations, are always an indication that something is wrong. When Gloucester describes Suffolk's *cloudy brow* in *Henry 6 Part 2*, he means 'sullen' or 'gloomy'. Edward in *Henry 6 Part 3* reports the Queen's forces as *a black, suspicious, threatening cloud*. And Agrippa in *Antony and Cleopatra* labels Caesar as having *a cloud in's face* – a 'troubled look on his face'.

*In clouds* is a good expression, meaning 'suspicious', 'filled with uncertainties', or 'hard to perceive': in *Hamlet*, Claudius uses it to depict the approach of Laertes, saying *he keeps himself in clouds*.

RICHARD III

The citizens are talking about what will happen now that King Edward is dead. All are gloomy, anticipating the worst. The First Citizen is the most optimistic – *All shall be well* – but the Third Citizen is a pessimist, and comes out with this series of analogies. The Third turns out to be the better prophet.

Sometime we see a cloud that's dragonish,
A vapour sometime like a bear or lion,
A towered citadel, a pendent rock,
A forked mountain, or blue promontory
With trees upon't that nod unto the world
And mock our eyes with air.

---

We sit out on a sunny day, we look up at the clouds, and at some point, someone will say, 'I can see a dragon …'

*Apophenia*, the word used to describe finding patterns where none exists, was first coined by the neurologist and psychologist Klaus Conrad in 1958, but evidently we have been finding patterns in clouds for hundreds of years: the fine combination of human imagination and an ever-changing canvas.

Trinculo in *The Tempest*, wandering around Prospero's island for the first time, hears a noise of thunder and looks up at the sky:

Yond same black cloud, yond huge one, looks like a foul bombard that would shed his liquor.

He says the cloud looks like a large leather wine jug. And Hamlet, in his assumed madness, teases Polonius, who is desperate to humour him:

Hamlet: Do you see yonder cloud that's almost in shape of a camel?
Polonius: By th'mass, and 'tis like a camel indeed.
Hamlet: Methinks it is like a weasel.
Polonius: It is backed like a weasel.
Hamlet: Or like a whale.
Polonius: Very like a whale.

(*By th'mass* – swearing by the Roman Catholic Mass that celebrated the Last Supper, when Christ used bread and wine as symbols of his body and blood.)

ANTONY & CLEOPATRA

Antony despairs that Cleopatra has left him for Caesar. He compares the changing shape of clouds to his own state of mind.

# A thousand businesses are brief in hand,
# And heaven itself doth frown upon the land.

— ∞ —

'There's a lot on, many brief *businesses* ('pressing tasks') to take care of. And now it's raining, too.'

*Thousand* has been a way of expressing an indefinite but large number for a long time (the King in *Henry 6 Part 1* says he rests *perplexed with a thousand cares*). And numbering increases in line with the strength of feeling being expressed. Juliet wishes Romeo *A thousand times good night*! Later in the play, when she hears of Romeo's banishment from Verona for murdering her cousin Tybalt, she says:

> ... that one word 'banished',
> Hath slain ten thousand Tybalts.

And faced with a distraught Romeo, the Friar soothes him that he will be allowed back to Verona

> **With twenty hundred thousand times more joy.**

In *Henry 4 Part 1*, Prince Hal promises to fight Percy to the death, and promises his father that he

> **... will die a hundred thousand deaths**
> **Ere break the smallest parcel of this vow.**

But even these numbers pale beside the characters who voice their feelings in millions. Falstaff has a useful line if you ever need to wriggle out of an accusation that you owe someone a thousand pounds. Simply assure them that *thy love is worth a million*.

KING JOHN

The French have invaded Britain. The Bastard is reflecting on the current times after discovering the death of Prince Arthur and hearing that some of the English nobles are going over to the French side. There are indeed many urgent tasks to be carried out.

# 'Tis like to be loud weather.

— ∞ —

We see clouds gathering of dark purple; the wind picks up and howls around the house; the leaves suddenly jump up and dance around the lanes; the sun sets in a particular way; and we gauge the weather that is about to visit us.

*Like* means 'likely' here. Sometimes the kings in Shakespeare feel they can predict and instruct the weather. Here's King John:

> **So foul a sky clears not without a storm;**
> **Pour down thy weather!**

King Lear thinks he can command the weather too, and so here's a line for when you're on top of a hill, the wind blows around you, and you want to encourage it:

> **Blow, winds, and crack your cheeks! Rage! Blow!**

The grief-stricken Constance in *King John* has a quote for when you want to make yourself heard – if no one will listen, then get a voice like thunder:

> **O that my tongue were in the thunder's mouth!**
> **Then with a passion would I shake the world.**

Talking of thunderous voices, Clarence in *Richard 3* describes one of the two murderers sent to kill him:

> **Thy voice is thunder, but thy looks are humble.**

Antigonus carries baby Perdita to the wild shores of Bohemia, where he intends to leave her, as he was ordered. A sailor tells him not to go too far inland, as it's a dangerous place, with fierce animals, and a tempest is brewing. Both dangers come to be: the storm will wreck their ship, and Antigonus will be torn apart by a bear …

MAY 16TH

Like an unseasonable stormy day
Which makes the silver rivers
        drown their shores
As if the world were all dissolved to tears.

— ∞ —

This line offers the most beautiful alternative to simply saying, 'It's raining', in answer to the question, 'What's the weather like?'

Othello offers a line of love-greeting, for anyone who makes it through a dreadful storm – meteorological or psychological – and back to loving arms. His happiness at seeing Desdemona makes him feel that any disturbance, no matter how ferocious, would be worth experiencing if only she were there at the end of it:

If after every tempest come such calms,
May the winds blow till they have wakened death.

Sir Stephen Scroop has brought tidings of calamity to King Richard, reporting Henry Bolingbroke's successful march through England. He compares Bolingbroke's rage to a river overflowing its banks after a great storm.

RICHARD II

# Many can brook the weather that love not the wind.

———— ✂ ————

Many are able to *brook* ('put up with, endure, tolerate') something they don't like. In *Henry 4 Part 1* Hotspur says to Prince Hal, just before they fight: *I can no longer brook thy vanities.*

And if you can gauge from the wind that there will be a day of *tempest* ('rain'), then call to mind this line of Hal's:

> The southern wind
> Doth play the trumpet to his purposes,
> And by his hollow whistling in the leaves
> Foretells a tempest and a blustering day.

In Shakespeare's day, there was a widespread belief that a south wind brought plague-carrying mists. So Coriolanus offers a great curse:

> All the contagion of the south light on you!

*Light* means 'descend, fall'. The other winds had different qualities too: the north wind is described as *tyrannous* in *Cymbeline*, as *sharp* in *The Tempest*, as *angry* in *Titus Andronicus* and as *rude and impatient* by Emilia in *The Two Noble Kinsmen*.

By contrast, Emilia says how much she likes a rose *when the west wind courts her gently*. Demetrius in *A Midsummer Night's Dream* describes how snow is *fanned with the eastern wind*. Aumerle in *Richard 2* tells how the north-east wind *blew bitterly against our faces*.

And Trinculo in *The Tempest* wonders where he might find shelter to *bear off* ('keep away') the approaching storm:

> Here's neither bush nor shrub, to bear off any weather at all,
> and another storm brewing. I hear it sing i'th' wind.

He then finds a place to hide – under the large loose cloak of the half-man, half-fish, Caliban ...

LOVE's LABOR's LOST

Nathaniel is reflecting on the stupidity he sees in Constable Dull, and concludes that even though he finds his ignorance irritating, he will have to put up with it ...

**Such wind as scatters young men
through the world
To seek their fortunes farther than at home,
Where small experience grows.**

— ∞ —

What makes people (not just *men*) want to travel and see the world?

Some say it's the wind that blows them around, others that it's the lure of fortune – that home grows only small experience.

Falstaff, in *Henry 4 Part 2*, asks Pistol, *What wind blew you hither, Pistol?* Shakespeare uses a proverb to form Pistol's reply: *Not the ill wind which blows no man to good.*

This duet is a fine way for two friends to greet each other.

Shakespeare also used the proverb a little earlier in his career, in *Henry 6 Part 3*, when a soldier hopes to find money in the purse of someone he's just killed:

**Ill blows the wind that profits nobody.**

In other words, it's *ill* ('bad luck') not to *profit* ('take advantage') of something that's happened 'naturally'.

Petruchio has arrived in Padua from Verona and visits Hortensio, who asks him why he has come: *what happy gale / Blows you to Padua?* This is his reply.

# What fates impose, that men must needs abide; It boots not to resist both wind and tide.

— ∞ —

You may or may not believe in 'fate' these days, but when the road is blocked, and the train breaks down, and the flight is cancelled, perhaps the universe is telling you not to go on holiday? Sometimes, it can feel pointless to resist – and useful to allow yourself a moment to regroup.

*Abide* is rarely used today, and perhaps has an archaic feel to it; you'll encounter it more in literary and religious settings. It usually means 'remain' or 'stay', but in today's lead quote it has the more emotional sense of 'endure', or 'remain steadfast'.

*Boot* has an interesting extra meaning that's no longer used today. Rather than just something you'd wear, *boot* could also mean 'help' or 'benefit'. So the second line can be read as: 'It's useless to fight against wind and tide.'

Hotspur turns this word into a joke in *Henry 4 Part 1*. Glendower reminds everyone that he has fought with the King and *sent him bootless home* – 'sent him home unsuccessful'. Hotspur ripostes:

> Home without boots, and in foul weather too? How 'scapes he agues, in the Devil's name?

If he's only wearing socks, how does he escape getting an *ague* ('a fever')?

Evidently, Shakespeare not only sometimes wrote bad jokes, he also wrote characters that told bad jokes. The degree to which Hotspur's attempt at humour was a chuckle, guffaw or belly laugh will remain lost to history (for more on jests, jokes and tomfoolery, see June 19th).

Edward Duke of York has been declared King, replacing Henry 6. But the Duke of Warwick attacks Edward's battle camp, takes the crown from his head, and sends him back home to York. Edward utters these lines before being forcibly led out – but his fortunes will take a turn for the better …

# This world to me is like a lasting storm, Whirring me from my friends.

—— ∞ ——

Sometimes, it can feel like the world – and all that loves you, and all you love in it – turns away. Or, as *Richard 2* offers, that

> Every tedious stride I make
> Will but remember me what a deal of world
> I wander from the jewels that I love.

Departure can sometimes feel wrong, in our gut, and we can reach for comforts:

> This must my comfort be
> That sun that warms you here shall shine on me.

And a third from *Richard 2*, a play full of heartbreak and parting. Lovers often rhyme, so Richard's rhyming reply to his estranged wife perhaps indicates his true feelings for her:

> Queen Isabel: And must we be divided? Must we part?
> Richard: Ay, hand from hand, my love, and heart from heart.

Want to express your reluctance to leave? This line from *Romeo and Juliet* comes after the two young lovers have spent their first night together, and the banished Romeo must leave Verona:

> I have more care to stay than will to go.

*Care* and *will* overlap a little in meaning: both words express 'desire' or 'inclination', with a hint of 'concern' in care, and 'intention' in will. *Parting*, as Juliet says, *is such sweet sorrow.*

PERICLES

Marina is walking alone, filling a basket with flowers, and thinking of the way she was born in a tempest and lost her mother. These words reveal her state of mind.

**But to stand stained with travel, and sweating with desire to see him, thinking of nothing else, putting all affairs else in oblivion, as if there were nothing else to be done, but to see him.**

—— ∝∞ ——

The lengths we'll go to, when we miss someone, can be beyond measure.

Talking of length, as we're approaching midsummer, the next three days feature longer pieces, especially for the more adventurous memorisers and wannabe sonneteers amongst you.

So here's the beginning of a sonnet. It explores the feeling that the person we miss is sending forth their *spirit* ('soul'), pushing their image into our eyes by the power of their *will* ('desire', 'intention'):

> Is it thy will, thy image should keep open
> My heavy eyelids to the weary night?
> Dost thou desire my slumbers should be broken,
> While shadows like to thee do mock my sight?

*Like to thee* means 'like you, that remind me of you'. The sonnet later continues:

> O, no, thy love, though much, is not so great:
> It is my love that keeps mine eye awake;
> Mine own true love that doth my rest defeat,
> To play the watchman ever for thy sake:

*Rest* means 'sleep'. (*Great* and *defeat* would have rhymed.)

HENRY IV:II

Falstaff has travelled to London to see the newly crowned Henry 5 as he passes by. Falstaff expects his old friend, now the king, will do him some good. But the meeting does not turn out as Falstaff hopes; Henry tells him, *I know thee not, old man …*

If the dull substance of my flesh were thought,
Injurious distance should not stop my way,
For then despite of space I would be brought
From limits far remote where thou dost stay.
No matter then although my foot did stand
Upon the farthest earth removed from thee,
For nimble thought can jump both sea and land,
As soon as think the place where he would be.
But ah, thought kills me that I am not thought
To leap large lengths of miles
    when thou art gone ...

— ∞ —

Today's quote continues our three-part celebration of longer pieces of an everyday character. *Injurious* means 'doing me injury'. If only the power of our thoughts could take us across oceans in moments, to the one we love. Thoughts in the poems and plays are often described as flying. Hamlet assures his father's ghost that he will revenge speedily,

    **... with wings as swift**
    **As meditation or the thoughts of love.**

The speed of thought is helpful to a Chorus (who narrates and asks the audience to use their imagination). In *Henry 5* we hear the Chorus say:

    **Thus with imagined wing our swift scene flies**
    **In motion of no less celerity**
    **Than that of thought.**

(*Celerity* means 'alacrity, rapidity, swiftness'.)

THE SONNETS

The poet reflects on his love, and wishes his body were like thought – he could be there immediately! Togetherness would then be possible no matter where he was on earth. These lines follow, before reality returns: *But ah, thought kills me that I am not thought.*

# When I was at home I was in a better place, but travellers must be content.

— ❧ —

Anyone feeling homesick will find it easy to relate to this one. And, having decided to go on a journey, travellers have to be patient or *content* ('accepting'), especially when there's no going back.

However, most travellers in the plays seem to be discontented. The poet in *Sonnet 50* is certainly not in a contented mood as he leaves his love behind:

> How heavy do I journey on the way,
> When what I seek (my weary travel's end)
> Doth teach that ease and that repose to say
> Thus far the miles are measured from thy friend.

And now, to end our three-day celebration where we offer longer pieces of an everyday nature, here's *Sonnet 27*. The poet is glad to get to bed – but can find no peace from missing a loved one there (*lo* means 'look, behold'):

> Weary with toil, I haste me to my bed,
> The dear repose for limbs with travel tired,
> But then begins a journey in my head
> To work my mind, when body's work's expired.
>
> For then my thoughts (from far where I abide)
> Intend a zealous pilgrimage to thee,
> And keep my drooping eyelids open wide,
> Looking on darkness which the blind do see,
>
> Save that my soul's imaginary sight
> Presents thy shadow to my sightless view,
> Which like a jewel (hung in ghastly night)
> Makes black night beauteous, and her old face new.
>
> Lo, thus by day my limbs, by night my mind,
> For thee, and for myself, no quiet find.

AS YOU LIKE IT

Rosalind, Celia and Touchstone have fled from the court, and have now entered the Forest of Arden. Touchstone thinks himself a fool to be in such a place, but decides with these words that he just has to put up with it.

## All places that the eye of heaven visits
## Are to a wise man ports and happy havens.

———— ⌁ ————

Every exit is an entrance elsewhere; every departure an arrival. And there's no place on Earth where the *eye of heaven* – the sun – fails to shine. So the best way to think about travel, today's quote suggests, is to see the places you'll visit as a true source of wonder, delight and nourishment.

This is what drove Petruchio to Padua in *The Taming of the Shrew*. He says he's *come abroad to see the world* – although *abroad* meant 'away from home', rather than the modern sense of 'overseas'.

Travel is the future lying before Pistol in *The Merry Wives of Windsor* as he prepares to leave Falstaff's service – although his plans sound both practical and potentially violent:

> Why then, the world's mine oyster,
> Which I with sword will open.

Not everybody responds well to being invited away, especially if the prospect of international travel is in conflict with an ongoing love affair at home. Proteus feels this way in *The Two Gentlemen of Verona*, and the absence doesn't make his heart grow fonder. Instead, he grows more distant to his love, and becomes rivalrous with his closest friend.

Thus we find Romeo reacting badly to the Friar's attempt at comforting him, following news of his banishment: *Be patient, for the world is broad and wide* – 'there is so much to do, and so many places to explore'. But for Romeo, the world is only where Juliet is …

John of Gaunt and his banished son, Bolingbroke, are saying farewell, and may never see each other again. Gaunt offers his son these lines as comfort, suggesting that absence can be reframed as a journey taken for pleasure. Bolingbroke isn't convinced, and indeed, this turns out to be their last meeting …

**As full of spirit as the month of May,**
**And gorgeous as the sun at midsummer.**

— ∞ —

Great lines to say when you want to speak of someone you know who's full of amazing energy. Or someone you once knew who was light, bright and always beaming warmth at you. Or someone you miss terribly.

Shortly before the battle of Shrewsbury, Vernon gives Hotspur a sharp description of Prince Hal and his comrades.

HENRY IV:I

## How many goodly creatures are there here! How beauteous mankind is!

— ❧ —

*Goodly* is hardly ever used these days (and when it is, it's in slightly antiquated set phrases like 'a goodly sum of money'). Shakespeare uses it here to mean 'good-looking' and 'attractive', though it can also mean 'excellent'.

An evocative use of the word occurs in *The Merchant of Venice*, when Antonio describes a villain as

**A goodly apple rotten at the heart.**

Use today's lead quote when arriving at a party, or anywhere you see people you think are beautiful!

Miranda sees all the shipwrecked folk together. Having lived on an island all her life, this is the first time she's ever seen so many people (all of whom are men). These words express her amazement, and are followed by one of Shakespeare's best-known lines:

O, brave new world,
That has such people in't!

THE TEMPEST

A good leg will fall; a straight back will
stoop; a black beard will turn white;
a curled pate will grow bald; a fair face
will wither; a full eye will wax hollow:
but a good heart … is the sun and the moon – or
rather, the sun, and not the moon; for it
shines bright and never changes, but keeps
his course truly.

— ∞ —

A testament for the worth, power and beauty of a good heart.

*Pate* meant 'skull, head'; *wax* means 'turn'. The moon was a symbol
of inconstancy, ever changing its appearance – whereas the sun always
appears the same.

Henry is wooing Princess Katherine. He contrasts
himself with those who can woo with flowery
eloquence, and says he will speak to her *plain
soldier* … but then produces this rhetorical flourish,
attempting to affirm his constancy.

HENRY V

Wherefore look'st thou sad,
When everything doth make a gleeful boast?
The birds chant melody on every bush,
The snake lies rolled in the cheerful sun,
The green leaves quiver with the cooling wind
And make a chequered shadow on the ground.

———— ∞ ————

These lines ask, 'Why do we ever look or feel sad or serious, when there is beauty in everything?'

*Wherefore* means 'why'; *sad* could mean 'feeling sorrow', but more often meant 'serious' or 'solemn'. Cleopatra, when she interrogates Alexas about Antony in *Antony and Cleopatra*, asks *What was he, sad or merry?*

This idea runs through Shakespeare's writing: whether at its worst or its best, life is, in and of itself, perfect. In its ups and downs, its infinite expanse and microscopic detail, its endless loop of birth and death ... – amid it all, it's important to stop, to listen to the wind in the trees and the birds singing, to feel the breeze on our faces.

With the snakes lolling around, these lines give an image of Eden-like perfection – it's almost too good. Birds chanting melody sounds like a description of a scene from a Disney movie.

The message is to not take everything so seriously: to ask someone who's frowning 'Why so serious?' when the weather is fine and nature is at its best – though perhaps not everyone would be so gleeful around the rolling snakes ...

Tamora (the former Queen of the Goths, now wed to Emperor Saturnine) encounters her lover Aaron in the forest. She's evidently in a romantic mood, but Aaron has only two things in mind: vengeance and murder.

# How still the evening is,
# As hushed on purpose to grace harmony!

— ⌒∞⌒ —

The time of day when the sun has set, there's no wind, and everything is quiet ...

The speaker is waiting for music to be played, and (evidently feeling poetic) suggests that the evening is so aware of the gracefulness of music that it's caused everything to fall silent in anticipation.

Often we see Shakespeare examine an idea and, in a different play, turn the jewel of thought ever so slightly, find fresh words and put it in a new setting. Lorenzo in *The Merchant of Venice* speaks to Jessica in a similar vein, as they sit outside Portia's house waiting for her musicians to begin playing:

> ... soft stillness and the night
> Become the touches of sweet harmony.

As these two eloped lovers sit in the moonlight on a very calm and clear night, the couple engage in a series of imaginative reflections about other night-times, recalling ancient tales about other lovers ... Lorenzo opens with this description:

> In such a night as this,
> When the sweet wind did gently kiss the trees
> And they did make no noise.

And finally for today, three lines for the end of something beautiful, from *Richard 2*. Whether it be a day, a storm, a rainbow, party, meeting or relationship – you know it'll stay in your memory forever:

> The setting sun, and music at the close,
> As the last taste of sweets, is sweetest last,
> Writ in remembrance more than things long past.

Claudio and Don Pedro are taking an evening walk in Leonato's garden, and are about to listen to Balthasar sing. Claudio remarks on how the stillness is a perfect setting for music – and it will also soon help them be easily overheard by Benedick ...

**The weary sun hath made a golden set**
**And by the bright track of his fiery car**
**Gives token of a goodly day tomorrow.**

— ∞ —

Proverbs about the weather can be found in the earliest records. One of the commonest is 'Red sky at night ...', where either shepherds or sailors have 'delight', as the next day promises to be fair. Today's lead quote offers a more powerful description of the golden glow that can accompany the *set* ('setting') of the sun – which has been out all day, for it's weary.

*Car* here means a 'carriage'. (In Greek lore, the god Apollo (or Helios) pulled the sun across the sky in a horse-drawn chariot. In the Roman tradition, the god was known as Phoebus.)

A nice sunset can give us hope that the next day will be a good one. Indeed, *Antony and Cleopatra* reminds us that if today doesn't go well, then there's always tomorrow:

> I will hope
> Of better deeds tomorrow.

And in *All's Well That Ends Well*, Helena reminds us that all bad will eventually come to good, in time:

> The time will bring on summer,
> When briars shall have leaves as well as thorns
> And be as sweet as sharp.

In *Henry 6 Part 2*, the King describes political dangers as thorns that can be cleared with a sharp blade:

> To mow down thorns that would annoy our foot,
> Is worthy praise.

The Earl of Richmond arrives at Bosworth Field to do battle with Richard. He thinks the weather is auspicious, and so is in a positive mood as he settles down to draw up plans for the fight.

# The dragon wing of night o'erspreads the earth.

— ⚬⚬ —

What sort of night is being captured? Looking at the way dragons are described in the plays, the quality of night becomes clearer.

Puck in *A Midsummer Night's Dream* tells Oberon they'll have to be quick to resolve the lovers' confusions, as dawn is approaching, and dragons (which carry the night) are fast:

> My fairy lord, this must be done with haste,
> For night's swift dragons cut the clouds full fast,
> And yonder shines Aurora's harbinger.

(*Haste* would have rhymed with *fast* in Shakespeare's time.) Aurora was the Roman goddess of the dawn; a *harbinger* is someone or something that signals the approach of another.

In *Cymbeline*, Iachimo, having managed to smuggle himself into Innogen's bedchamber (so he may describe it to Posthumus, and win a horrible bet), returns to his hiding place in a trunk. Fearful of discovery, Iachimo urges that same dragonish speed and hopes the night will be over soon:

> Swift, swift, you dragons of the night.

The size of dragons is implied by Gloucester in *Henry 6 Part 1*, describing the dead Henry 5:

> His arms spread wider than a dragon's wings.

And an assassin is hinted at in *Pericles* by Antiochus:

> ... deathlike dragons here affright thee hard.

It would seem, then, that dragons are huge, move very quickly and aren't very pleasant. So neither is the night described in today's lead quote.

The authors of this book have sadly never seen a dragon, aside from the red one protecting the flag of their home country of Wales.

TROILUS &
CRESSIDA

The Trojan and Greek armies are retiring for the night. Achilles, who has just killed Hector, provides this ominous description of the close of a long day of fighting …

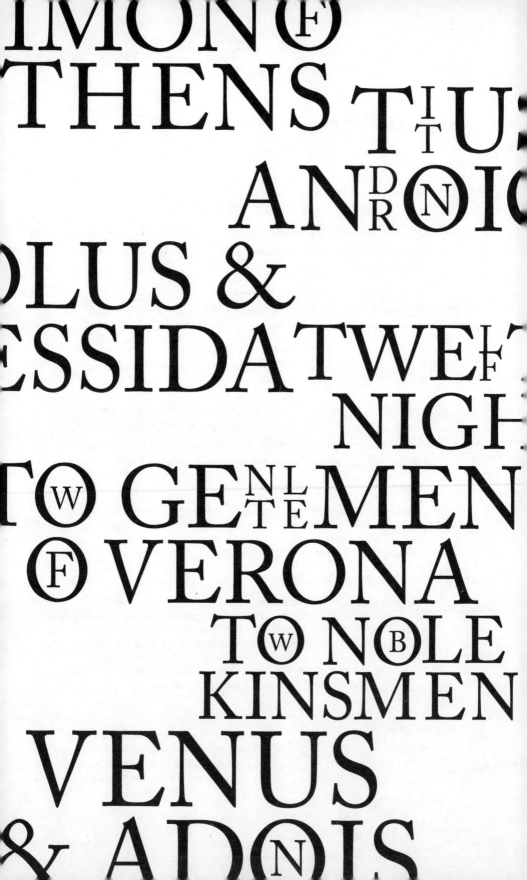

**Thou hast no more brain than I have in mine elbows.**

—— ∞ ——

Thersites is throwing a series of insults at the Greek warrior Ajax, who keeps beating him. Despite being beaten, Thersites keeps on insulting him …

TROILUS & CRESSIDA

## As much foolery as I have, so much wit thou lackest.

———— ∞ ————

'As foolish as I may be, that's how much cleverness you don't have.'

An equivalent to the feeble retaliation to an insult, famed in British schoolyards, 'I know you are, but what am I?'

Shakespeare still says it better.

A Fool is engaged in conversation with Apemantus and a group of servants …

TIMON ℗F ATHENS

# Y' have got a humour there
## Does not become a man; 'tis much too blame.

— ∞ —

A quote for when you meet someone (man or woman) whose turn of phrase, personality or sense of humour is mean or overly critical.

*Humour* used to mean 'mood' and in this line means a mood that doesn't *become* ('befit') a (hu)man, as it's too *blame* ('too blameworthy').

Timon has invited a group of lords to dinner. Apemantus arrives, and his host bids him welcome, but Apemantus gives a surly reply; these words follow from Timon …

TIMON OF
ATHENS

## Worse than the sun in March,
## This praise doth nourish agues.

—— ⚭ ——

*Ague* (pronounced 'EH-gyou', to rhyme with 'glue') meant 'fever', but was also used more generally to mean 'illness', 'discomfort' or 'sores'.

The sun in England's late winter and early spring is weak; its warmth barely melts the frosted dew on the grass. Everything stays mildewy, towels out to dry remain damp – everything that keeps a sore from healing, in other words.

So, this line is for anyone who gives you weak praise, a compliment weaker than the winter sun. Perhaps the praise had been intended to make things better, but instead ends up making things just a little bit worse, in just the worst way.

Hotspur has been listening to Vernon describe Prince Hal and his companions. What he hears irritates him so much that he tells Vernon to stop, as the praise is making him feel ill …

HENRY IV:I

# Small winds shake him.

— ∞ —

Words are powerful; their cut can feel deeper than any sword's; and some words, however lightly expressed, can really tear someone apart. The slightest 'wind' can blow the strongest building down.

Indeed, without realizing it, we can find ourselves incensing someone we're trying to calm. In which case, reach for this line from *Coriolanus*:

> This is the way to kindle, not to quench.

Or, as *Richard 2* offers:

> How fondly dost thou spur a forward horse!

In other words, how *fond* ('foolish') are you to provoke a *forward* ('high-spirited') person! So, if you find you've kindled the fire of someone's rage, take wise advice from *Henry 8*:

> Heat not a furnace for your foe so hot
> That it do singe yourself.

*Furnace* is a really strong word for Shakespeare. He uses it in the plays only four times: twice for anger and twice for love. One of the love instances comes in *Cymbeline*, when Iachimo describes seeing a Frenchman in Rome, in love with a girl in France:

> He furnaces
> The thick sighs from him.

The Frenchman sends out the sighs of love like smoke from a furnace.

Arcite and Palamon discuss whether they ought to leave Thebes, which has become a wicked place under the rule of King Creon. Creon calls for them, in a huge fury. Palamon knows of his moods, and says these words. But it turns out to be a large 'wind' that is the cause of Creon's rage: the news that Theseus is advancing against him in war.

## Rumour is a pipe
## Blown by surmises, jealousies, conjectures.

— ∞ —

The *pipe* is a musical instrument with finger-holes, a relatively easy instrument to play, like a recorder. Hamlet, accusing his friends Rosencrantz and Guildenstern of trying to manipulate him, asks them: *do you think I am easier to be played on than a pipe?*

The idea in the play that provides today's lead quote is that rumour is so quick to circulate, anyone can 'play' it, and thus spread the sound of *jealousies* ('mistrusts') and *conjectures* ('suspicions'). In the same play, Warwick doubts the number of soldiers reported to be on the rebel side:

Rumour doth double, like the voice and echo,
The numbers of the feared.

Indeed, Rumour personified appears in the opening scene and sums up its role:

Upon my tongues continual slanders ride,
The which in every language I pronounce,
Stuffing the ears of men with false reports.

Rumour, personified, greets everyone at the beginning of the play with this image. The many tongues of Rumour *bring smooth comforts false, worse than true wrongs.*

# 'Tis not the many oaths
## that makes the truth,
## But the plain single vow that is vowed true.

—⋘—

A truth about truth, and swearing oaths (or making promises).

The honest and true Juliet hears Romeo swear by the moon that he loves her, but she interrupts him, telling him not to swear by something so *inconstant* – as the moon changes every day. At a loss, Romeo asks:

> **What shall I swear by?**

And she tells him:

> **Do not swear at all**
> **Or, if thou wilt, swear by thy gracious self,**
> **Which is the god of my idolatry,**
> **And I'll believe thee.**

In other words, 'Only make promises on your own sense of grace and elegance, which is the part of you I worship.'

In other other words: be true to yourself. You don't need to promise anyone a thing, as promising over and over is no guarantee of sincerity.

Bertram swears to Diana that his love for her is true, but she doesn't trust him. He repeats that he has sworn that he is true – but it's all part of a plan to get him to make love to Helena. (It's an unusual play …)

ALL'S WELL THAT END WELL

**I learn you take things ill which are not so,
Or, being, concern you not.**

— ∞ —

Antony has arrived in Rome for an important
(but awkward) meeting. As soon as he sits down,
Antony broaches the subject of the contention
between him and Caesar, with these words …

ANT⊙NY &
CLE⊙ATRA

# One doth not know
# How much an ill word may empoison liking.

—— ◦⧒◦ ——

*Ill* meant 'unfavourable'; *empoison liking* meant 'destroy desire'.

Those last two words had much stronger senses in Shakespeare's day. The *em-* of *empoison* adds a nuance of motion – as it were, to 'inject poison into something, so as to destroy it'. And *liking* could mean 'desire' or 'sexual attraction', as in *Venus and Adonis* when the poet personifies Adonis's dimples, turning them into beings with mouths that can swallow her sexual desire:

> ... these round enchanting pits,
> Opened their mouths to swallow Venus' liking.

We hear *liking* again in the first Chorus to *Pericles* when Gower describes Antiochus' incest with his daughter: *With whom the father liking took.*

*Ill* is rarely heard today, but in Shakespeare's time the sense of 'bad' or 'unfavourable' was very common, with phrases like *ill fortune, ill luck, ill news, ill counsel* or an *ill request.* When talking to Polonius about the visiting actors, Hamlet says:

> After your death you were better have a bad epitaph
> than their ill report while you live.

Beatrice is eavesdropping on Hero and Ursula, who are discussing how Benedick is fully in love with her. Hero says that rather than tell Beatrice, she thinks it better to go to Benedick and advise him to fight against his passion. She thinks this advice will go over all the better by making up some innocent slanders which will make Beatrice seem less attractive. But Hero herself will soon fall victim to made-up slanders.

MUCH ADO ABOUT NOTHING

# It is the disease of not listening, the malady of not marking, that I am troubled withal.

———∞———

*Mark* means 'hearing with attention', and is evidently distinct from listening. So, this quote is a 400-year-old way of highlighting the difference between 'hearing' and 'listening'.

*Malady* is an old word for 'disease'. Shakespeare often uses a difficult word, but helps us by using a similar (but easier) word nearby. The Duke in *Othello* talks about a *grise or step*, and you guessed it, *step* is another word for *grise*.

If you find yourself overhearing something that catches your interest, and you want to stop to listen, say this line of Hamlet's: *Couch we awhile, and mark – couch* meant 'rest', 'crouch' or 'hide'.

Falstaff meets the Lord Chief Justice in the street, who questions the drunken knight. The Justice accuses him of being deaf, *for you hear not what I say to you.* Falstaff replies that he *hears him well*; the problem is rather one of not being able to pay attention …

# Would thou wert clean enough to spit upon!

— ⌘ —

Today we have a run of brilliant insults to sling (only for fun, of course).

In the opening scene of *The Tempest*, the ship carrying King Alonso is about to sink. Some of the nobles come up on deck in great distress, and like many novices at sailing, speak to the sailors as if they're experts. The Boatswain curses them for being there and howling so much, and Sebastian swears at him for being so rude:

A pox o' your throat, you bawling, blasphemous, incharitable dog!

*Pox* was a word for any disease that gave the skin horrible pustules – 'give your throat sores with your shouting', in other words.

Here's another great one from *Henry 6 Part 1* (*minister* here means 'messenger', or 'servant'):

Break thou in pieces and consume to ashes,
Thou foul accursed minister of hell!

'Shatter to pieces and burn to dust, you demon of hell!' And from *Henry 4 Part 2*, a great wagging of the tongue from Falstaff's page:

Away, you scullion! You rampallian! You fustilarian!
I'll tickle your catastrophe!

A *scullion* is a servant. A *rampallian* is a ruffian. A *fustilarian* is a smelly old person. A *catastrophe* is a conclusion or ending – here being used as a description of a body part. So use this quote sparingly, as you'll be threatening to make someone's bottom tingle.

Try all four quotes together – just be careful who you say them to!

TIMON ⓕ ATHENS

Apemantus visits Timon, who has abandoned humanity. They trade a series of insults, and each tries to outdo the other. This is one of Timon's most forceful efforts, but Apemantus hits back with *A plague on thee! Thou art too bad to curse.*

# I understand a fury in your words,
# But not the words.

—⚬✤⚬—

A calm and clear response to any intense outlay of passion when the words make no sense to you, but the general emotional state is obvious.

And here's a defusing response to furious or *foul* ('harsh, rough, hard') words, from *Much Ado About Nothing*:

> Foul words is but foul wind, and foul wind is but foul breath,
> and foul breath is noisome.

*Noisome* means 'harmful'.

This is one for when you don't have words to send back to someone … at least, not yet …

> You shall hear from me still; the time shall not
> Outgo my thinking on you.

*Still* means 'always'. So, 'Oh you'll hear back from me! Time itself won't outdo how much I'll think about this.'

These lines could also be used when you're saying farewell to someone you love. So, 'I'll write to you every day; I'll think of you every second.'

That's the main thing to remember with these quotes: there's no single way to read Shakespeare. It's whatever it means to you that counts.

Othello addresses Desdemona in a cold and forceful way. She cannot understand why he is so angry, and on her knees she asks him what he means.

Thy wit, that ornament to shape and love,
Misshapen in the conduct of them both,
Like powder in a skilless soldier's flask
Is set afire by thine own ignorance,
And thou dismembered
    with thine own defence.

— ∞ —

*Wit* meant your 'reasoning', 'intelligence', 'mental sharpness', your 'mind' or 'brain'. *Ornament* meant 'special quality' or 'distinction'. *Shape* meant 'to give shape to', but also meant your 'appearance'. *Conduct* meant 'leadership', 'guidance', 'care, protection'. *Powder* meant 'gunpowder', which was stored in a flask.

In other words, 'Your reasoning, that looks after and loves you, has been bent out of shape, and like gunpowder in a fool's hands, you've set yourself on fire with your own stupidity, and hurt yourself trying to protect yourself.'

'Don't cut your nose off to spite your face,' our gran used to say. Today's quote will make for a pretty clever-sounding insult, said in the right way …

Romeo has come to see Friar Lawrence, distraught. He goes to stab himself, but the Nurse snatches the dagger from him, and the Friar remonstrates with the young man …

# You play the spaniel,
# And think with wagging of your tongue
# to win me.

— ∞ —

Today's lead quote will be useful for when someone is clearly trying to persuade you of something, with a lot of flowery, complimentary or persuasive words, and seeks your favour like a doggie when it wags its tail.

To *wag your tongue* was to 'speak foolishly', or 'utter silly remarks'. It turns up again in *Hamlet*, with this line fit for anyone who shouts a lot at you:

What have I done that thou darest wag thy tongue
In noise so rude against me?

'What have I done to deserve this?', or 'Why are you shouting at me?' we might say today, when someone harangues us and we don't know why.

*Rude* here doesn't have its modern meaning of 'offensive' or 'indecent', senses that arose only in the 20th century. *Rude* had a very wide range of uses in Shakespeare, and here it means 'violent', 'harsh' or 'unkind'.

The Bishop of Winchester and other members of King Henry's council have been plotting the downfall of Archbishop Cranmer. But Cranmer has Henry's support, and the King is unimpressed when Winchester offers an elaborate speech of welcome.

# HENRY VIII

# I begin to be aweary of thee, and I tell thee so before, because I would not fall out with thee.

— ⁂ —

Sometimes, direct honesty (and kindness) is the best policy. Such directness isn't always nice to hear, suggests this quote, but can be better than finding yourself in an argument.

Honesty can also be funny, as in *Henry 4 Part 1* (*railing* means 'haranguing'):

> He is as tedious
> As a tired horse, a railing wife,
> Worse than a smoky house.

And sometimes, simple, plain frankness is the only way. This line, from *As You Like It*, is best for when it's evident you're not getting on with someone:

> I do desire we may be better strangers.

It could also be said in great irony, for when it's crystal clear you need to spend the rest of your life together.

The court Clown engages Lafew in a jokey back-and-forth, until he tires Lafew out. Lafew then tells him to go away and look after his horses …

ALL'S WELL THAT ENDS WELL

# How now, rain within doors, and none abroad?

—— ∞ ——

You step into a room and quickly perceive the mood is low. Either everyone's faces are gloomy, or the atmosphere is thick – have you walked into an argument?

For better or for worse, this line offers help if you're trying to lighten the mood (*how now* is an exclamation of surprise; *abroad* here means 'outside').

If your attempt to improve the ambience falls flat – if everyone starts shouting at you – then here's a follow-up from *Richard 3*:

> **What! Were you snarling all before I came,**
> **Ready to catch each other by the throat,**
> **And turn you all your hatred now on me?**

If that seems to catch the flame of their upset, and the room rolls into a rage, use Hamlet's lines to see how far everyone's willing to go:

> **Woo't weep? Woo't fight? Woo't fast? Woo't tear thyself?**
> **Woo't drink up eisel? Eat a crocodile?**

*Woo't* was a colloquial way of asking 'would you?' *Eisel* (pronounced 'EYE-sel') is 'vinegar'.

Then, not having any crocodiles to hand, perhaps you might hurry away from the storm inside, and head for the fairer weather *abroad* ('away from here'), offering this pithy line from *King Lear* before you leave:

> **I am guiltless as I am ignorant**
> **Of what hath moved you.**

Prince Hal arrives to visit his sick father. Hal's brother Clarence says he feels full of *heaviness* – 'sadness'. As he has only heard good news, the Prince gives this response in surprise, and then asks after the King …

## Art thou obdurate, flinty, hard as steel?
## Nay, more than flint, for stone at rain relenteth.

— ∞ —

A quote for anyone stubborn and sulking.

Then, if you made them crack a smile, here's a line from *Coriolanus*, to tease them in their sullen obstinacy:

> You are no surer, no,
> Than is the coal of fire upon the ice,
> Or hailstone in the sun.

*Sure* meant 'certain, definite, steadfast', as well as 'safe, harmless, loyal', or 'trustworthy' – so this line could also be used if you don't trust someone.

The goddess has approached Adonis, who shows no interest in her. This puzzles her, and she asks him whether he is *obdurate* ('stubborn') and hard like flint – but then realises that flint isn't a strong enough comparison, for it eventually *relenteth* ('gives way') under the gentle, persistent force of rain.

VENUS & ADONIS

## Like a dull actor now
## I have forgot my part and I am out,
## Even to a full disgrace.

— ∞ —

The perfect quote for when you're in the middle of an argument, you know exactly what you want to say, and – and – and then – you can't remember it ...

*Dull* means 'stupid', 'lifeless', 'inattentive' or 'dim, lacking keenness'. *Out* means 'in error', 'at a loss' or 'unable to remember your lines'. Actors in Shakespeare's time didn't carry around a full copy of a play; like musicians in a modern orchestra, they only carried their own *parts*, just the lines for their character.

This is also a great quote to have on hand or in the back of your mind if you ever have to give a speech, or are suddenly asked to say something at an event.

Just remember that it's from *Coriolanus* – and throw in the context below for good measure; if nothing else, everyone will quickly forget that you couldn't remember what to say ...

The banished Coriolanus, leading a Volscian army, is about to launch a revengeful attack on Rome, having rejected all previous pleas to get him to change his mind. His mother, wife and child now come to him to beg for mercy, and suddenly he doesn't know what to say.

CORIOLANUS

# It is not well done, mark you now, to take the tales out of my mouth, ere it is made and finished.

—— ∞ ——

Interruption in a conversation is generally felt to be unwelcome, even if the interrupter is making a point that reinforces what the speaker is saying. *Mark* means 'listen'.

It can feel worse if someone finishes your story for you, or tells the punchline of a joke. Rather than get upset, bring these lines to mind, from *Pericles*:

> **Patience, good sir,**
> **Or here I'll cease.**

As ever, feel free to replace 'sir' with 'madam', 'fellow', 'friend' ... And a *fit* ('appropriate') reply for your fellow or friend?

> **I'll hear you more, to the bottom of your story,**
> **And never interrupt you.**

The Welsh captain Fluellen has launched into a story about Alexander the Great, and mentions that Alexander killed his best friend in a quarrel. The English captain Gower interrupts – and Fluellen doesn't take too kindly to the interruption ...

HENRY V

# Turning these jests out of service, let us talk in good earnest.

— ∞ —

'Joking aside, let's change the subject.' Or perhaps: 'The conversation may have been flippant until this point, but now let's be serious.'

A *jest* in Shakespeare can be anything from a joke or trick to an idle tale or mocking speech, to a fully fledged pageant or play.

Jests have to be made in the right time and place. If they aren't, jesters get into trouble. Antipholus of Syracuse tells Dromio so in *The Comedy of Errors*:

> These jests are out of season.
> Reserve them till a merrier hour than this.

And this, from Lucentio in *The Taming of the Shrew*:

> 'Tis no time to jest,
> And therefore frame your manners to the time.

And in *Henry 4 Part 1*, when Falstaff gives Prince Hal a bottle of booze instead of a gun at the Battle of Shrewsbury, Hal is furious:

> What, is it a time to jest and dally now?

*Dally* could mean 'flirt' or 'delay', but here means 'play' or 'muck about, tease'. So now, let's find time to dally and jest in good earnest!

Celia and Rosalind have been watching Orlando defeat Charles the Wrestler in a fight. Rosalind says she's suddenly fallen in love with Orlando, and her cousin Celia quickly becomes serious, with these words …

AS YOU LIKE IT

# These are but wild and whirling words.

—— ∞ ——

A great reply to anyone in a highly excited or emotional state, speaking with great passion, but not necessarily clearly or calmly.

*Wild* can mean 'furious', 'erratic' or 'agitated, upset', as well as 'savage, cruel'.

If the wild and whirling wordsmith doesn't immediately calm, then perhaps these firm words from *Coriolanus* may help:

> 'Tis fit
> You make strong party, or defend yourself
> By calmness or by absence.

*Fit* means 'appropriate'; *party* meant 'faction'.

This line teeters into the territory of threat: inviting someone, in other words, to 'get backup'. But it pulls back from the brink of violence, with the invitation to defend oneself either by being calm, or by leaving.

Firm, peaceful, de-escalation – the Shakespearean way to fend off a fight.

Hamlet has just seen the ghost of his father. Horatio and Marcellus meet him and ask what happened. Hamlet gives a number of replies that don't make sense to them, and Horatio responds with this line.

# This is very midsummer madness.

— ⁂ —

This line describes the weird behaviour or sudden bouts of foolishness that can visit us all with the high temperatures in summertime. Shakespeare is the first recorded user of this turn of phrase, but it was the effect of heat on the brain that was thought to lead to strange behaviour

When Macbeth sees a dagger floating in front of him, he wonders if it's a hallucination caused by heat:

> ... art thou but
> A dagger of the mind, a false creation,
> Proceeding from the heat-oppressed brain?

The association of heat with midsummer is acknowledged by Rosalind, in *As You Like It,* as she recalls the story of how Leander died for love on a *hot midsummer night.*

> Leander is a character from classical mythology: a young man in love with Hero, a priestess of Aphrodite (the Greek goddess of sexual love; Venus, in Roman mythology).

> Hero lived on the opposite side of the Hellespont (a narrow strait connecting the Aegean Sea and the Sea of Marmara, in Turkey), and each night Leander swam across to her, guided by her lamp.

> But one night the lamp blew out in a storm and he was drowned – and poor Hero committed suicide by throwing herself into the sea, to be with her love ...

TWELFTH NIGHT

Malvolio appears before Olivia, dressed in a bizarre way, speaking strangely and smiling broadly – quite unlike his normal, restrained (and very much unsmiling) behaviour. Olivia is at a loss to explain this weird conduct, and leaves him with these words.

# Talkers are no good doers.

— ✺ —

In Shakespeare, it's the *doers* who get the praise. And this line is the kind of comment all politicians fear: that they are 'all words and no actions'.

It's a criticism that can apply to anyone we feel is procrastinating, putting off an action or decision, while still promising an outcome (whether that promise is written or verbal).

The Prince criticises himself in *Hamlet* for not doing anything (yet) to avenge his father's murder, other than *unpack my heart with words*.

The ideal, of course, is to be both talker and doer, as Prospero intends to be in *The Tempest*, when he says:

> I will pay thy graces
> Home both in word and deed.

*Graces* here means 'the sense of duty you've shown'; *home* means 'fully'; and *pay* here means 'repay'.

Richard instructs two murderers to kill his brother Clarence. He advises them to do the deed quickly, and not give the man a chance to plead for his life:

> For Clarence is well-spoken, and perhaps
> May move your hearts to pity if you mark him.

*Mark* meant 'listen to'. The First Murderer assures Richard with these words that they won't waste time …

## RICHARD III

# The lady doth protest too much, methinks.

— ∞ —

Whenever you hear someone (not only a lady) going on and on, saying more than they need to, trying to sell their case too earnestly – whisper this to someone nearby.

When people *protest* today, it's to 'express disapproval or dissent'. It used to have the more positive meaning of 'making a formal or emphatic declaration'. We still use it in this way, when people say, 'I protest', in the sense of 'I really mean what I'm about to say.'

So the word is closer to our modern 'avow' or 'affirm', 'swear' or 'promise'. In other words, 'the lady's making too many promises'.

We hear *protest* again in *Much Ado About Nothing* when Benedick tells Beatrice *I protest I love thee*. Later in the play he issues a challenge to Claudio: *Do me right, or I will protest your cowardice*. In other words, he intends to make Claudio's cowardliness (his refusal to fight) known in public, which would be a terrible loss of honour for a young soldier.

As ever, when adapting a lead quote to an everyday situation, do feel free to adapt the words, which means a co-author can easily say 'Ben doth protest too much, methinks.'

A play is being performed, in which a queen assures her husband that, were she a widow, she'd never marry again, and makes extreme statements about never marrying in the future. Hamlet asks his mother whether she likes the play he's staged, and then Queen Gertrude responds with today's lead quote. ...

HAMLET

**To wail friends lost**
**Is not by much so wholesome-profitable**
**As to rejoice at friends but newly found.**

— ∞ —

In a situation where we've lost or are about to lose a friend, it's natural to *wail* ('grieve') for them; but it's much more *wholesome-profitable* ('beneficial to our well-being') if we can take delight in the friendships that will come to us, or return to us, in time.

Friendship is a really popular theme in the plays. Shakespeare refers to it over a thousand times – although a 'friend' could also refer to a relative.

The Princess of France has learned of her father's death, and is about to leave for home. The King of Navarre says that his love for her is sincere, and hopes that her cloud of sorrow won't push his love out of her mind, nor prevent her from taking delight in her new friends.

LOVE's LABOUR's LOST

# It were a goot motion if we leave our pribbles and prabbles.

— ∞ —

'It'd be a good idea to stop arguing.'

*Goot* is 'good'; *pribbles and prabbles* are 'silly quarrels'. They're written that way to capture a (supposedly) Welsh pronunciation.

*Brabble* (or *prabble*) was a 'brawl or noisy quarrel', and a *brabbler* was a 'braggart, brawler or quarreler', as heard in *King John*:

> We hold our time too precious to be spent
> With such a brabbler.

Peace comes to those who wish it, especially after a difficult conversation or unpleasant disagreement, and it's healthy not to go to bed unhappy. So follow these words from *Julius Caesar*, after Cassius and Brutus finish a long and bitter disagreement, and part on good terms:

> This was an ill beginning of the night;
> Never come such division 'tween our souls!

It's the opening scene of the play, and Shallow is complaining to his friends of the bad treatment he has received from Falstaff. The argument might even come to a fight. The Welsh parson, Evans, suggests they stop chattering idly about silly quarrels.

MERRY WIVES OF WINDSOR

# I hold it cowardice
# To rest mistrustful where a noble heart
# Hath pawned an open hand in sign of love.

—— ∞ ——

It's the work of a coward to stay suspicious when someone has pledged or promised peace.

And yet, it's only natural to be unsure when someone we think of as an adversary comes to us showing a sign of friendship. Perhaps these lines remind us that there's a risk on both sides. For the one who *pawns* ('pledges') their heart, there's a risk that the open hand won't be accepted. And for the one who must decide whether to believe the gesture is sincerely meant, there comes the risk of behaving like a coward, when faced with genuine openness.

*Pawn* isn't being used here to mean 'deposit something with a pawnbroker' (*pawnbroker* is first recorded in 1658); nor is it the chess piece (first recorded in about 1400, meaning a 'walker'); but since the 15th century *pawn* has had the more general sense used in today's lead quote, of 'pledging' or 'security'.

Hands and hearts often go together in Shakespeare. *Give me your hand* turns up a lot in the plays, and one of the finest is when Cassius says it to Brutus after their fierce quarrel in *Julius Caesar*:

> Brutus: When I spoke that, I was ill-tempered too.
> Cassius: Do you confess so much? Give me your hand.
> Brutus: And my heart too.
> Cassius: O Brutus!

A fine end to any argument.

HENRY VI:III

The Duke of Warwick is leading an army against King Edward. He's surprised to see Edward's brother, the Duke of Clarence, approaching him, accompanied by the Duke of Somerset. They say they come as friends, so he welcomes them warmly with these words. A new political alignment follows ...

## With all the gracious utterance thou hast
## Speak to his gentle hearing kind commends.

—— ∞ ——

Bearing in mind that you can switch *his* for 'her' or 'their' or any other pronoun you desire, these lines offer an elegant alternative to the conventional sending of 'best wishes' to someone.

*Commends* is a very formal greeting; the closest modern equivalent would be 'my compliments'. In *Richard 2*, we hear Bolingbroke wanting to send reassurance to the Queen, and asks his uncle to *Tell her I send to her my kind commends*.

The usual practice was to say simply: *Commend me to* … whomever. 'Give David my kind regards' would be a present-day version. Isabella asks Lucio in *Measure for Measure* to *Commend me to my brother*, and Coriolanus asks his mother Volumnia to *Commend me to my wife*.

Some characters amplify their greeting with extra words of warmth. In *Troilus and Cressida*, Pandarus tells Helen that her brother Troilus *commends himself most affectionately to you*.

And Hamlet adds an extra note to Horatio and Marcellus: *With all my love I do commend me to you* – a great message to text someone out of the blue.

Northumberland has brought a greeting from Bolingbroke. King Richard acknowledges the greeting, and returns it with these careful words …

RICHARD II

# I will be the pattern of all patience.

—— ❦ ——

Most characters appreciate the value of patience. A gentleman in *Henry 8* praises Buckingham for displaying *a most noble patience* in the face of adversity.

Still, for some, circumstances don't allow for patience. In *Henry 6 Part 3* the King asks Clifford, who wants revenge against the Yorkist faction, to be patient. He's in no such mood: *Patience is for poltroons* – 'worthless cowards'.

And in such cases, the following words from *Hamlet* can be used in an attempt to calm an angry person, someone who seems to be raving or suffering from a *distemper* (a 'bad mood', 'strange behaviour', 'mental imbalance'):

> **Upon the heat and flame of thy distemper**
> **Sprinkle cool patience.**

The sense of 'mental instability' is there in *The Two Noble Kinsmen* when the Gaoler describes his poor daughter with the words *She is continually in a harmless distemper.*

Lear and his Fool are in the midst of a great storm. After shouting and raving at the winds, and listening to the complaints of his companion, Lear seems to calm with these words …

# KING LEAR

## What, ho! Peace here, grace and good company.

— ∞ —

A fine greeting, fit for when you arrive somewhere and want to wish peacefulness, goodwill, and seek *gezellig*, the untranslatable Dutch word describing that warm, comfortable, cosy feeling you get when you're in good company.

The wishing of peace upon arrival at a house or a meeting isn't common today, but it was a popular expression in Shakespeare's time, used as a greeting and a farewell. In *Henry 4 Part 2*, Prince John greets the King with the words *Health, peace, and happiness to my royal father.*

And the King greets the French leaders in *Henry 5* with a fine quote for any virtual conference: *Peace to this meeting, wherefore we are met!* – 'a state of calm to this meeting, which is the reason why we have all gathered'.

*Peace* was also a word used to command someone to be quiet or to calm them. In *Othello*, Iago tries to stop his wife telling the truth about his lies (*zounds* means 'God's wounds'): *Zounds, hold your peace!*

In *Twelfth Night*, Feste's response to *Hold your peace* has often been misinterpreted lewdly, as he says, *I shall never begin if I hold my peace.* (The similar-sounding 'piece' could be used as a euphemism for genitalia.) As we'll see on December 29th, Shakespeare sometimes uses his first name in a similar way, especially in *Sonnet 135*.

Isabella has come to visit her condemned brother Claudio in prison. She calls at the door with these words, and the Provost acknowledges her greeting and invites her in with *The wish deserves a welcome.*

MEASURE
FOR MEASURE

But since all is well, keep it so:
Wake not a sleeping wolf.

— ∞ —

The Lord Chief Justice wants to question Falstaff
about his part in a robbery (an event in *Henry 4
Part 1*), but now thinks that Falstaff's service at the
recent Battle of Shrewsbury, and what he calls the
current *unquiet time*, will allow him to overlook
the matter. He advises Falstaff not to get into any
more trouble.

HENRY IV:II

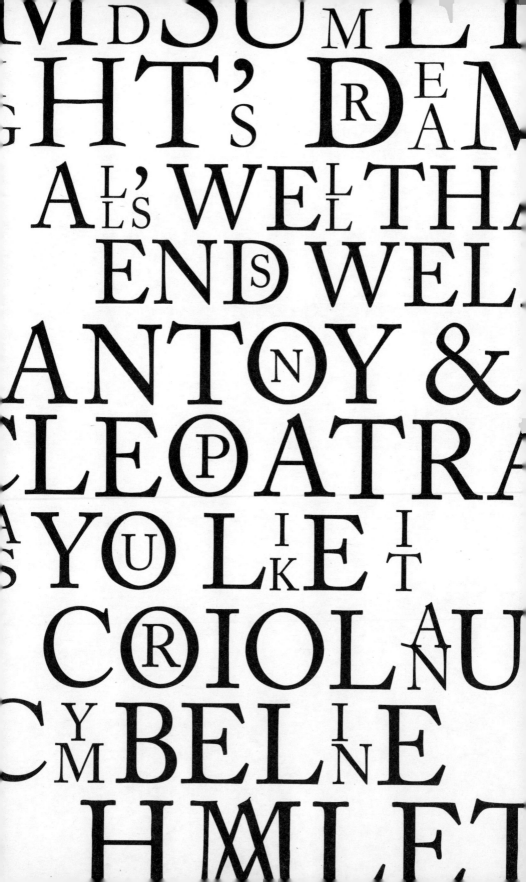

**Humanity must perforce prey on itself**
**Like monsters of the deep.**

———∞———

Albany condemns his wife, Goneril, for her awful treatment of her father. He tells her that the heavens will seek revenge, if not soon, then in due course. He ends his attack on her with this reflection: that human beings *perforce ('violently')* *seize and devour each other, like monsters.*

KING LEAR

JULY 1ST

# The devil knew not what he did when he made man politic – he crossed himself by't.

———⧜———

*Politic* here means 'crafty', 'self-serving' – as well as the normal, modern senses of 'devious', 'indirect' – sorry, of course we mean 'inspiring', 'wise' and 'judicious'.

So, the greatest tempter to 'evil', the devil, *crossed himself* ('screwed himself over', or 'gave himself a problem') when he instilled craftiness in mankind – both because he put himself out of a job, and because wickedness can be made to appear virtuous. In other words, humankind can argue its way out of any corner, even out of hell, by using the language of politics.

You may think that politics might have changed in the last centuries; though this line from *King Lear* might deflate that thought:

> Get thee glass eyes,
> And like a scurvy politician seem
> To see the things thou dost not.

*Scurvy* meant 'worthless', 'contemptible', 'despicable', 'disagreeable'. Or 'wretched'. Shakespeare's words, not ours.

Timon has sent his servant to Sempronius, whom he has treated generously in the past, to now ask him for financial support. Sempronius refuses, on the basis that he wasn't the first person to be asked for help. The servant is horrified at his ingratitude, and reflects on it with these words.

TIMON ⓄF ATHENS

# My true eyes have never practised how
# To cloak offences with a cunning brow.

— ∞ —

Perhaps, if you're truly good and pure of heart, these lines from *The Rape of Lucrece* might resonate with you.

Do your friends show their emotions or keep them hidden? This is a question that has been on people's minds since long before Shakespeare's time.

The duplicitous, lying crook Iago in *Othello* says *I will wear my heart upon my sleeve*. It's an expression that probably originated in the medieval sport of jousting: knights would wear their love's *favour* (a 'token of affection, like a ribbon') on their sleeve.

Hotspur in *Henry 4 Part 1* accuses King Henry of hiding his true character before he was crowned, saying he seemed

> ... to weep
> Over his country's wrongs – and by this face,
> This seeming brow of justice, did he win
> The hearts of all that he did angle for.

*Angle*, like you would with a rod, when fishing for a catch.

By contrast, in *The Two Gentlemen of Verona*, Julia acknowledges the battle between how she feels on the inside, and how she has expressed herself. She tears up a love letter she's received from Proteus without reading it – and then immediately regrets it:

> How angerly I taught my brow to frown,
> When inward joy enforced my heart to smile.

After being attacked by Tarquin, Lucrece wonders how she can face the forthcoming day. She would like to hide her disgrace, as she sees it, from the world, but knows she won't be able to. She reflects in these words a truth born of self-knowledge: her face will give her away.

# There's daggers in men's smiles.

———— ✤ ————

There are those whose smiles don't reach their eyes. The ones who are only being pleasant out of necessity, because they want something from you. Those who'd rather shove you out of the way rather than beg for your approval.

Today's lead quote comes from Donalbain, talking with his brother Malcolm after the murder of their father, the King. Malcolm then offers this line:

> To show an unfelt sorrow is an office
> Which the false man does easy.

A *false* ('treacherous') person finds it an *office* ('easy task') to put on a show of sorrow – especially one *unfelt* ('one they haven't experienced').

How often is a smile genuine? Perhaps someone is neurodiverse and struggles to 'feel' things in the 'normal' day-to-day of life. Perhaps society has become really good at faking agreeableness. Perhaps, as someone opens one hand to shake yours, the other is clenched into a fist.

No matter what the intention might be, we can be read the wrong way, as *Henry 4 Part 1* acknowledges:

> Look how we can or sad or merrily,
> Interpretation will misquote our looks.

*Sad* means 'serious'; *misquote* means 'read a mistaken meaning into something'. So this next line from *The Merchant of Venice* is for that person in your life who, no matter what is actually meant, always takes things the wrong way:

> I pray thee understand a plain man in his plain meaning.

Exchange *man* for *woman, person, dog, aircraft pilot* ...

Not knowing who killed the King, Donalbain speaks to his distrust of everyone around him, with these words.

# All hoods make not monks.

— ⁂ —

Or, as Feste the Fool says in *Twelfth Night* (and Lucio does similarly in *Measure for Measure*), *Cucullus non facit monachum\**. It's Latin for 'the hood does not make the monk'. In other words, wearing the cloth is not all it takes to be good, do good, live good, and sometimes even those wearing the symbols of trustworthiness can't be trusted. 'Walking the walk is not talking the talk.'

*Measure for Measure* takes the point further:

> Thieves for their robbery have authority
> When judges steal themselves.

When there's corruption in high places, especially when the wrongdoers are themselves the custodians of justice, then it's as if *authority* ('permission') is given to anyone to commit crime.

Such wrongdoing was evidently well recognised in Shakespeare's day, judging by the remark of Claudius in *Hamlet*:

> In the corrupted currents of this world
> Offence's gilded hand may shove by justice;
> And oft 'tis seen the wicked prize itself
> Buys out the law.

*Gilded* meant 'gold-bearing'. The worst offenders can buy their way out of trouble with the law. The world changes every moment – and still some things never change.

---

\* pronounced something like 'ku-KOOL-us non FASS-it mon-AH-kum'

Cardinals Wolsey and Campeius have come to see Queen Katherine. She is suspicious about their motives and wonders if they are good men, with these words …

# 'Tis time to fear when tyrants seem to kiss.

— ∞ —

A *tyrant* is a 'cruel and oppressive ruler', and tyranny is a kind of leadership that seems to have fascinated Shakespeare, especially in the last years of his writing life.

This line from *Measure for Measure* puts it neatly:

O, 'tis excellent
To have a giant's strength, but it is tyrannous
To use it like a giant.

Many characters probe and explore the qualities of a tyrant. *Timon of Athens* recognises that pity, empathy and mercy are the traits of good leadership – they are the qualities that maintain our laws:

For pity is the virtue of the law,
And none but tyrants use it cruelly.

Here's a line from *Pericles* that acknowledges the fear that's at the heart of all tyrants; any hope of them getting better, becoming kinder, is foolishness:

Tyrants' fears
Decrease not, but grow faster than the years.

And here's one from *Henry 4 Part 2*, for the soap opera of modern politics, or any organisation where foes and friends are *enrooted* ('intertwined'):

His foes are so enrooted with his friends
That, plucking to unfix an enemy,
He doth unfasten so and shake a friend.

In acting against your enemies, you're likely to lose those close to you, too.

PERICLES

Pericles tells his counsellor Helicanus that he solved the riddle of Antiochus, the murdering, incestuous ruler of Antioch. Now Antiochus is afraid of Pericles, but has spoken to him in a flattering way. Pericles knows all too well that this is a façade.

The eagle suffers little birds to sing,
And is not careful what they mean thereby,
Knowing that with the shadow of his wings
He can at pleasure stint their melody.

*Suffer* often describes a physical or mental state, as when Miranda in *The Tempest* tells Prospero how she suffered at the sight of a sinking ship with all its sailors on board. That's the dominant meaning today, but in Shakespeare's world the word could also convey 'permission'.

In today's quote, the meaning is 'allow' or 'tolerate'. That sense is little heard nowadays, except occasionally in literary use and some regional dialects. *Careful* is another word that can catch us out. If I'm being careful, I really have no cause to be concerned (which is the mood of the eagle in today's lead quote). If I am literally 'care-full', then I'm anxious or worried.

The *eagle*, of course, stands for anyone in a position of power – a political or military leader, a boss, a parent, an older sibling … Such people can *stint* ('stop') the words or activities of those beneath them. As *Twelfth Night* offers:

If one should be a prey, how much the better
To fall before the lion than the wolf!

If you're going to be something's dinner, better it be the dinner of the king of the jungle – the prideful, graceful lion – than the savage wolf. In other words, if you're going to get taken down, get taken down by the best, rather than the most merciless and cunning.

Emperor Saturnine has heard that the Goths are rising up against him, led by Lucius Andronicus, son of Titus. He thinks the Romans will welcome Lucius and depose him. His wife Tamora calms him with these lines, implying he is the eagle and the citizens of Rome are the little birds.

# I do love
# My country's good with a respect more tender,
# More holy and profound, than mine own life.

—— ∞ ——

Most people have love for the country they belong to, and take pride in it; this speaker is affirming his willingness to die for it. (He's speaking in a time of war, when many characters speak in this patriotic way.)

It can be hard to hear such strong words without suspecting them to be hyperbole. Timon's steward in *Timon of Athens* agrees, having seen his master give away everything he has:

> His promises fly so beyond his state
> That what he speaks is all in debt. He owes
> For every word.

*State* here means his 'estate' – what his property is worth – though it could also mean 'mental state' or 'reasoning'. A line for any politician making promises they can't keep.

*The Merchant of Venice* offers a complementary line, good for anyone who talks a lot, while also not saying very much of substance:

> His reasons are as two grains of wheat hid in two bushels of chaff: you shall seek all day ere you find them, and when you have them they are not worth the search.

Here *reason* means not only 'points' but 'sensible points'. A *bushel* was a measurement for grain; *chaff* was the leftover husks and leaves that are removed from the grain.

The tribunes, with the support of the people, are banishing Coriolanus. Cominius intervenes and tries to say something in his support, including these lines, but they don't allow him to continue.

# Runs not this speech like iron through your blood?

— ∞ —

It's a shame there aren't more times in life when we hear someone give a great speech; one whose very sound makes you feel strong inside.

Instead, too often, we hear speeches made about events and decisions so awful it would seem the world may stop turning. A chill goes through you. For Shakespeare's audience, the image was more one of an iron weapon tearing through your body – a common way to die, in those days.

Lewis the Dauphin gives a speech-worthy slogan in *King John*:

> **Strong reasons makes strong actions!**

But in *Macbeth*, Banquo reminds us that not all of the most pernicious ideas we hear are said in the nastiest way; sometimes the worst is covered over with *trifles* ('little bits') of worthless honesty:

> **Oftentimes, to win us to our harm,**
> **The instruments of darkness tell us truths;**
> **Win us with honest trifles, to betray's**
> **In deepest consequence.**

And then there are some events (especially in modern politics) that are so unlikely, so orchestrated, that this line from *Twelfth Night* might well be necessary:

> **If this were played upon a stage now, I could condemn it**
> **as an improbable fiction.**

Borachio is admitting his part in the plot to slander Hero and destroy her plan to marry Claudio. Don Pedro and Claudio have been listening to him, and now realise the depth of their error in accusing Hero of being disloyal.

MUCH ADO ABT NOTHING

**The fashion of these times,**
**Where none will sweat but for promotion.**

———— ⧜ ————

Adam offers to follow Orlando as he escapes into
the Forest of Arden and continue as his servant
without payment. Adam reminds him of olden
times, *when service sweat for duty, not for meed*
(*meed* here means 'reward') and with these lines,
contrasts the old ways with the state of things
today …

AS YOU LIKE IT

**And art made tongue-tied by authority,**
**And folly (doctor-like) controlling skill,**
**And simple truth miscalled simplicity.**

— ✿ —

And creativity stifled by bureaucracy.

And foolishness (in the guise of wisdom) in place of expertise.

And loss of faith in the media.

The poet reflects on the things that are wrong with the world. The only thing that keeps him going, he says in the final line of his sonnet, is love.

T<sup>H</sup><sub>E</sub> SONNETS

## Say what you can, my false o'erweighs your true.

———∞———

A line from someone who believes their greatness will protect them when they commit atrocities against another; that their *false* ('wrongful') proposal will *outweigh* ('prevail over') the truth of another's accusation.

Today's quote – and the play it comes from – have taken on a special resonance since the advent of the #MeToo movement.

Angelo (the Duke's deputy) will release Claudio from the death penalty if Claudio's sister Isabella will sleep with him. And Angelo knows that if Isabella were to accuse him of this proposal in public, nobody would believe her.

MEASURE
FOR MEASURE

# Nothing emboldens sin so much as mercy.

— ∞ —

There are people who see compassion, and forgiveness, as an opportunity for abuse and cruelty.

The same sort of person feels, as Pericles does, that

> Vice repeated is like the wandering wind,
> Blows dust in others' eyes, to spread itself.

A person's faults, crimes and terrible secrets will scatter, be blown around like dust in the wind. The salacious truths people desperately try to keep hidden will spread like weeds in a bank of flowers.

Portia makes a memorable statement about the overriding quality of mercy, in an attempt to persuade Shylock to have pity on Antonio, the 'merchant of Venice'. She argues that mercy is stronger than a monarch's temporal power:

> But mercy is above this sceptred sway,
> It is enthroned in the hearts of kings
> It is an attribute to God himself,
> And earthly power doth then show likest God's
> When mercy seasons justice.

Humans on Earth most strongly resemble the power of God when we demonstrate compassion and forgiveness, while we practise fairness.

And yet, there are those who are thought to be without mercy. Sicinius hopes that the fearsome warrior Coriolanus will show some mercy towards the city, and Menenius describes his character with these words:

> There is no more mercy in him than there is milk in a male tiger.

The Athenian senators have decided that one of Alcibiades' soldiers should be executed for breaking the law. Alcibiades asks them for mercy but they reject any plea, using these words as justification. They will come to regret their decision …

# Didst thou never hear
# That things ill got had ever bad success?

— ∞ —

A quote about karma. Achievements or objects *ill* ('badly') obtained *ever* ('always') have a *bad success* ('bad outcome').

As we saw on *Star Wars* day (May 4th), Escalus in *Measure for Measure* wisely points out the unfair way of the world:

> **Some rise by sin, and some by virtue fall.**

Some make their way to the top by committing atrocious acts; and some fall to the bottom, even though they've only ever been good.

The unfairness can perhaps make it easier to understand why Shakespeare's characters (and audience) believed in higher powers, beyond the religious gods:

> **There's a divinity that shapes our ends,**
> **Rough-hew them how we will.**

A line from *Hamlet*, for those who don't believe in coincidence, who feel there has to be a supernatural explanation for the way things turn out, despite human attempts to be in control.

The Prince of Morocco in *The Merchant of Venice* wisely acknowledges that those who *hazard all* ('give everything up' – or to go 'all in', to use the poker term) only do it in the hopes of winning back at least half of what they've ventured:

> **Men that hazard all**
> **Do it in hope of fair advantages.**

As usual, for *men* read 'humans'.

King Henry is planning to give away his throne and thereby disinherit his son's right to the crown. Clifford attempts to persuade Henry to think of his son's future, but Henry maintains that the crown wasn't his in the first place (Henry Bolingbroke having taken it from *Richard 2*).

Could great men thunder
As Jove himself does,
    Jove would ne'er be quiet,
For every pelting, petty officer
Would use his heaven for thunder,
Nothing but thunder.

— ∞ —

Greatness is a subject Shakespeare often returns to – and equally often challenges. Here, we're offered the idea that great people should exercise their authority wisely. If they were as powerful as Jove, the god of thunder, then every *pelting* ('worthless') jobsworth would abuse their power, and all we'd hear would be thunder.

One of the most famous commentaries on greatness is in *Julius Caesar*:

> Th' abuse of greatness is when it disjoins
> Remorse from power.

Brutus is perhaps saying that greatness – and power itself – is tied to empathy, mercy, pity and, most importantly, *remorse* ('deep regret') for having made a decision that affects people badly.

There's insightful wisdom in *Coriolanus* – a warning for today's leaders, as much as it was for the leaders of centuries ago:

> There hath been many great men that have flattered the people,
> who ne'er loved them; and there be many that they have loved,
> they know not wherefore.

*Wherefore* means 'why':

And *Henry 4 Part 2* counsels that greatness comes with a price:

> Thou seekest the greatness that will overwhelm thee.

MEASURE
FOR MEASURE

Isabella confronts Angelo in a bid to save her brother Claudio from execution, and tries these words to persuade the Deputy to use his power wisely …

**The King is but a man, as I am:**
**the violet smells to him as it doth to me;**
**the element shows to him as it doth to me;**
**all his senses have but human conditions.**

— ∞ —

A good quote for anyone worried about meeting 'someone important', and a reminder that we're all human, no matter what status someone has been given.

*Element* here means 'forces of nature'.

Henry walks through his camp the night before the Battle of Agincourt. He's disguised himself, and he meets some of his soldiers, who ask him how the commanders are feeling. He says that the King feels the same as anyone else, which starts something of an argument amongst his men …

HENRY V

# There's many a man hath more hair than wit.

—— ∞ ——

*Wit* today usually refers to 'the ability of someone to make amusing remarks, effective because of their ingenuity or unexpectedness'.

It's a sense that emerged in English in the 16th century, and Shakespeare uses it in the opening scene of *Much Ado About Nothing*: Beatrice and Benedick are described as never meeting without *a skirmish of wit between them*.

It's in *As You Like It* too, in these lines that seem to anticipate modern stand-up comics being rebuked for speaking truth to power:

> **Touchstone: The more pity that fools may not speak wisely what wise men do foolishly.**
> **Celia: By my troth, thou sayest true: for since the little wit that fools have was silenced, the little foolery that wise men have makes a great show.**

In today's lead quote, though, *wit* has a much more general meaning. It means 'intelligence', 'good sense', 'wisdom' and 'good judgement', as well as 'humour'.

Polonius's aphorism in *Hamlet* perhaps holds all meanings of wit in one punchy line:

> **Brevity is the soul of wit.**

Antipholus of Syracuse is having a playful exchange with his servant Dromio, who has just said that men who don't have a lot of hair often have a lot more wit (are funnier or cleverer than more hirsute types), and this is his master's counter-point …

THE COMEDY OF ERRORS

## Uneasy lies the head that wears a crown.

———∞———

King Henry reflects on the difference between someone in his position and the *many thousand of my poorest subjects* who are able to fall asleep without difficulty – presuming they don't carry as big a burden.

A line for anyone in a position of power, leadership or control, struggling with that burden, that responsibility, that privilege.

Whether you're the prime minister, a local councillor, a chief executive, a manager, a headteacher, a leader of a community group, this line affirms that beyond any glitter and glamour, any fame and fortune, a great deal of worry will keep you awake at night.

This line perhaps also speaks to the invisible crown that is universally worn: many of us believe our problems are the biggest when we're going through them. That *we're* the only ones who can't sleep, and spend our nights lying awake, jealous of our fellows supposedly sleeping peacefully without anything to worry about.

These next lines, spoken in *Henry 6 Part 3* by the deposed King Henry, now crown-less, remind us that any physical crown that we might reach for is secondary to the one in our hearts. (*Content* means 'peace of mind, happiness, satisfaction'):

> My crown is in my heart, not on my head;
> Not decked with diamonds and Indian stones,
> Nor to be seen; my crown is called content;
> A crown it is that seldom kings enjoy.

Contentedness. The hardest crown to reach for, and yet within everyone's grasp.

HENRY IV:II

King Henry, now very ill, hears news of a rebellion, and takes to his bed to sleep – but he can't …

So doth the greater glory dim the less.
A substitute shines brightly as a king
Until a king be by, and then his state
Empties itself, as doth an inland brook
Into the main of waters.

— ∞ —

*Substitute* here has the sense of 'deputy' or 'subordinate'.

We see something that amazes us, a thing that we can only describe as 'beautiful'. It shines out at us – and then something even more beautiful is placed next to it. Suddenly, the bright light of the first object of our amazement seems slightly dim, by comparison.

And yet, great worth was considered to be found in the everyday, among common folk. *Henry 8* offers:

> A beggar's book
> Outworths a noble's blood.

The Duke of Buckingham thinks that a beggar's possessions, being few, have more value to them than rich ancestry (at least to the beggar); that merit and personal achievement are more valuable than what comes naturally; and thereby that learning from books is worth more than noble heritage.

Books are held in great appreciation in the plays. 80 per cent of people in Shakespeare's London were illiterate, and books were thought to hold magic, especially from the point of view of those who could not parse them.

The Lady Portia is on her way home in the dark and sees a candle shining from her house; she's impressed by how far its beams travel. Her maid Nerissa adds that they weren't able to see the candlelight when the moon was out, and this makes Portia reflect on the nature of greatness …

**Why, what is pomp, rule, reign,
but earth and dust?
And, live we how we can, yet die we must.**

— ∞ —

*Pomp* means 'splendour', as in the modern phrase 'pomp and circumstance' – which comes from *Othello*. (*Circumstance* means 'ceremony'.)

Shakespeare is perhaps suggesting in today's quote that few on their deathbed wish they'd worked more in life.

Warwick, fatally wounded, is reflecting on the power he had, and how it now means nothing.

HENRY VI:III

## Why should the private pleasure of some one Become the public plague of many moe?

— ∞ —

There is always Us and Them. Those keen to be famous, known, spoken about, and those uninterested in 'fame'.

(*Moe* was a way of saying 'more in number'.)

There are those who see through this lifting up of others, and point it out. In *The Winter's Tale*, King Polixenes discovers the relationship between his son Florizel and Perdita, the shepherd's daughter, and he bans their marriage. This is Perdita's response – the difference in their ranks does not matter:

> The selfsame sun that shines upon his court
> Hides not his visage from our cottage, but
> Looks on alike.

(This is also a good quote to remember if you miss someone who's on the other side of the planet; it's nice to remember they can feel the warmth of the same sun on their skin.)

Gossip about celebrities seems to have been as common in Shakespeare's time as it is today, judging by this line from *Twelfth Night*:

> What great ones do, the less will prattle of.

*Prattle* is one of several words expressing the notion of 'chattering and idle talk'. *Gossip* in its modern sense was just coming into use in Shakespeare's day – in *Titus Andronicus*, Aaron calls the Nurse *a long-tongued, babbling gossip*. And the Nurse in *Romeo and Juliet* is told to *Smatter with your gossips, go!* (*smatter* meant 'chatter').

THE RAPE OF LUCRECE

Lucrece is in despair and looks at a picture of the Trojan War, when this thought comes to her mind ...

They ne'er cared for us yet.
Suffer us to famish, and their storehouses
crammed with grain; make edicts for usury,
to support usurers; repeal daily any
wholesome act established against the rich,
and provide more piercing statutes daily
to chain up and restrain the poor.

— ∞ —

A group of Roman citizens have been complaining
about their country's leaders, and one of them
makes their point very clearly.

CORIOLANUS

# Distribution should undo excess
# And each man have enough.

— ∞ —

In all of the quotes for today, read 'human(s)' for *man* or *men*.

If everyone shared, it would *undo* ('eliminate') excessive wealth, and no one would ever have to go without.

There is a seam that runs through Shakespeare that reaches towards a call for equality, which holds that each human life is valuable. There's also a bemusement – or at least an acknowledgement, teetering towards a question – that such equality is within our power, and yet we, as a species, do not pursue it.

But as Portia recognises in *The Merchant of Venice*, doing good isn't as easy as knowing what's good to do:

> If to do, were as easy as to know what were good to do,
> chapels had been churches, and poor men's cottages
> princes' palaces.

A *chapel* was a 'sanctuary or place of worship' – but didn't have the status of the main church in town.

*Timon of Athens*, though not so well known, is the play that looks hard at the way wealth corrupts people and can cause a great many problems. Timon himself offers this thought, after making himself penniless through his own generosity:

> Bounty, that makes gods, does still mar men.

*Bounty* meant 'an act of kindness'; *still* meant 'always'; *make* meant 'prosper'; and *mar* meant 'harm'.

KⁱNG LEAR

Gloucester has been blinded, and wants to get to Dover to find Lear. On his way, he meets his son Edgar, disguised as the beggar Poor Tom. Gloucester hopes that his wretched state will make Edgar/Tom feel better about his lot.

**Men must learn now with pity to dispense,**
**For policy sits above conscience.**

— ∞ —

When *policy* ('statecraft, diplomacy') is given priority over *conscience* ('that which we know to be right'), then we'll need to learn to share pity with each other.

As ever, swap *men* with 'women', 'humans', 'everyone', what you will …

Three strangers have been observing the way Timon has been treated by his 'friends' since asking for their help. The First Stranger sums up their shared disquiet with these words.

TIMON ᴼF
ATHENS

## Think'st thou that duty shall have dread to speak When power to flattery bows?

— ∞ —

Our most powerful rulers need people like Kent in *King Lear* around them.

They could use some advice from Master Page, in *The Merry Wives of Windsor*, too:

> **Be not as extreme in submission**
> **As in offence.**

Know when to submit and when to strike – and never be extreme in either reaction.

The loyal Kent is appalled at Lear's treatment of Cordelia, and publicly tells him so. Lear threatens him, but the loyal Kent is unafraid to speak his mind.

KING LEAR

# Wisdom cries out in the streets and no man regards it.

— ⁓ —

Today's quote will perhaps be appreciated by anyone who takes to the streets to demonstrate in support of a cause they believe in – but finds their protests fall on deaf ears. It's an adaptation of a quotation from the *Book of Proverbs*. The *Geneva Bible* – published in England from the 1570s, and probably the one Shakespeare used – reads 'Wisdom crieth without: she uttereth her voice in the streets'.

It can be hard to divine the truth from the lies, the worthy media from the false (and indeed, 'hard' can feel an understatement). While wisdom is ignored on the streets, *fair terms* ('great deals') are everywhere, riddling the internet and world politics, and often hiding monstrous intentions. In which case, reach for this line from *The Merchant of Venice*:

**I like not fair terms and a villain's mind.**

And remember this line from *Cymbeline*, for a friend who refuses to commit to something – or when, no matter what you do or say, the idea, the project, the homework wriggles out of your grasp:

**As slippery as the Gordian knot was hard.**

The Gordian knot is a Greek legend, symbolic of a task of extreme difficulty. This was a knot tied by Gordius, King of Phrygia: it could only be untied by the one who was to rule Asia. (Similar to the legend of King Arthur's sword, Excalibur, which could only be pulled from the stone by the one who was to rule Britain.)

HENRY IV:II

Falstaff tells Prince Hal about someone in the street who disapproved of Hal's behaviour. Falstaff says he paid him no attention, even though he talked very wisely. Hal responds with this biblical quotation (which Falstaff recognises, though he considers Hal's ability to quote scripture *damnable* – 'deserving to be sent to Hell').

> As I travelled hither through the land,
> I find the people strangely fantasied,
> Possessed with rumours, full of idle dreams,
> Not knowing what they fear, but full of fear.

— ∞ —

If ever there was an observation that anticipates the state of a nation – or a world – during a pandemic, it's this one.

Time was, that in order for news to spread, it had to be carried by word of mouth, on horse or foot, from town to town, village to village, city to city, country to country.

Now, we travel through our communities and countries online; news is spread and rumours become amplified on social media – once the place for idle dreams and opinions, and more often now a receptacle for hatred and fear-mongering.

The newly banished Martius in *Coriolanus* rails against those who have condemned him:

Let every feeble rumour shake your hearts.

A threat and a warning against those waiting to take advantage of weakness.

With war between England and France looming, the Bastard describes a people *fantasied* ('full of strange imaginings'), with rumours spreading about the fate of the young Prince Arthur at the hands of King John …

KING JOHN

# Now this ill-wresting world is grown so bad,
# Mad slanderers by mad ears believed be.

— ∞ —

To *wrest* something is to give it a twisting movement – the word relates to 'wrestle' and 'wrist'. *Ill-wresting* thus means 'distorting', and, in this context, of *slanderers* – 'twisters of the truth'.

This is Shakespeare suggesting that when the truth is twisted into lies, people can start to feel maddened; such a mental state can open the door to believing the most hateful commentators.

The Fool in *King Lear* describes a world where truth, rather than being celebrated, is hard to distinguish from lies. It's treated the way some punish a badly-behaved dog – making it sit, cold and alone, outside in the rain, in a leaky doggie-house:

**Truth's a dog must to kennel.**

These lines are part of a plea to the poet's beloved that she stay faithful. He knows the world is full of people whose eyes stray – but he asks that her heart remains true.

THE SONNETS

# 'Tis the time's plague when madmen lead the blind.

— ∞ —

Calamity comes to those who listen to an out-of-date sat-nav. And of course, this line can apply to modern politics, a country's leader and its people.

*Plague* means 'calamity, affliction, trouble'.

Claudius in *Hamlet* offers further wisdom about those who become 'mad':

> Madness in great ones must not unwatched go.

And next, a line for those who cannot be trusted. *The Merchant of Venice* suggests that anyone without music in themselves (whether a metaphorical internal rhythm, the creative arts in general, or an actual love of music) falls into the 'unreliable' category:

> The man that hath no music in himself,
> Nor is not moved with concord of sweet sounds,
> Is fit for treasons, stratagems, and spoils.
> The motions of his spirit are dull as night,
> And his affections dark as Erebus.
> Let no such man be trusted.

Music, the *concord* ('harmony') of *sweet* ('pleasing') sounds. Those without music in them are only fit for committing treasons, *stratagems* ('violent deeds') and *spoils* ('the stolen goods of others').

Their spirit is full of *motions* ('evil inward promptings'), and their *affections* ('state of mind') are as *dark* ('gloomy') as Erebus, the son of Chaos in Greek mythology. There is no darker place in classical literature.

(*Erebus* is a personification of the place of darkness that people pass through on their way to the underworld, after they die.)

All three quotes today use *man/men* to mean 'people'.

KING LEAR

Gloucester has been blinded, but then encounters his son Edgar, disguised as the beggar Poor Tom and often called 'mad'. This is Gloucester's reply.

# The time is out of joint.

——— ∞ ———

*Out of joint* is defined in the *Oxford English Dictionary* as 'disordered, out of order, disorganised'. As in, when a bone disjoints.

*King John* offers a line for when times get really bad, when we have to find a solution immediately before the cancer takes hold:

> The present time's so sick,
> That present medicine must be ministered,
> Or overthrow incurable ensues.

*Physic* overlaps with *medicine* in meaning; a serving man in *Henry 6 Part 1* goes off to see *what physic the tavern affords.*

And *King Lear* reminds us that during terrible moments in history, it can be difficult to respect traditions or aspects of social *compliment* ('etiquette') with each other. The courteous and civil ways of social interaction must be abandoned, for the greater good:

> The time will not allow the compliment
> Which very manners urges.

These lines were useful to the authors during the pandemic of the 2020s.

After seeing his father's ghost, Hamlet reflects on his new responsibility (to avenge his father's murder) and recognises that his world and the times have shifted …

## – Time to be honest.
## – That time serves still.

*Serves* means 'be of use'. There will *still* ('always') be time for honesty. Some may deny its power, or even its existence, as Isabella in *Measure for Measure* affirms:

> For truth is truth
> To th' end of reck'ning.

Truth just 'is', even to the end of time. In the same play, Mariana tells us that there is sense and goodness in truth, just as the sun shines and words are made of breath:

> As there comes light from heaven and words from breath,
> As there is sense in truth and truth in virtue.

*King Lear* suggests that, in serious or sad times, we might wear our hearts on our sleeve, speak to how we feel, and not get weighed down or constrained by form, etiquette, politics:

> The weight of this sad time we must obey;
> Speak what we feel, not what we ought to say.

Passionate times call for passionate words. *A Midsummer Night's Dream* offers a rejoinder:

> It is not enough to speak, but to speak true.

When someone talks about 'speaking true' in the plays, they usually mean 'speaking truthfully'. And yet, there's a second sense of *true* that was around in Shakespeare's day (which we still use): when we say that something is 'true north', *true* means 'correct or accurate, in accordance with a standard'.

That's the sense here: a 'pureness', or 'absolute quality of truth'. Truth that has been fact-checked, counter-checked, and hermetically sealed in a barrel of liquid truth.

Honesty and truth will see us through life's difficult moments.

TIMON ⓕ ATHENS

A Lord has asked Apemantus what time it is, and he responds (sarcastically) with these words.

**Come what come may,
Time and the hour runs through
the roughest day.**

—— ❧ ——

A combination of despair and hope – 'whatever will be, will be'.

There may be challenging times ahead, but console yourself with the thought that even the worst of moments or days will pass, and come to an end.

Macbeth is reflecting on the meaning of his encounter with the three Witches. In a series of asides we hear what he's thinking, as the prospect of becoming king dawns on him, along with the dangers that may lie ahead ...

MACBETH

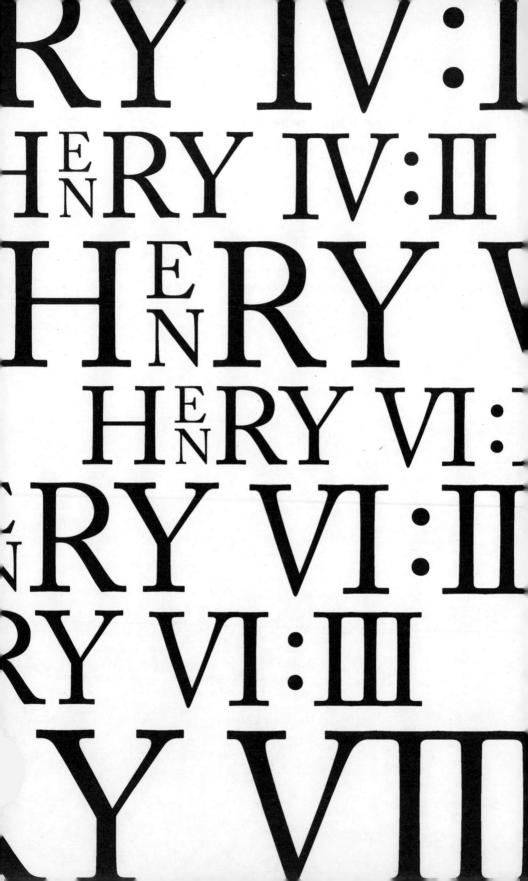

# No evil lost is wailed when it is gone.

— ∞ —

Luciana tells her sister Adriana how Adriana's husband Antipholus seems to have declared his love to her (neither know that it is in fact not Adriana's husband at all, but his twin). Adriana then lists all that is wrong with her husband, which makes Luciana wonder who would be jealous of such a man, and so she says these words.

THE COMEDY OF ERRORS

**A little fire is quickly trodden out;**
**Which, being suffered, rivers cannot quench.**

———— ❀ ————

A line for dealing with any sort of trouble, actual fires or metaphorical ones. Arguments between friends, strife with publishers, problems while producing plays – the best way is to deal with 'fires' quickly before they get out of hand, and not let situations fester or let the flames spread.

*Suffer* here doesn't mean 'feel pain', but rather 'tolerate, put up with'.

Henry and his nobles hear that the invading Edward is marching towards London, gaining support along the way. Henry thinks they should raise an army and beat him back, before the challenge becomes too great. Clarence agrees, with these lines – although their hope for success is short-lived …

# The sweets we wish for turn to loathed sours
# Even in the moment that we call them ours.

— ∞ —

You strive to be rich, then find money makes you miserable. You want that holiday, then spend most of your time away wishing you were home.

Today's lead quote was written for a horrific assault, but shines a light on a wider truth: Shakespeare seems to think we are a fickle species. Wonder where he gets that idea from …

Tarquin has raped Lucrece and then reflects on his actions.

# THE RAPE OF LUCRECE

# The strongest oaths are straw
# To th' fire i'th' blood.

——— ∞ ———

The most passionate promises we make can be like straw, quick to catch the fire of our hearts.

Longaville makes a similar point in *Love's Labour's Lost*. Having fallen in love, he tries to persuade himself to break the vow he has made to study hard and avoid women:

> **What fool is not so wise**
> **To lose an oath to win a paradise?**

Having decided on a course of action, one must move quickly:

> **Celerity is never more admired**
> **Than by the negligent.**

*Celerity*, used here in *Antony and Cleopatra*, means 'swiftness of movement'. In other words, those who procrastinate often wonder at those who finish tasks quickly; or, those who make their fortune creating a business are admired by those who neglect to take any action at all.

Macbeth has a similar line on his way to kill Duncan, having just seen a dagger float in front of him. Understandably, he spends some time talking about what he's just seen, and then realises all his words are allowing Duncan to live and cooling the heat of his purpose:

> **Words to the heat of deeds too cold breath gives.**

The breath used to speak isn't hot enough to make deeds happen. While we can talk ourselves into doing things, just talking about it isn't necessarily going to make an event take place. 'Keep your breath to cool your porridge', some might say.

THE TEMPEST

Prospero warns his daughter Miranda's suitor, Ferdinand, to control himself in his advances towards her, even though the young prince has sworn that he will act in a proper way.

# No perfection is so absolute
# That some impurity doth not pollute.

— ∞ —

Nothing and nobody is perfect. Look closely enough and the most perfect jewel will have a micro-imperfection. In *Venus and Adonis*, Venus describes how Cynthia (a name often given to Diana, the Roman goddess of the moon) bribed the Destinies:

> To cross the curious workmanship of Nature,
> To mingle beauty with infirmities
> And pure perfection with impure defeature,
> Making it subject to the tyranny
> Of mad mischances and much misery.

*Infirmities* means 'defects, flaws', or 'a physical or mental weakness'; *defeature* means 'loss of beauty'. The Fates were persuaded to meddle with the way nature makes us, mixing beauty with flaws. Cleopatra is evidently an exception, according to Enobarbus:

> I saw her once
> Hop forty paces through the public street,
> And, having lost her breath, she spoke, and panted,
> That she did make defect perfection.

She was perfection in exhaustion. Like a movie star with perfectly arranged hair in the morning.

Contrast that with *Sonnet 130*, where the poet describes his perfect imperfect love, who moves not like a goddess, but walks the earth:

> My mistress' eyes are nothing like the sun,
> Coral is far more red than her lips' red …
> I grant I never saw a goddess go;
> My mistress when she walks treads on the ground.

THE RAPE OF LUCRECE

After being attacked by Tarquin, Lucrece reflects on the way evil enters into nature. She thinks of worms infecting the buds of flowers, cuckoos hatching in the nests of sparrows, and concludes with these words.

Guiltiness will speak
Though tongues were out of use.

There has been a sword fight, instigated by Iago. Roderigo has been killed and Cassio wounded. Iago implicates Bianca, to avoid blame, and tries to convince everyone that her paleness implies guilt …

# Beauty is bought by judgement of the eye,
# Not uttered by base sale of chapmen's tongues.

— ∞ —

Whether it's a house, a car, a piece of furniture, or any object where we praise appearance to the skies, most people realise they need to experience it rather than just hear about it.

We put great trust in our judgement, and are reluctant to be persuaded solely by the *base* ('dishonourable') chatter of *chapmen* ('merchants'). *Utter* not only meant 'speak', but also 'make available'.

The point is affirmed again in *The Rape of Lucrece*:

> **Beauty itself doth of itself persuade**
> **The eyes of men without an orator.**

And yet, beauty, and the value of judgement by eye alone (including distinguishing people by race), is challenged in *Coriolanus*:

> **Not that our heads are some brown, some black, some abram,**
> **some bald, but that our wits are so diversely coloured.**

*Our wits*, our intelligence as humans, are as diverse as our skin colour. *Abram* means 'golden brown' – a variant of 'auburn'.

Boyet lavishes praise on the Princess, but she rejects his fine words. Her beauty, she says, *Needs not the painted flourish of your praise.* And then she gives him a short lesson about where beauty lies, with these words.

# Beauty provoketh thieves sooner than gold.

———— ⁂ ————

Rosalind and Celia recognise that they'll be in
danger if they travel alone to the Forest of Arden.
Celia, knowing that some qualities are prized
more highly than money, comes up with the idea
of disguising themselves.

AS YOU LIKE IT

To gild refined gold, to paint the lily;
To throw a perfume on the violet,
To smooth the ice, or add another hue
Unto the rainbow; or with taper-light
To seek the beauteous eye
    of heaven to garnish,
Is wasteful, and ridiculous excess.

— ∞ —

The first line is still in modern use. You may have heard the turn of phrase *to gild the lily* – to add a layer of gold to a white flower.

The other lines sit well together, and haven't turned into proverbs like their sister, but all express the same sentiment – that it isn't worthwhile to add something extra when the job's already done. Unnecessary ornamentation. Putting a hat on a hat, some might say.

*Taper* has narrowed its meaning: today it's a long wax-coated wick used as a spill to light a candle or a fire, whereas it used to refer to the candle itself (the sleepwalking Lady Macbeth enters *with a taper*).

The lily was Shakespeare's flower of choice to express beauty, with 'lily-whiteness' being a highly desirable feature, especially for parts of the body. Venus has *lily fingers* in *Venus and Adonis*, and Thisbe has *lily lips* in *A Midsummer Night's Dream*. Lavinia has *lily hands* in *Titus Andronicus*; and the writer's love steals whiteness from the lily in *Sonnet 99*.

King John has happily celebrated a second coronation. With these words, Salisbury tells his king that while one coronation may not have been enough, two is too many.

# KING JOHN

## On the finger of a throned queen
## The basest jewel will be well esteemed.

— ∞ —

The worth of something can shift, depending on who's holding it, and on whether we admire and respect whoever claims it's valuable.

The line can also be read to mean: if we love someone we will make allowances for any faults they may have and see them as merits. None of us is perfect, it suggests, and our imperfections should be loved, rather than polished away. Even a jewel of the *basest* ('poorest') quality, when it's worn by someone we admire, increases its splendour.

Beauty is often compared to a jewel: Innogen describes Posthumus as *this jewel in the world* in *Cymbeline*; for Hortensio, Bianca is *the jewel of my life* in *The Taming of the Shrew*. And the sonneteer describes his love as *the fairest and most precious jewel* in *Sonnet 131*.

The comparison can go in other directions. For Miranda in *The Tempest*, her chastity is *the jewel in my dower* – the most valuable part of the gift that comes with her hand in marriage. For Mowbray in *Richard 2* the equivalent of a jewel in a heavily locked safe or vault is a courageous soul in a loyal person:

> A jewel in a ten-times barred-up chest
> Is a bold spirit in a loyal breast.

Whereas to Macbeth, the soul is an *eternal jewel*.

The poet talks to the young person he loves, whose faults he sees as 'graces'. Any errors in him will appear as truths. He uses this analogy to drive his point home.

THE SONNETS

## The crow doth sing as sweetly as the lark
## When neither is attended.

———∞———

If a tree falls in a forest, when no one's around, does anyone care what it sounds like? When people aren't paying attention to sounds, they lose their distinctive character, and these lines suggest that even the harsh cawing of a crow and the musical notes of a lark are the same, if no one listens to them.

Benvolio draws a similar contrast in *Romeo and Juliet*, telling Romeo to look beyond his current love, Rosaline:

> Compare her face with some that I shall show,
> And I will make thee think thy swan a crow.

The crow family is usually shown in a negative light – as in many mythologies. Crows, ravens, rooks and magpies all create a sense of foreboding. Macbeth brings two together as he plans *a deed of dreadful note*:

> Light thickens
> And the crow makes wing to the rooky wood;
> Good things of day begin to droop and drowse
> While night's black agents to their prey do rouse.

*Rooky* meant 'filled with rooks', or 'dark'; *rouse* means 'startle from their lair'.

To call someone a *crow* would therefore be quite an insult. The writer Robert Greene complained in 1592 about a young up-and-coming actor – 'Shakescene' – who aspired to write as well as established playwrights. Greene called him an 'upstart crow'.

Not a bad first review, Master William Shakespeare – it's when they *stop* talking about you that you have to worry.

It's the end of the play. Portia and Nerissa return to their house in the dark, after their eventful time at the Duke's court. Portia hears her musicians playing and reflects on how much sweeter music sounds at night than during the daytime. She goes on to consider other instances where sounds change their character.

# There is differency between a grub and a butterfly, yet your butterfly was a grub.

— ∞ —

A simple sentiment: change is the only constant.

And, even the worst situations (or creatures that lack charm, like grubs) can blossom into the most beautiful, fragile examples of life, even if only for a brief moment. If we have started out in life with few prospects, and since done well through our own efforts, we can reflect with pride on our origins.

For the lepidopterists among you, Shakespeare refers to butterflies only four more times. Their beauty is noted in *A Midsummer Night's Dream*, by Titania who describes them as *painted*; the same sentiment can be found in *King Lear*, when Cordelia and her father, together in prison, laugh at *gilded* butterflies.

On the other hand, in the same play as today's lead quote, the poor insects are in danger from children: Cominius talks about *boys pursuing summer butterflies*, and a gilded one described by Valeria is teased to death by the son of the fearsome warrior, Coriolanus.

Menenius and Sicinius are discussing the changes in Coriolanus, since his banishment. Menenius believes Coriolanus will show no mercy to Rome. Sicinius wonders if it's possible for someone to change so much in such a short time, and Menenius replies with these lines, adding that Coriolanus has grown from man to dragon … (For more on dragons, see May 31st.)

CORIOLANUS

There is a tide in the affairs of men,
Which, taken at the flood,
　　leads on to fortune;
Omitted, all the voyage of their life
Is bound in shallows and in miseries.

———— ∞ ————

A decision needs to be made, with time a-ticking. It's a turning-point moment, so ... grab life with both hands; don't let golden opportunities pass you by; *carpe diem* – seize the day.

These are common modern phrases; today's lead quote goes one further. It doesn't describe the tides but a tide – singular. *The* juncture in life when a path to fortune comes your way. You must take it, because if you miss it, your life will become stuck (as a boat can get trapped in shallow waters) and miserable.

The *flood* is when the tide reaches its maximum point of flowing in; when you sail, you take the tide at its highest point, so as it ebbs it can carry you out to sea (or fortune) without too much extra effort needed on your part. If you miss that tide, or *omit* ('forget about' or 'ignore') that opportunity, then a lifetime of regretful 'what if I hads' and 'should I haves' is probably going to follow, unless you're good at acceptance, and seeing silver linings in clouds.

Shakespeare's usual word for a decision is *doom*. It was beginning to develop its modern connotations of 'ruin' and 'death' in Shakespeare's time, as in *Sonnet 14*: *Thy end is Truth and Beauty's doom and date.*

JULIUS CAESAR

Brutus and Cassius have been arguing about the best military strategy for their forthcoming battle against Antony. Cassius thinks they should stay where they are and let the enemy seek them out. Brutus argues that they need to press on to fight at Philippi. Which way to go ...?

Life's but a walking shadow, a poor player
That struts and frets his hour upon the stage,
And then is heard no more. It is a tale
Told by an idiot, full of sound and fury,
Signifying nothing.

*Shadow* here means 'imitation'; *player* means 'actor'.

We make a lot of fuss and noise, but none of it means anything. These words are spoken by Macbeth who has only recently said these equally sad words:

And that which should accompany old age,
As honour, love, obedience, troops of friends,
I must not look to have.

Powerful lines; ones that we hope we'll never have to say. Shakespeare doesn't always show us the people or situations that we want to emulate; he also likes to show us the worst constellations of the heart.

Macbeth waits for a final battle with the English army. He has just heard of the death of his wife, and reflects on what life is to him.

MACBETH

## Manhood is called foolery when it stands Against a falling fabric.

———— ⚮ ————

A line for whenever we walk into a rake.

*Against* means 'close to'; *fabric* means 'building'. In other words, 'Don't lean against a building that's falling down'; 'Don't go into a burning house'; 'Don't try to drink an ocean'; 'Don't try to fly using weather balloons' ... This applies to all humanhood.

Today's quote could be the slogan for the Darwin Awards: the annual virtual prize-giving for those judged to have done humanity the biggest favour, by leaving it in some extraordinarily daft (although often, well-intentioned) way. Their innately stupidity-related departure from life is considered evolutionarily useful to the species, by 'keeping their genes out of our pool'. The first winner was crushed to death by a vending machine, having tried to break into it.

It's important not to read in the most common modern sense of 'fabric' which developed in the 18th century, of manufactured textiles, and the products they've brought with them, like 'fabric softener'. The line loses some of its force if someone chooses to stand under a piece of falling cloth.

A related sense is still heard: *fabric* as in, the 'basic structure of something', as when we talk about the 'fabric' of a building. This is how the wizard Prospero uses the word in *The Tempest*, when he tells his daughter Miranda and her suitor, Ferdinand, that the vision they've just seen was a *baseless fabric*. *Baseless* meant 'unsubstantial, lacking a foundation' – its basic structure lacked substance, it had no basis in reality.

Cominius advises Coriolanus not to confront a mob of citizens, since they have turned against him. The odds, he says, are *beyond arithmetic* ('beyond mental computation'). Coriolanus agrees to go – although it is a temporary departure. He'll be back.

**When once our grace we have forgot,
Nothing goes right.**

— ∞ —

*Grace* here means 'virtue, goodness, gracefulness, charm, clemency, personal duty, respect …'.

Angelo recognises that he broke the very law that he himself introduced, but thinks he is safe from discovery. Now his conscience begins to prick him, and he reflects on how it goes when we lose our grace.

MEASURE
FOR MEASURE

# Nothing will come of nothing.

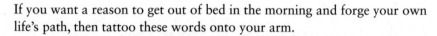

If you want a reason to get out of bed in the morning and forge your own life's path, then tattoo these words onto your arm.

If you're pondering creationism (that everything came from someone) or the Big Bang (that everything came out of something) then you're in luck: the concept of nothing is repeatedly chewed over in the plays.

Feste the Fool in *Twelfth Night* offers a global truth, that nothing is quite what it seems, when you put it under close examination:

> Nothing that is so, is so.

These words were written just as the microscope was being invented.

And Richard, in *Richard 2*, welcomes the idea that we will not truly find contentment as humans until we have moved past our egos and accepted our relative insignificance in the universe:

> But whate'er I be,
> Nor I, nor any man that but man is,
> With nothing shall be pleased, till he be eased
> With being nothing.

Coriolanus's mum puts living fully and contentedly as a person in the simplest and wisest terms (as mothers always do):

> You might have been enough the man you are
> With striving less to be so.

As ever with these quotes, read 'human' instead of *man*.

> Lear has asked Cordelia to put her love for him into words, in order to receive a third of his kingdom. She is unable to say anything other than the word, *nothing*. This is Lear's response.

# KING LEAR

# In peace there's nothing so becomes a man
# As modest stillness and humility.

— ✥ —

*Stillness* here means 'restraint', 'sobriety', 'generally quiet behaviour'. Only one character in the plays is actually described in this way: Montano, the governor of Cyprus in *Othello*. He's praised by Othello:

> The gravity and stillness of your youth
> The world hath noted.

Life, and all its unexpected turns, invites and invokes different qualities of behaviour. Asked why he killed the guards of the murdered King Duncan, Macbeth tells of his competing emotions, which pulled him in different directions at once:

> Who can be wise, amazed, temperate and furious,
> Loyal and neutral, in a moment?

Who can be logical, surprised, keep their temper and also be furious, loyal to someone you care for and objective, all at the same time? Arguably – when in shock, and passionate – none of us.

Frightening to think we might all have a little something in common with a murderous warrior like Macbeth.

King Henry gives his troops a rousing speech before the Battle of Harfleur, encouraging them to storm the gap in the walls again with the words, *Once more unto the breach* ... Peacetime is contrasted with wartime when he tells them to *imitate the action of the tiger.*

HENRY V

# Virtue is bold, and goodness never fearful.

— ∞ —

*Virtue* means 'courage', 'integrity'; *goodness* has been so highly valued over the centuries that it has become part of the everyday idiom in 'for goodness' sake', and lost its force as a consequence – it's now just an exclamation of irritated impatience.

The ancestor of the idiom – indeed, its first recorded use in English – is there when Cardinal Wolsey appeals to Queen Katherine in *Henry 8*:

> For goodness' sake, consider what you do.

Here, the Cardinal is making a serious entreaty, not informally expressing irritation.

In Shakespeare's time, *goodness* retained a meaning of 'natural kindness' or 'generosity'. We hear it used in that way when a merchant praises Timon in *Timon of Athens*:

> A most incomparable man, breathed, as it were,
> To an untirable and continuate goodness.

He only breathes, he's only alive, so that he can continue to be inexhaustibly, naturally, kind and generous.

MEASURE
FOR MEASURE

The Duke of Vienna is disguised as a friar, and is advising Isabella about a way to save her brother from execution. She tells him she has the spirit to do anything that appears not *foul* ('false, hypocritical, shameful') and he commends her with these words.

# I have learned that fearful commenting
# Is leaden servitor to dull delay.

— ∞ —

Don't be slow to speak. 'Get to the point', we might say, if we find ourselves impatient with someone who talks around a subject. *Fearful* meant 'timid'; *commenting* meant 'pondering'; *servitor* meant 'servant'. In other words, 'indirect speech is a slow servant to boring delay'. Perhaps Cymbeline says it better:

> I stand on fire.
> Come to the matter.

*Matter* here means 'subject matter', just as Queen Gertrude interrupts Polonius's verbosity in *Hamlet* with the words *More matter, with less art* – less flourish and unnecessary bits. *The Merry Wives of Windsor* says it well:

> Come, to the forge with it, then.
> Shape it. I would not have things cool.

Work out a plan of action quickly before enthusiasm – the fire for an idea – cools, and like metal in a forge, can no longer be shaped. Reignier in *Henry 6 Part 1* also advises Charles to take action quickly:

> Defer no time; delays have dangerous ends.

And Antonio in *The Merchant of Venice* almost loses patience with his friend Bassanio (who has come to ask him for financial help):

> You know me well, and herein spend but time
> To wind about my love with circumstance.

*Wind about* meant 'pursue an indirect course' – pronounced to rhyme with 'find' rather than 'binned'. *With circumstance* – with 'circumlocution' or 'unnecessary verbiage'. Cut to the chase, Bassanio.

Ratcliffe has brought Richard news of his followers. Some have abandoned him, including his former closest adviser, the Duke of Buckingham. Richard pulls himself together with these words.

# They whose guilt within their bosoms lie
# Imagine every eye beholds their blame.

— ∞ —

We're so worried that people will perceive our guilt, that in desperately trying not to appear guilty, we feel even more guilty, and imagine everyone's slightest reaction to be an indication that we've been found out.

A similar line occurs in *Hamlet*:

> **So full of artless jealousy is guilt**
> **It spills itself in fearing to be spilt.**

Guilt is full of such *artless* ('uncontrollable') *jealousy* ('suspicion') that it *spills itself* ('makes itself known') in the careful attempt to not 'spill a drop' of guilt.

We're used to *jealousy* meaning 'envy' or 'fear of rivalry', rather than 'suspicion' – a sense that has largely disappeared, though it will still be heard in some regional dialects, as in 'it's only my jealousy'.

A sister quote to May 6th.

Lucrece fears her servant will see her shame, and the poet reflects on guilt with these words.

T<sub>HE</sub> RAPE <sub>OF</sub> LUCRECE

We do pray for mercy,
And that same prayer
   doth teach us all to render
The deeds of mercy.

———∞———

Whether we pray or hope for mercy from those in power, the very act of seeking mercy teaches us to become merciful in our own actions.

In other words, the mirror neurons in our brains (which fire when we see someone laugh, and make us feel a little happier thereby) teach us empathy, and make us feel merciful, when we see others act benevolently, kindly, compassionately.

This reciprocal wish is rarely encountered in the plays. Acts of mercy tend to be rejected, or have dangerous outcomes. *Sweet mercy is nobility's true badge*, says Tamora in *Titus Andronicus*, pleading for the life of her son; but she receives none, and will give none herself later in the play.

*Mercy* was frequently part of an exclamation, with several uses. *I cry you mercy* was very common, basically meaning 'I'm sorry'. Also common was *God-a-mercy* ('God have mercy'), used to express thanks, surprise, and other positive attitudes.

Henry responds to a greeting with it in *Henry 5*:

> Erpingham: The Lord in heaven bless thee, noble Harry!
> Henry: God-a-mercy, old heart, thou speak'st cheerfully.

Portia speaks these words to Shylock the Jew. He has denied her request to show mercy to the merchant Antonio, and asks, *On what compulsion must I?* Portia replies *The quality of mercy is not strained*, and these words follow shortly after. (See July 12th for more about mercy.)

# Where the greater malady is fixed,
# The lesser is scarce felt.

— ❦ —

*Malady* means both physical and mental ill health. *Fixed* means 'firmly in place'.

When there is anguish of mind so firmly in place, no attention is paid to the troubles which would normally be a cause of distress.

In other words, if you cut your hand off (a fairly fixed injury), you probably won't be worrying about your tax return for a while.

A little later in the same play, a balancing line is offered:

> When the mind's free,
> The body's delicate.

When you're free of worry, the body will be *delicate* – sensitive to the slightest issue, which then can't be ignored. In other words, only in a moment of (relative) peace might we notice our nails need trimming.

Lear and his companions are in a huge storm; Kent tries to get the aged king to take shelter. Lear says that although Kent finds the storm a great trouble, it isn't so to him because something much greater *beats there* – 'preoccupies him':

This tempest in my mind
Doth from my senses take all feeling else
Save what beats there.

KING LEAR

# The apprehension of the good
# Gives but the greater feeling to the worse.

The anticipation of something good can make you feel worse when you're down.

It's only natural to try to comfort someone who feels they're in a bad situation that isn't going to change. Comfort or support can feel like a hindrance rather than a help, and some will push back against anyone attempting to sympathise with them. In *Romeo and Juliet*, the newly banished Romeo firmly rejects Friar Lawrence's attempts to advise:

> Thou canst not speak of that thou dost not feel.

Banishment is also the driving force behind the words of today's quote. Bolingbroke is adamant that it's useless to think about good times ahead – that the power of positive thinking, manifesting and reframing will only take you so far.

> O, who can hold a fire in his hand
> By thinking on the frosty Caucasus,
> Or cloy the hungry edge of appetite
> By bare imagination of a feast,
> Or wallow naked in December snow
> By thinking on fantastic summer's heat?

(The Caucasus is the range that contains Europe's highest mountain.)

John of Gaunt has been offering solace to his son, Bolingbroke, who has just been sent into exile for six years and can't see the bright side of his situation. His father points out the benefits that a time abroad could bring, but Bolingbroke rejects his father's thoughts with these words.

RICHARD II

The passions of the mind,
That have their first conception by misdread,
Have after-nourishment and life by care,
And what was first but fear
    what might be done
Grows elder now and cares it be not done.

———— ∞ ————

It's easy to find yourself getting into a *passion of the mind* (an 'emotional state') over a *misdread* (a 'fear of something that doesn't actually happen').

Instead of relaxing, most of us will keep worrying about it, letting *care* ('anxiety') give the worry *after-nourishment* ('sustenance'). So what begins as fear of the possibility of Something happening *grows elder* ('worsens with time'), turning into great anxiety – and much energy is spent ensuring that the Something never happens.

Today's quote is for the worriers. *Worry*, in the sense of 'mental distress', is actually a very recent usage in English – 19th century. In Shakespeare's time, the word meant 'maltreated' or 'savaged', as when in *Richard 3* Queen Margaret says Richard is a *dog ... to worry lambs* – a usage still with us. *Care* was the usual word to express the notion of worry: the King in *Richard 2* perhaps says it best when he asks Scroop:

> Say, is my kingdom lost? Why, 'twas my care;
> And what loss is it to be rid of care?

PERICLES

King Antiochus knows Pericles solved the riddle revealing an incestuous relationship with his daughter, and fears Pericles will tell everyone about it. Pericles thinks the King will go to war against Tyre. So he decides to travel abroad and escape his new enemy – and Pericles' misfortunes truly begin.

## Adversity's sweet milk, philosophy.

— ∽∞∾ —

*Adversity* – 'hardship', or 'difficulty'. *Sweet milk* – the kind of drink that you might give to calm someone, or help them sleep at night. And *philosophy* – the 'way of thinking about things', as in a 'philosophy of life'.

So: philosophical reflection can help soothe the pain of misfortune.

*Sweet are the uses of adversity*, says Duke Senior in *As You Like It*. But not everyone agrees about the power of philosophy. Failing to use one's philosophy can lead to distress. Brutus in *Julius Caesar* complains of being *sick of many griefs*. Cassius attempts to give him some advice:

> **Of your philosophy you make no use,**
> **If you give place to accidental evils.**

And in *King John* we hear philosophy being employed in an unusual way: Lady Constance begs the Cardinal to *preach some philosophy* that will madden her so much that she might forget her grief.

Romeo is distraught at the news of his banishment. Friar Lawrence offers him philosophy as an armour to keep off that word. But Romeo says *Hang up philosophy!* – as in, take philosophy to the hangman's gallows – a feeling many of us may recognise when in the heat of an upset, and temporarily blind and deaf to the grounding nature of philosophical, objective advice.

## Music oft hath such a charm
## To make bad good, and good provoke to harm.

— ∞ —

*Provoke* could mean 'incite', but here means 'make tremble, cause to shake'.

Music can make you feel good if you're down, or lift an awkward atmosphere, turning it into a pleasant and agreeable one; thus, music can shake and disintegrate anything of harm.

The healing power of music is a recurring theme in the plays. For some, it's a way out of sadness. Lucentio in *The Taming of the Shrew* asks why music was *ordained* ('created') and answers his own question:

> **Was it not to refresh the mind of man**
> **After his studies or his usual pain?**

Man stands for 'human'; you can replace *his* with 'her' or 'their'. The sentiment is echoed by the Gentlewoman singing to Queen Katherine in *Henry 8*:

> **In sweet music is such art,**
> **Killing care and grief of heart.**

But others may find themselves like Jessica in *The Merchant of Venice*, where music – especially *sweet* ('pleasant') music – can have the opposite effect:

> **I am never merry when I hear sweet music.**

Perhaps Jessica would like thrash metal?

Mariana has been listening to a sad love song. The Duke arrives (disguised as a friar), and she welcomes him as someone of comfort, and apologises that he found her so musical. She explains that the sad music actually helps her: *My mirth it much displeased, but pleased my woe …*

# He that stands upon a slippery place
# Makes nice of no vile hold to stay him up.

— ∞ —

*To make nice* is to 'be fastidious' or 'overscrupulous'; *no*, unusually, here means 'every' or 'any'; *vile*, as today, is 'despicable' or 'abhorrent'; and *stay* means 'prop' or 'hold'. As ever, replace *he/him* with 'she/her' or 'they/their' to suit.

So: those who feel unsafe, for whatever reason, are never fussy about clutching at anything that will help them, even if it's something they'd usually avoid. If you were falling off a cartoon cliff, you'd grab a snake or a panther's tail to stop your fall.

Or, for anyone who finds themselves faced with a great difficulty in life, actions normally avoided can quickly become temptingly attractive.

Cardinal Pandulph is advising Lewis the Dauphin how the French cause could still succeed, despite losing a recent battle. He knows that in order for King John to feel safe in his reign, he must do something most would consider vile – have young Prince Arthur killed: *That John may stand, then Arthur needs must fall.*

KING JOHN

**We turn not back the silks upon the merchant
When we have soiled them;
    nor the remainder viands
We do not throw in unrespective sieve
Because we now are full.**

— ◦⁂◦ —

We don't send a purchase back to the seller once we've used it; nor do we waste *remainder viands* ('leftover food') by throwing it away into a *sieve* ('bin') in which everything is *unrespective* ('mixed up').

If we value something, we want to keep it and take responsibility for looking after it. It's an argument that might seem unnecessary, but shopkeepers have had the experience of a customer trying to return something for no other reason than they've taken a dislike to it. And if good food is left over after a satisfying meal, most people would want a doggy-bag or some Tupperware, to conserve it for another occasion, and might look askance at anyone who didn't seem to care about food waste.

People who waste or squander in Shakespeare are usually referred to as *prodigals*. Maria in *Twelfth Night* describes Sir Andrew Aguecheek as *a very fool and a prodigal*, and Shylock in *The Merchant of Venice* says the same of Antonio: *A bankrupt, a prodigal*. Anyone who is foolishly extravagant attracts the term.

TROILUS &
CRESSIDA

The Trojans are having second thoughts about the wisdom of protecting Helen, whose abduction caused the war. Hector thinks she isn't worth the cost (measured in lives) they've had to pay for keeping her, and they should send her back. Troilus uses these analogies to reinforce the opposite view.

Time, whose millioned accidents
Creep in 'twixt vows, and change decrees
   of kings,
Tan sacred beauty, blunt the sharp'st intents,
Divert strong minds to th' course
   of alt'ring things.

— ∞ —

The poet reflects on time. How many *accidents* ('happenings') take place as time goes by. Anything can change, even the strongest of intentions – and not always for the worse. It can divert a *strong* ('firmly set') mind, to alter the *course* ('direction') of things.

Shakespeare is suggesting here that it would be good if the leaders of our countries were amenable to changing their minds over time, especially if they're causing untold and horrific damage.

The poet writes that his earlier poems lied, as they said he could not love any more than he already has – but now he feels the flame of his love burns even more strongly. He puts the blame on Time – a Shakespearean 'Absence makes the heart grow fonder'.

THE SONNETS

## The words of Mercury are harsh after the songs of Apollo.

—∽—

This is a line for whenever a happy event has been disturbed by the sudden arrival of bad news.

Apollo was the Greek sun god, who pulled the sun across the sky in a horse-drawn chariot; he had many functions, including being the god of prophecy and music.

Mercury was the messenger of the Roman gods. He was also the god of commerce, and could thus be seen as representing the real world, whereas Apollo has more to do with the world of make-believe. So today's quote would also work well in the context of a fantasy which is 'brought down to earth' by reality, and the 'songs' attributed to Apollo could be any kind of happy event.

Messengers in the plays are sometimes described as Mercuries. Richard, in *Richard 3*, claims that bad news – a death warrant – was brought to Clarence by a winged Mercury. And Falstaff in *The Merry Wives of Windsor* gets some good news from Mistress Quickly, whom he calls a *she-Mercury*.

And while messengers in Shakespeare are almost always people, occasionally the word is used metaphorically. In *The Two Gentlemen of Verona* Julia describes Proteus' tears as *pure messengers sent from his heart*.

A play is put on for entertainment, and actors perform as Ver (springtime, the cuckoo) and Hiems (winter, the owl). When their songs are over, Don Armado says this line as Marcade (Mercury) arrives with a message informing the Princess of her father's death. Understandably, this breaks up the poetic revelry (of Apollo).

LOVE's LABOR's LOST

## O Lord, I could have stayed here all the night
## To hear good counsel. O, what learning is!

— ⚮ —

A line for when you have been saturated with wisdom.

Before we leave August, here's one more, from *As You Like It*. This quote is for when someone is desperately trying to show off their wisdom, or is heavy-handed with its distribution. The melancholic Jacques has been listening to the Fool Touchstone's conversation with the milkmaid Audrey. Touchstone makes a reference to Greek mythology, which prompts this caustic comment from Jacques:

O, knowledge ill-inhabited, worse than Jove in a thatched house!

Juliet's Nurse has been listening to Friar Lawrence's grounding advice to the recently banished Romeo; evidently the Nurse is very impressed by the wisdom that can come from *learning* ('education, study').

JULIUS
CAESAR
KING JOHN
G LEAR
LOVE'S LABOUR
LOST
MACBETH
MEASURE
FOR MEASU

## Is there more toil?

— ∞ —

Ariel has performed all the tasks Prospero has asked – wrecking the King's ship, sending the rest of the King's fleet back to Naples, and the mariners to sleep, while bringing the nobles safely to different parts of the island. When Prospero says there's more work to be done, Ariel begins to question the wizard, with these words.

THE TEMPEST

# A while to work, and after, holiday.

— ∞ —

Few of us enjoy the return to work.

Prince Hal in *Henry 4 Part 1* offers the best balance to this 'back-to-school-blues' feeling as an analogy for his behaviour, which he says has so far been *loose* ('casual', 'unrestrained', 'uninhibited'), anticipating a reformation that will by contrast appear even more impressive:

> If all the year were playing holidays,
> To sport would be as tedious as to work;
> But when they seldom come, they wished-for come,
> And nothing pleaseth but rare accidents.

Forget the modern sense of *accident*, meaning a 'mishap, or an event that incurs an injury'; here it simply means 'an event or happening', without any hint of danger.

With this work–life or work–holiday balance, the *rare* ('unusual or exceptional') events cause pleasure, as they stand out from the routine of daily living.

Shakespeare repeatedly illustrates there has to be bad, for there to be good. That there need to be moments of down and difficulty, in order to perceive the moments of up and ease. That we need tragedy for there to be comedy, binary for there to be non-binary, and nothing once, for there to be everything now.

Bolingbroke, after a successful arrival in England, is ready to sort out his ailing country …

RICHARD II

# 'Tis no sin for a man to labour in his vocation.

— ❧ —

The Japanese word *ikigai* describes the place where vocation, mission, passion and profession overlap – where that which the world needs, that which you love, that which you're good at, and that which you can be paid for, meet.

Few of us get to experience this place, as there is usually one part missing. Either you're good at it, paid for it, and the world needs it – but you don't love it; or you love it, you're good at it, and the world needs it – but you don't get paid for it.

And it is no bad thing to pour time and energy into something that you feel is your *vocation* – your 'professional calling'. So, next time you're happily working late, either in the office or on your shed-hobby, call out today's lead quote if anyone chastises you. Or mutter this line from *Macbeth*:

> The labour we delight in physics pain.

'If we're doing a job we like to do, any effort feels easy'. *Physic* meant 'cure', or 'dose with medicine'. And *pain* has a meaning of 'effort' or 'endeavour' – as when we say we 'take pains' to do something.

And a more romantic alternative, from *The Tempest*, for any task undertaken for your love, not just when you're bringing firewood in for the winter:

> For your sake
> Am I this patient log-man.

As ever, with these quotes, *man* stands for 'human', and is easily replaced with woman, person, being, lover, what you will …

HENRY IV:1

Falstaff has announced his intention to give up his life of thieving, but when Prince Hal suggests there's a chance to take another purse, Falstaff jumps at it. Hal teases him about his change of heart, and Falstaff responds with these words (he's quoting a proverb, well-known in Shakespeare's day). He's essentially arguing that thievery is his vocation!

## The hand of little employment
## hath the daintier sense.

— ∞ —

This doesn't quite have the same meaning as the modern phrase, 'the Devil makes work for idle hands', but it's close.

Those of us with little to do have a *daintier sense* – 'possess a more delicate sensibility'. The line perhaps suggests that those who don't use their hands very much have a greater opportunity to develop refined tastes – perhaps because their hands aren't made rough through hard work, or because someone with little work to do has more time and energy to be creative.

There's another reading of this line that means something like, 'Those who don't take their job too seriously have a lightness of touch in their work.'

We can get bored or complacent about the most challenging or fascinating jobs, if they don't change and we do them for too long. Corin, the self-admittedly simple shepherd in *As You Like It*, offers the following pragmatic approach to his work (*harm* means 'misfortune'):

> I am a true labourer: I earn that I eat, get that I wear,
> owe no man hate, envy no man's happiness, glad
> of other men's good, content with my harm.

Hamlet and Horatio have watched the gravediggers as they prepare a grave. One of them sings and chats as he works; the other goes off for something alcoholic to drink – and all this leads Hamlet to wonder how gravediggers can do this while performing such a morbid job.

# Leave no rubs nor botches in the work.

— ∞ —

*No rubs nor botches* means 'neither unevenness nor clumsiness'. Be thorough, in other words.

There's good advice throughout the plays for anyone working on a project. Thoroughness and specificity, even scrupulousness, are important when you work – but up to a point, suggests King John:

> When workmen strive to do better than well,
> They do confound their skill in covetousness;
> And oftentimes excusing of a fault
> Doth make the fault the worse by th' excuse.

*Skill* ('craft') can be *confounded* ('ruined') by being *covetous* ('overzealous, greedy for perfection'); and trying to *excuse* ('correct') a little mistake can make everything much worse.

Or as Albany in *King Lear* succinctly puts it:

> Striving to better, oft we mar what's well.

Overdoing something, or making work where none is needed, might be a familiar frustration to any holidaymakers, as *The Merchant of Venice* wryly observes:

> Why, this is like the mending of highways
> In summer, where the ways are fair enough.

Macbeth is talking to the men he wants to carry out the murder of Banquo; with these words, he instructs them to be thorough in the killing of his friend ...

**Like a man to double business bound
I stand in pause where I shall first begin,
And both neglect.**

———— ⚮ ————

Ah! I've overcommitted myself – which project do I attend to first?

Ah! I'm overcooking two things – which do I save first?

Ah! I'm carrying something that's heavy and can't get wet and it's started raining and the umbrella's in my bag – what do I do first?

Which road do I take? Which insurance company? Which TV series tonight?

And by resting in that dithering indecision, we invariably end up getting everything soaked, ordering take-away, and watching trailers all evening.

(As ever, *man* here stands for 'human'.)

Claudius is alone, reflecting on what he has done. He feels he should pray but finds he cannot. He is uncertain about what to do next, and recognises he is *in pause* ('a state of hesitation').

## 'Tis not sleepy business,
## But must be looked to speedily, and strongly.

— ∞ —

A nice way of telling someone that you need them to hurry to finish a task, but still take care of it well, or *strongly*.

Macbeth – on his way to commit murder, and regicide at that – has an offer for anyone tending towards procrastination. If you're going to do something then it's best you do it straight away:

> If it were done when 'tis done, then 'twere well
> It were done quickly.

*Richard 3* warns of thinking too far ahead, focusing on the deadline instead of the task at hand:

> But yet I run before my horse to market.

We might say today, 'I'm getting ahead of myself', or, 'I'm counting chickens before they're hatched'. *Venus and Adonis* also invites us to be mindful when rushing a task, while home or heart is bothering us:

> For oft the eye mistakes, the brain being troubled.

Venus is looking *steadfastly* ('unwaveringly') at the body of Adonis (who has been fatally wounded by a boar). She sees three wounds instead of one, then two faces, and each limb doubled. The poet sympathises with these words, that 'our eyes can't always be trusted when we're in grief'.

An Italian proverb offers a similar idea: 'The eye is blind if the mind is absent.' To this end, a disturbed Achilles in *Troilus and Cressida* offers:

> My mind is troubled, like a fountain stirred,
> And I myself see not the bottom of it.

(*Bottom* could mean 'full extent', or 'gist, main point'.)

War is in the offing between Rome and Britain. Cymbeline says the British must prepare for a battle, and the Queen agrees, with these words.

# Frame the business after your own wisdom.

— ❦ —

Creative freedom in one's work can be liberating, exciting, terrifying. As Lady Northumberland in *Henry 4 Part 2* says to her husband:

Do what you will; your wisdom be your guide.

Or you might decide to gift that kind of freedom to your employees, just as the grief-stricken King (in *Henry 6 Part 2*) says to his nobles to carry on without him:

My lords, what to your wisdoms seemeth best
Do or undo, as if ourself were here.

Gloucester has just learned from Edmund of the supposed wickedness of Edgar, and is desperate to find out the truth. Gloucester says he'd give up everything to get some certainty: *I would unstate myself to be in a due resolution.* He gives Edmund free rein to find a way forward, with these words.

KING LEAR

**Away, and glister like the god of war
When he intendeth to become the field.
Show boldness and aspiring confidence!**

———— ∞ ————

These lines were spoken to urge a king to go to war, but they could easily be adapted to any situation where someone is in need of encouragement – entering a competition, sitting an exam, running a marathon, giving a speech, competing on *The Great British Bake Off*, acting on stage … Any challenge might be metaphorically described as a battle to be won.

*Become the field* doesn't mean turn into earth and grass; *become* means give a 'pleasing appearance'. In other words, make the field look prettier, or the work better, because of what you're doing in it. The glittering allusion is to the helmet and armour of Mars, the god of war, sparkling in the sun, as he *becomes* ('graces with his presence') a battlefield.

In other words, don't just play the game, make the game look better in your playing of it. The most important thing is to do it proudly, boldly and with great confidence: *glister* ('sparkle') like the god of war. And we're invited to remember, as *The Two Gentlemen of Verona* says:

> Experience is by industry achieved,
> And perfected by the swift course of time.

*Experience* had a sense of 'knowledge of the world'. *By industry* means 'by being conscientious, diligent'. Doing something new or without guidance will likely take time and experience before it goes well. The good news is, it won't take long (time is swift), and experience is the beginning of gaining craft and skill in something.

The message is simple: go and sparkle.

KING JOHN

The Bastard has brought news to King John: his nobles have defected to the French. He tries to revive his king's drooping spirits, saying, *Be great in act, as you have been in thought.* He continues with these words.

# The task he undertakes
# Is numbering sands and drinking oceans dry.

— ⚭ —

Next time you're faced with a seemingly impossible task, reach for today's lead quote. Or indeed, this one, from *Henry 5*:

> You may as well go about to turn the sun to ice,
> with fanning in his face with a peacock's feather.

(*His* refers to *the sun*.) If you do find yourself overloaded, remember this advice from Cassius in *Julius Caesar*:

> Those that with haste will make a mighty fire
> Begin it with weak straws.

Go step by step: focus on the footfall in front of you, not the mountain above you, as Ben's mother says.

Shakespeare writes to those beset by doubts about their ability or suitability to make an enterprise come to fruition – those who might consider themselves to be weak straws. But straws are still the basic ingredients to make a mighty fire burn.

*Straw* has the modern meaning of 'a hollow tube used to suck down a cool refreshing drink' – a meaning that didn't emerge until the mid-19th century. Here it refers to the dry stem of a cereal plant – something that would very easily start a fire, though it's weak in its structure. Its relative uselessness leads to a meaning of 'trivial matter'; in *The Winter's Tale*, Hermione rejects Leontes' threats and says, of her life: *I prize it not a straw.*

Bushy, Bagot and Green think they will not meet again in the face of Bolingbroke's progress. Bushy thinks there's a possibility that the Duke of York will beat back the invading Bolingbroke, but Green thinks he hasn't a chance, and says so.

RI<sub>CH</sub>ARD II

**If you saw yourself with your eyes, or knew yourself with your judgement, the fear of your adventure would counsel you to a more equal enterprise.**

— ∞ —

In other words, 'I wouldn't do that if I were you.'

*Adventure* here simply means a 'venture' or 'enterprise', especially one that's hazardous. It lacks the sense, dominant today, of a 'novel or exciting experience'.

And yet, it's inevitable that there will be *checks* ('setbacks'), especially when people are engaged in a really ambitious project:

> Checks and disasters
> Grow in the veins of actions highest reared.

This line is from *Troilus and Cressida*. After seven years of war, the Greeks have been unable to break through the walls of Troy, and they're evidently gloomy. Agamemnon, the Greek commander, acknowledges that everything they've done so far has failed to achieve their aim, but insists that such setbacks are an inevitable part of any ambitious enterprise.

*Disasters*: the intended meaning needs to be carefully evaluated, for people can call an event 'a disaster' in an ironic or jocular way. The word has various degrees of force, from 'calamity' and 'catastrophe' through 'misfortune' and 'failure' to 'unfavourable appearance'.

AS YOU LIKE IT

Orlando has volunteered to fight Charles, the Duke's wrestler, renowned for his prowess and ferocity against opponents. Rosalind and Celia are horrified at the unequal nature of the contest, and are trying to persuade Orlando not to proceed. But the young man will surprise them all …

# What to ourselves in passion we propose,
# The passion ending, doth the purpose lose.

— ◦∞◦ —

Get all excited about an idea, commit to it … and then lose energy for it.

For those of us familiar with that routine, especially when the Great Idea might also have been a bit daft, *As You Like It* asks:

> How many actions most ridiculous
> Hast thou been drawn to by thy fantasy?

These words are originally spoken by a young man called Silvius, telling an old shepherd called Corin how much he is in love. Silvius wonders if others have loved as ardently as he, and asks Corin about his own former *fantasy* (er, let's say 'amorous fancies'). In other words, 'How many stupid things have you done in the name of love?' Corin's perfect reply is: *Into a thousand that I have forgotten.*

Love is said to conquer all. And those that are able to hold love in their hearts, and not become a slave to their emotions – those are the people that Hamlet prizes most dearly:

> Give me that man
> That is not passion's slave, and I will wear him
> In my heart's core, ay, in my heart of heart,
> As I do thee.

The actors at Elsinore are performing a play before the court. One character insists that she will never marry again when her husband is dead. The other character points out that people with the best of intentions can break their promises, especially when their intentions are expressed while in a *passion* (a 'highly emotional state').

HAMLET

## Now does my project gather to a head.

— ∞ —

All the parts are in place; just the finishing touches to add. Or, as a line in *Hamlet* goes:

> **Everything is sealed and done**
> **That else leans on the affair.**

Final arrangements have been made for all else that this idea depends on. (The original sense of *seal* was to close a document by melting a piece of soft wax on it, with a personalised symbol or letter, which showed it was authentic.)

At a final point in any creative process, it's easy to ruin the end product; to panic-add or -take away too much. Hairdressers and landscape gardeners, painters and sculptors, woodworkers and musicians, directors and designers, and many others know this very well. Still, when considering that final pruning, remember that Timon of Athens suggests simpler can often be better:

> **Let it go naked, men may see't the better.**

It is the last scene of the play. Prospero is satisfied that his magic is working, and that his plans will come to fruition at long, long last.

**Why good ladies
This is a service, whereto I am going,
Greater than any war; it more imports me
Than all the actions that I have foregone
Or futurely can cope.**

— ❦ —

Sometimes, a project makes you feel so proud that, as you come to finish it, its importance is second-to-none. In that case, reach for these lines, where a character is on their way to the most important thing in their life to date.

Saying the words out loud feels awesome. Try it now. It's like giving voice to a Marvel superhero, but, y'know, written by Shakespeare.

Wouldn't it be great if we all got to say something like this in real life, and mean it, just once? (*Ladies* can be replaced with 'gentles', or 'people'.)

Duke Theseus (the same one as in *A Midsummer Night's Dream*) is on his way to attend his wedding ceremony. Three widowed queens arrive, begging him to avenge their dead husbands. He says what he's about to do is more important than anything else before or since – but he is eventually persuaded …

TWO NOBLE KINSMEN

If to have done the thing you gave in charge
Beget your happiness, be happy then,
For it is done.

———— ∞ ————

*Beget* ('give birth to', 'produce') seems to be going out of use, apart from in religious texts, where one character is said to 'beget' another or someone is said to be 'begotten'. It has a literary use, like a formula, 'x begets y': 'violence begets violence', or 'industry begets wealth'.

A line for anyone who wants to acknowledge that a requested task has been satisfactorily performed.

Tyrrel agreed to arrange the murder of the two young princes in the Tower of London, at the instigation of Richard. He goes to see King Richard, who asks, *Am I happy in thy news?* Tyrrel takes up the theme of happiness in his reply.

RI<sub>H</sub><sup>C</sup>ARD III

## He is well paid that is well satisfied.

— ∞ —

Portia is disguised as a male lawyer. Bassanio tries to give him/her three thousand ducats for his/her services, but he/she refuses. Saving Antonio's life is satisfaction enough, he/she says. Portia then asks instead to have Bassanio's ring (which she gave him upon their marriage). Trouble, as you might imagine, later ensues.

THE MERCHANT OF VENICE

# A greater power than we can contradict
# Hath thwarted our intents.

—— ∞ ——

And if a project fails? If, no matter what else you do, it falls apart? Then you get to use this quote. *Intents* ('plans') have been defeated by something you're unable to *contradict* ('oppose').

For some, the *greater* ('higher') *power* in question must be a god; for others it might be supernatural beings, cosmic energies, or universal forces of some kind. A soothsayer in *Cymbeline* declares:

> The fingers of the powers above do tune
> The harmony of this peace.

Whatever you feel them to be, characters in the plays often call on them. Ophelia asks for help for Hamlet, who appears to be deranged: *O heavenly powers, restore him!*

And Emilia in *The Two Noble Kinsmen*, distraught at the way the contest between Arcite and Palamon has ended, calls out:

> O all you heavenly powers, where is your mercy?

This is an especially useful one when your cake doesn't rise, says Ben's gran.

Friar Lawrence has arrived in the family burial vault where Juliet has been sleeping, drugged to look as if she's dead. The Friar, though, is too late to explain to Romeo that she didn't actually die. Juliet wakes, hears with these words that their plans have failed, and (spoiler) finds her love lying dead next to her.

# SEPTEMBER 17TH

**One good deed dying tongueless
Slaughters a thousand waiting upon that.
Our praises are our wages.**

— ✦ —

Whenever you read this, it's important to remember that good deeds, and hard work, need to be appreciated with words, and not acknowledged *tongueless* ('in silence'). Someone may have a store of worthy initiatives in mind, but failing to acknowledge just one can be enough to make the good angel lose all inclination to do more.

The King in *Henry 5* also condemns tonguelessness. He's determined to have victory in France, so that history with full mouth will acclaim his actions; the alternative will be a grave with no epitaph – a *tongueless* mouth.

Richard in *Richard 3* also uses the word, bitterly complaining about the citizens, calling them *tongueless blocks*, because they didn't join in the applause to acclaim him as king.

People look for praise – as long as the praise is for them, and not for someone else. 'Whenever a friend succeeds, a little something of me dies', as the modern quote goes.

King Leontes praises his wife, Queen Hermione, for persuading King Polixenes to stay with them longer. She says she was only ever praised by Leontes once before. She's probably joking – and certainly doesn't know this will be the last praise she'll get from him for many years …

THE WINTER'S TALE

**It is a good divine that follows his own instructions. I can easier teach twenty what were good to be done, than be one of the twenty to follow mine own teaching.**

— ∞ —

Are you great at offering advice about relationships, or the benefits of exercise, but terrible at following your own counsel?

A *divine* is an older way of describing a clergyman. (Escalus in *Measure for Measure* asks for Claudio to be *furnished with divines* before his execution.) The implication is that those who give sermons, advising people every week how to behave, often don't live up to their own recommendations. They don't 'practise what they preach'.

The hypocrisy of 'Do as I say, not as I do' extends well beyond the sphere of religion. We can replace *divine* with 'politician', or any other role where people advocate behaviour they fail to respect themselves.

Hypocrisy is reserved for characters who clearly don't act as they should, as in *Love's Labour's Lost*. Berowne is in no doubt that his companions haven't lived up to the oaths they made: *Now step I forth to whip hypocrisy* – though the same charge will shortly be made against him.

> The Lady Portia complains about her state of mind, which Nerissa finds problematic, especially when Portia has such fine fortune. She agrees that Nerissa's advice is good, but her friend and maid says that simple agreement is not enough; action is needed. *If only it were so easy*, Portia replies.

THE MERCHANT OF VENICE

# God give thee the spirit of persuasion, and him the ears of profiting, that what thou speakest may move, and what he hears may be believed.

———— ⚮ ————

It can feel impossible to persuade someone to your way of thinking. Indeed, common wisdom says that you can't, that they have to find their own way.

Some characters are aware they aren't good persuaders. Hotspur is one in *Henry 4 Part 1*. Before the Battle of Shrewsbury he tells his fellow-soldiers:

> Better consider what you have to do
> Than I that have not well the gift of tongue
> Can lift your blood up with persuasion.

'Persuade yourself', in other words; 'I'm no good at it'. Those trying to dissuade Leontes from his tragic course of action in *The Winter's Tale* have one final idea: Paulina intends to show Hermione's new-born child to Leontes, in the hope that this will turn his jealous mind:

> The silence often of pure innocence
> Persuades when speaking fails.

– though perhaps those of us who wish to persuade need to be more like the condemned Claudio's sister, Isabella, in *Measure for Measure*. He hopes she'll be able to appeal to the deputy Angelo on his behalf:

> She will play with reason and discourse,
> And well she can persuade.

And the king's counsellor Gonzalo in *The Tempest* is described by Antonio as a professional persuader: *a spirit of persuasion*.

Falstaff has invited Prince Hal to rob some travellers. Hal has refused, but Poins thinks he can persuade the Prince to go along. Falstaff wishes him well with these words, and the Prince does join in the robbery – but not in the way Falstaff expects.

For I know thou'rt full of love and honesty,
And weigh'st thy words before
   thou giv'st them breath,
Therefore these stops of thine
   affright me more:
For such things in a false disloyal knave
Are tricks of custom; but in a man that's just,
They're close dilations, working
   from the heart,
That passion cannot rule.

— ∞ —

To *weigh thy words* means to 'consider what you say (before you say it)'.

*Stops* meant 'pauses'; *affright* meant 'frighten'; *false* meant 'faithless' or 'traitorous'; *knave* meant 'scoundrel'; *tricks of custom* meant 'skill of habit'.

*Just* meant 'honourable, faithful, loyal'; *close dilations* meant 'secret expansions' or 'hidden allegations'.

Pauses in someone known to be a liar are part of their instinctive habit and skill in cheating. In someone known to be true, a sudden pause indicates something truthful, pressing on their heart, that they want to say, but hold back from saying.

A useful, 400-year-old litmus test when someone gives you feedback, or an appraisal of your work.

Iago has been hinting at Desdemona's infidelity, and his pauses are now frightening Othello ...

> – I will tell you a thing, but you shall
> let it dwell darkly with you.
> – When you have spoken it, 'tis dead,
> and I am the grave of it.

— ∞ —

A great opportunity to bring some Shakespeare into an everyday relationship with a close friend. Here, *darkly* means 'secretly', so the first line runs, 'I'll tell you something, but you must let it live a secret within you'. In other words, 'You mustn't tell anyone'. The *dwell darkly* metaphor used here needs an equally portentous response, and an allusion to *the grave* conveys it nicely.

Secrets are quite often told in the plays. In *Hamlet*, Laertes tells his sister Ophelia to remember his advice, and she replies:

'Tis in my memory locked,
And you yourself shall keep the key of it.

*Measure for Measure* offers a similar line: *'Tis a secret must be locked within the teeth and the lips.*

Less convincing might be these lines from *Henry 8*:

2nd Gentleman: This secret is so weighty, 'twill require
            A strong faith to conceal it.
1st Gentleman: Let me have it; I do not talk much.

Truthfulness, honesty, and promises were evidently of great importance to Shakespeare's audience. *Swearing* – making an oath – was an even stronger form of promising. And finally for today, *Henry 6 Part 2* offers a line for when a promise is being doubted:

Had I but said, I would have kept my word;
But when I swear, it is irrevocable.

Two lords are gossiping about Bertram's behaviour towards Helena, and how he has now incurred the King's displeasure. The First Lord says he knows something about Bertram, and the Second Lord can't wait to hear it.

## Pour out the pack of matter to mine ear,
## The good and bad together.

— ∞ —

Today's lead quote is useful when someone says 'I've got good news and bad news. Which would you like to hear first?' But be careful how you bring your news. The King in *Richard 3* is abrupt when Ratcliffe bursts in: *Good or bad news, that thou com'st in so bluntly?*

It isn't always easy hearing both types of news. In *Macbeth*, Macduff has heard many different types of news, pretend-lies and deep truths, and is having a tough time taking it all in:

> Such welcome and unwelcome things at once
> 'Tis hard to reconcile.

Some, as in *Othello*, want nothing but the truth, however bad it may be:

> Speak to me as to thy thinkings,
> As thou dost ruminate, and give thy worst of thoughts
> The worst of words.

And when something intense takes place, Macbeth suggests it is deserving of reflection, time, space to *weigh it* ('consider it'), before sharing your *free* ('unconstrained, free of worry') heart's thought with someone else:

> Think upon what hath chanced, and at more time,
> The interim having weighed it, let us speak
> Our free hearts each to other.

A messenger has brought Cleopatra news of Antony. He begins with good news, but then hints of bad with a *But yet* … This angers Cleopatra, and she tells him to say what the rest of the news is at once.

## – Shall I say more?
## – I would hear you still.

— ∞ —

'I could have listened forever.'

*Still* means 'always' or 'constantly'. 'Do go on', we might say, when someone pauses in the middle of a fascinating narrative, and asks 'Shall I carry on?'.

*Still* in the sense of 'constantly' or 'continually' is used a great deal by Shakespeare. It's one of his everyday words. It looks forwards rather than backwards in time, to mean 'now and forever', rather than 'once'.

Prince Hal in *Henry 4 Part 1* tells Falstaff, *I must still be good angel to thee.* Claudius in *Hamlet* tells Polonius: *Thou still hast been the father of good news.*

Anne in *The Merry Wives of Windsor* begs her suitor Fenton: *Yet seek my father's love, still seek it.* And in *Sonnet 76*, the poet assures his sweetheart: *You and love are still my argument* (my 'subject').

*Still*, what all these characters are emphasising, in a word, is 'always'.

Arcite and Palamon are in prison. Arcite has been trying to make the best of their situation. Palamon follows him with an even more effusive affirmation of their plight, then pauses with these words. They continue to reframe their fortune for a few more lines, but then Emilia appears – and changes everything.

TO NOBLE KINSMEN

Be thou assured, if words be made of breath,
And breath of life, I have no life to breathe
What thou hast said to me.

—∞—

Today's quote offers us a perfect response to anyone who asks, 'Can you keep a secret?'

It's a brilliant verbal pyramid: words are made of breath; breath is made of life; and so my promise is I have no life *to breathe* ('to speak') your words.

The link between words and breathing is very common in Shakespeare. *Breath* often means 'utterance', 'speech', 'voice'. Cardinal Pandulph in *King John* comments on the conflict between England and France: *It was my breath that blew this tempest up.*

*Breathe* has a similar range of meanings: 'speak', 'utter', 'talk'. *I have toward heaven breathed a secret vow*, says Portia in *The Merchant of Venice*. The word appears in its most succinct form when the Host in *The Merry Wives of Windsor* demands, *Speak, breathe, discuss!* (We'll see this again on November 11th.)

*Richard 3* offers a line to those who promise to help *effect* ('make happen') an intention, as well as swear themselves to secrecy:

Thou art sworn
As deeply to effect what we intend
As closely to conceal what we impart.

Hamlet asks his mother Gertrude never to reveal what has passed between them, and especially that he is *not in madness, but mad in craft*. The Queen strongly reassures him, with these words.

HAMLET

The truth you speak doth lack some
    gentleness,
And time to speak it in. You rub the sore,
When you should bring the plaster.

— ⬡ —

It's good to be direct and straightforward with someone, perform the duty
of a friend or colleague, and not keep things from those you care about.
And yet, there are times – perhaps when they're exhausted, in grief, half-
awake or asleep, hungry, or doing something complicated or dangerous –
when the news might be better received a little later.

There's a balance to be struck, a time and a place for truth and honesty.
With today's lead quote, timeliness is only part of the issue; the truth
hadn't been sugar-coated; it lacked some gentleness.

And *Richard 2* counter-offers, *Truth hath a quiet breast*. (*Quiet* means
'calm' – in other words, 'Truth doesn't need to step forward and proclaim
itself.')

King Alonso and his companions find themselves
shipwrecked on an island. Sebastian blames the
King for their desperate situation, even while
Alonso expresses grief for his son who, it seems,
was drowned. The badly timed blame-shaming
prompts Gonzalo to criticise Sebastian's lack of
empathy.

THE TEMPEST

Corruption wins not more than honesty.
Still in thy right hand carry gentle peace
To silence envious tongues. Be just,
and fear not.

— ∞ —

*Being just* meant 'being true', or 'being honest'. Honesty is a prize quality in Shakespeare – although it can get in the way. Othello warns Iago that his honesty *minces* ('plays down') the seriousness of their subject:

Thy honesty and love doth mince this matter.

*Honesty* can also mean 'chastity'. In *As You Like It*, Touchstone praises Audrey, his new love, and articulates succinctly that being beautiful and 'honest' can be too much of a good thing:

Honesty coupled to beauty, is to have honey a sauce to sugar.

Cardinal Wolsey is facing up to his downfall from grace. He advises Cromwell, his secretary, how to behave to avoid the same fate.

# O, reason not the need!

— ✸ —

If someone asks for something they feel they really need ('I really need another Ferrari') then they may be asked in return, 'Do you *really* need another Ferrari?' – implying that there's something unnecessary about their desire.

*Reason* here means 'debate the pros and cons', and O is the sound of breath being exhaled, or an emotional wail of some kind, be it frustration or impatience or surprise or …

When the feeling of need is in response to a plea for an extra dessert, or the necessity of doing something burdensome ('I need to go to my ex's birthday party') then reach for the reply 'reason not the need' – don't debate doing something out of necessity, in other words.

Lear has had an angry confrontation with his daughters Goneril and Regan, who have objected to the number of followers he's brought to their houses. They tell him he must cut their numbers, and repeatedly question him about his reasons:

What need you five-and-twenty, ten, or five
To follow … What need one?

It's this final denial that prompts Lear's emotional response.

KING LEAR

# Haply your eye shall light upon some toy
# You have desire to purchase.

— ∞ —

Planning a stroll around the shops? Unexpectedly given some money to spend?

*Haply* (which is often taken to mean 'happily', whereas it actually meant 'perhaps') you'll see something you'd like to buy.

*Toy* meaning a 'child's plaything' was only just coming into use in Shakespeare's time. (It might be the sense at the end of *Twelfth Night*, when Feste sings, *When that I was and a little tiny boy … A foolish thing was but a toy*.)

Usually *toy* meant a 'trinket' or 'trivial ornament'. This is probably what Cleopatra intends when she lies to Caesar that she's given up everything she owns, at the end of *Antony and Cleopatra*:

> I, some lady trifles have reserved,
> Immoment toys.

*Immoment* means 'unimportant' – she's kept back some womanly bits and pieces, trivial and unimportant, perhaps nostalgic but value-less (in fact, she's kept more than enough to buy back what she's admitted to).

And if you find yourself in a haggling situation, or if someone is being reluctant to help you – remember this line from *The Winter's Tale*:

> Show the inside of your purse to the outside of his hand,
> and no more ado.

Or as *The Merry Wives of Windsor* claims:

> If money go before, all ways do lie open.

TWELFTH NIGHT

Antonio and Sebastian have arrived in Illyria. Sebastian suggests that they explore the town, but Antonio declines – he's known as an enemy there. He suggests Sebastian take his purse, and gives these words as reason.

# Who would not wish to be from wealth exempt, Since riches point to misery and contempt?

— ⌀ —

*Timon of Athens* tackles money, wealth, generosity, and how all of that affects people and the society we live in. *Measure for Measure* also has severe things to say about wealth, addressing the common theme that 'you can't take it with you':

> If thou art rich, thou'rt poor,
> For, like an ass, whose back with ingots bows,
> Thou bear'st thy heavy riches but a journey,
> And death unloads thee.

Nor does age help:

> ... and when thou art old and rich,
> Thou hast neither heat, affection, limb, nor beauty
> To make thy riches pleasant.

The feeling of 'I don't know where the money goes' may be familiar. This last quote (from *Henry 4 Part 2*) is for any spender who sees the habit as an 'incurable disease'. Here, Falstaff discovers he has seven groats and two pence (a very small amount) in his wallet:

> I can get no remedy against this consumption of the purse;
> borrowing only lingers and lingers it out, but the disease
> is incurable.

*Consumption* was a disease characterised especially by severe weight loss – and an appropriate metaphor for a purse that's continually losing its weight.

TIMON ℗
ATHENS

Flavius, Timon's steward, has been bidding farewell to the servants of the household, and sharing what little money he has with them. He reflects on the nature of glory and wealth, with these words.

# He that wants money, means, and content is without three good friends.

— ∽ —

*Wants* means 'lacks'; *content* means 'contentment, peace of mind'. Swap *he* for any friend (or foe). The Fool in *King Lear* offers similar advice, for anyone in pursuit of peace of mind:

> Have more than thou showest,
> Speak less than thou knowest,
> Lend less than thou owest.

And Polonius offers further sage words, for those who are unsure about how to handle their finances:

> Neither a borrower nor a lender be,
> For loan oft loses both itself and friend,
> And borrowing dulleth edge of husbandry.

The first line has virtually become a modern proverb. The second tells a familiar truth: that a loan, even when made with the best of intentions by both parties, is sometimes never paid back, and a good relationship thereby destroyed.

The third line is aimed at those who continually live off borrowed money and have lost the inclination to do something about whatever circumstances originally led them to take a loan. Their *edge* ('keen motivation') for *husbandry* ('careful management') will become *dulled* ('blunted') over time.

AS YOU LIKE IT

Touchstone has asked Corin if he has any philosophy in him. Today's lead quote is the beginning of Corin's reply. He continues with the following words:

That the property of rain is to wet and fire to burn; that good pasture makes fat sheep; and that a great cause of the night is lack of the sun ...

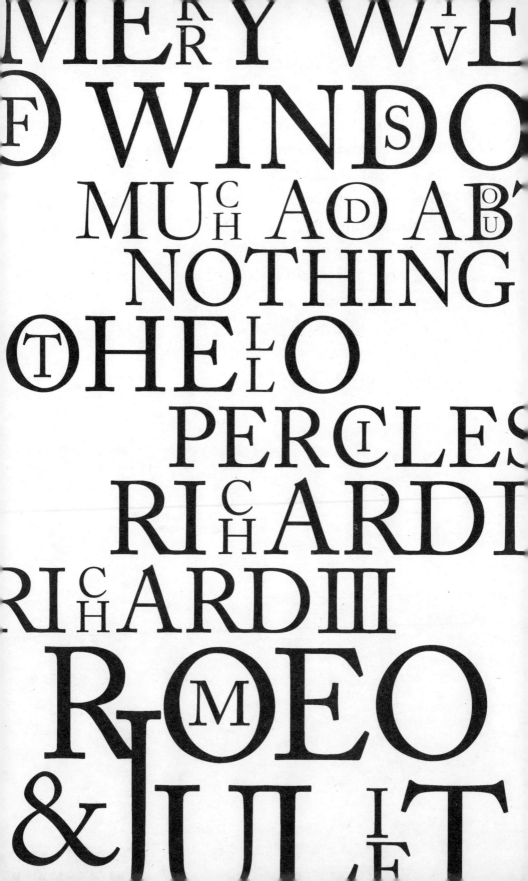

OCTOBER

Here being thus together,
We are an endless mine to one another;
We are one another's wife, ever begetting
New births of love; we are father, friends,
    acquaintance;
We are, in one another, families.
I am your heir, and you are mine; this place
Is our inheritance; no hard oppressor
Dare take this from us; here with
    a little patience
We shall live long and loving.

— ∞ —

Arcite and Palamon have become prisoners in
Athens, and have decided to make the best
of their lot. This is Arcite's account of their
relationship.

THE TWO NOBLE KINSMEN

## We are born to do benefits.

—— ∞ ——

Timon has given a banquet, and one of his guests hopes to do something in return. Timon affirms the value of friends (his optimism will turn out to be misplaced) with the words, *What need we have any friends if we should ne'er have need of 'em?*, and then says today's line.

TIMON ⒡ ATHENS

**Thou hast made me now a man; never before**
**This happy child, did I get anything.**

— ∞ —

The speaker is a male character, but the sentiment can apply to a new parent of any gender (just replace *man* with 'human'). *Get* as in 'beget'.

Another from *The Tempest*, for a parent to their child (here too, *father* can be replaced by 'mother'):

**Now all the blessings**
**Of a glad father compass thee about!**

And one more for a parent, speaking of their child (*he* and *his* can be replaced with any pronouns you prefer):

**He makes a July's day short as December,**
**And with his varying childness cures in me**
**Thoughts that would thick my blood.**

This is from *The Winter's Tale*. *Varying* meant 'changing'. The different energies that come every moment with a young child mean that you're often taken away from the turgid thoughts of adulthood.

And this last, also from *Henry 8*. Very little pleases proud parents of a new-born more than to be told their child looks like them, so learn this one before you next visit your exhaustedly happy friends:

**'Tis as like you**
**As cherry is to cherry.**

At the end of the play, King Henry speaks to his joy at the birth of his daughter, Elizabeth (who will become Shakespeare's Queen Elizabeth 1).

# I never knew so young a body with so old a head.

———— ❧ ————

This observation is apt for whenever we hear innocent wisdom produced by a young one, of any age.

In the plays, young children are usually wise beyond their years. The tiny page Mote in *Love's Labour's Lost* is one of the most precocious, taking on his master Don Armado in rapid exchanges of wit, leading Armado to exclaim *thou art quick in answers*.

Mamillius in *The Winter's Tale* is said by Camillo to be *a gallant child; one that indeed physics the subject, makes old hearts fresh*.

In *Richard 3*, however, we see the dangers of the wisdom of youth. Buckingham is impressed with the conversation of the young Prince of York:

> With what a sharp-provided wit he reasons!
> … So cunning, and so young, is wonderful.

And although Richard is equally impressed by Prince Edward, he adds a quiet, sinister note:

> So wise so young, they say, do never live long.

Shylock and Antonio meet in court. The Duke says he has heard from a lawyer, Bellario, that he is sick, but has sent *a young and learned doctor* to the court to try the case. The Clerk reads out a letter from Bellario which praises the young doctor Balthasar (in reality, a disguised Portia).

THE MERCHANT OF VENICE

## A decrepit father takes delight
## To see his active child do deeds of youth.

— ∞ —

The sentiment, of course, isn't restricted to old and feeble parents – and certainly not just fathers – but applies to the pride taken by parents of any age and state of health in the achievements of their children.

*Decrepit* had a sense of 'powerless', rather than the modern 'feeble, frail or old'. So, the line captures that feeling of pride taken by anyone who has passed skills on to the next generation. Adapting the quote a little, 'Decrepit teachers take delight to see their active students do deeds of youth', too.

Lack of pride in a son is a major theme in *Henry 4 Part 1*, notes the decrepit co-author. King Henry contrasts Prince Hal's riotous behaviour with Northumberland's son Hotspur, and even wishes

> That some night-tripping fairy had exchanged
> In cradle-clothes our children where they lay.

But by the end of the play his mind is changed.

The sonneteer draws a contrast between himself, imagined as an old man, and the youth and beauty of the person to whom the sonnets are addressed. These lines begin the sonnet.

THE SONNETS

# Is this the promise
# that you made your mother?

— ∞ —

Haunting to hear a scolding line that was written 400 years ago, but could have been said yesterday, and probably was, thousands of times around the world, in hundreds of different languages.

Here's another, from *Richard 2*:

> An if I were thy nurse thy tongue to teach,
> 'Pardon' should be the first word of thy speech.

*An* meant 'and'; a *nurse* was a 'nanny'; the elder co-author tells the younger that *pardon* should have been the first word of his *speech* (his 'language acquisition').

Coriolanus has promised his mother that he will stay calm when meeting the plebeians and the tribunes, but he quickly becomes angry. Menenius tries to remind him, with these words, but he is ignored.

CORIOLANUS

# I will chide no breather in the world but myself, against whom I know most faults.

— ∞ —

If you're ever asked to be critical of the world, reach for this line, which responds with a lesson in humility: you will reprove no *breather* ('living being') on earth other than yourself.

*Chide* here means 'scold' or 'rebuke', and is very common in Shakespeare. We hear it when Hamlet sees the ghost of his father for a second time, and recognises that he's *tardy* ('he's late', or 'he has done nothing yet') to carry out his promise of revenge:

Do you not come your tardy son to chide?

Another son is scolded in *Henry 4 Part 2*, when the King asks Warwick to find Prince Hal and *chide him hither*.

And Romeo asks his spiritual father Friar Lawrence not to tell him off for his new infatuation: *I pray thee chide me not.*

Orlando and Jacques have been talking together while walking through the Forest of Arden. Jacques suggests the two of them take a moment to complain about the world and their misery. Orlando the lover refuses, with these words, and soon after, the melancholy Jacques leaves his company.

AS YOU LIKE IT

# Courage mounteth with occasion.

—— ✻ ——

*Occasion* here means 'requirement' or 'need', and is reminiscent of such modern expressions as 'Needs must', when we're about to take a course of action that requires courage.

Like, for example, proposing marriage to someone. Or going for a job interview. Or asking someone out. Or quitting a job. Or ending a bad relationship. Or …

Shakespeare actually uses the 'Needs must' line in its full form in *All's Well That Ends Well*, when the Clown says *he must needs go that the devil drives*.

'Opportunity' is the most common sense of *occasion* in Shakespeare. We hear it in *Othello*, when Iago calls Cassio *a finder-out of occasions* (this would look good on a business card).

The English army has arrived in France and the French aren't ready for them. King Philip bemoans this fact, but the Archduke of Austria reassures him that they're ready to defend themselves, and offers this line shortly before a fierce exchange ensues at the city gates of Angiers.

# KING JOHN

OCTOBER 8TH

**I have a motion much imports your good,**
**Whereto if you'll a willing ear incline,**
**What's mine is yours and what is yours is mine.**

— ∞ —

Not a bad line for a wedding *motion* ('proposal') …

Just ignore the source material.

It is the last speech of the play, and the Duke suddenly makes a *motion* to Isabella (who started the play wanting to become a nun, and spent most of the play battling a lecherous man in a position of power). The lines appear to be an offer of marriage. We are left in the dark as to whether Isabella accepts, as she is given no verbal reply, and the play ends with her silence.

MEASURE
FOR MEASURE

## I am your own for ever.

— ∞ —

A simple, beautiful testament of love and fidelity.

As with yesterday's quote, best to enjoy the line in isolation, and not reflect too carefully on its origins …

Iago has convinced Othello of Desdemona's unfaithfulness. Othello rewards him by making him his lieutenant, replacing the disgraced Cassio. Iago accepts the promotion with these words.

# Hang there like a fruit, my soul,
## Till the tree die.

— ❧ —

Words to whisper to a loved one, as you embrace. Here's another, from *Richard 2*:

**Your own is yours, and I am yours and all.**

'Everything that is yours, is yours, including me.' Another good 'hug' quote comes from the last scene in *Pericles*. King Pericles has finally found his wife, Thaisa, whom he had thought to be dead. He embraces her with these words:

**Be buried
A second time within these arms.**

And one from *The Winter's Tale*. Perdita is gathering flowers to make into garlands, some of which she will throw over Florizel, her love. He jocularly asks her if this is how she'd act for a dead body at a funeral. Not at all, she replies, unless the burial were one of love, in which he was *quick* ('alive') and being embraced by her:

**If, not to be buried,
But quick and in mine arms.**

In other words, 'If you're not going to die, then be alive, and in my arms.'

Innogen, previously disguised as a page, has finally revealed who she is, and embraces her lover Posthumus, who greets her embrace with these words.

CYMBELINE

## My salad days,
## When I was green in judgement, cold in blood.

— ∞ —

There are decisions we make when young – like who we sleep with, or marry – that we can blame on our being *green* ('immature').

The greenness of these days makes them our *salad days*, naive in judgement, and *cold in blood* – perhaps implying prudishness, or frigidity in choice of partner.

Cleopatra asks if the love she felt for Caesar when she was younger was as great as her present love for Antony. She's upset when Charmian praises Caesar, but Charmian protests that she was only saying what Cleopatra herself once said. Today's lead quote is Cleopatra's appraisal of her own youth …

ANTONY &
CLEOPATRA

## For youth is bought more oft than begged or borrowed.

———— ❧ ————

This line points towards the extremes people will go to in an attempt to buy youth – either to gain the attention of young people, or to stay young themselves.

*Amazing* to think this line was written just under 400 years before cosmetic surgery became popular.

The word 'amazing' gives us an appropriate moment to comment on Shakespeare's creative vocabulary. For many years it was thought that he coined this word, as its first recorded use was thought to be in *Richard 2*. John of Gaunt talks of blows falling *like amazing thunder* on the helmet of an enemy (he uses the word to mean 'terrifying') – but it's now been found to have been used earlier, by other writers.

Shakespeare certainly did coin many words and phrases – as all dramatists did at the time – and there are several in this book that show his creativity. According to the historical *Oxford English Dictionary*, as of 2023 he's still the first recorded user of around 1,500 words and phrases.

For example, *gnarling* (see March 26th), *midsummer madness* (see June 21st), and *shog* (see December 27th). And yet, most of them would very likely have been words in daily use that he was just the first to employ in dramatic writing. Shakespeare the magpie!

Olivia has sent for Cesario (the disguised Viola) to come and see her. As 'he' is young, Olivia wonders if gifts will be a better way of persuading Cesario to love her.

TWELFTH
NIGHT

## My age is as a lusty winter,
## Frosty, but kindly.

— ∞ —

*Lusty* means 'strong'; *frosty* means 'creaky' or 'white-haired'; and *kindly* means 'good natured'. A line to offer anyone that might be daunted by you, if you're of older years.

Hopefully they will then reply with a line like Hector's, from *Troilus and Cressida*, when he meets Nestor, who is renowned for his great age and wisdom:

> Let me embrace thee, good old chronicle,
> That hast so long walked hand in hand with time.

A *chronicle* was a 'historical account'. It's a lovely, sweet, slightly mocking name for someone advanced in years (like the chronicling co-author).

The old servant, Adam, begs his master Orlando to let him be a companion when he leaves Duke Fredrick's court. Adam points out that as a young man he didn't drink wildly and lived carefully, so now, as an old man, he is still strong.

AS YOU LIKE IT

# Thou shouldst not have been old till thou hadst been wise.

— ∞ —

Old age and wisdom do not always go hand in hand, and this line suggests it helps to become old having already become wise. Then you've got something to lose.

To which, reply with this line from *Henry 4 Part 2*:

**I am only old in judgement and understanding.**

And if weakness or illness is suggested by the youth in your world, then reach for this line from *Twelfth Night*:

**Infirmity, that decays the wise, doth ever make the better fool.**

At least, while we're getting older and frailer, we're getting funnier.

The Fool has been chiding Lear about his foolishness in dealing with his daughters. This is one of the Fool's pointed 'jokes that aren't really jokes'.

KING LEAR

Crabbed age and youth cannot live together:
Youth is full of pleasance, Age is full of care;
Youth like summer morn,
    Age like winter weather;
Youth like summer brave, Age like winter bare.
Youth is full of sport, Age's breath is short;
Youth is nimble, Age is lame;
Youth is hot and bold, Age is weak and cold;
Youth is wild and Age is tame.
Age, I do abhor thee; Youth, I do adore thee;
O, my love, my love is young!
Age, I do defy thee.

---

The contrast between youth and age forms the entire content of a poem in the collection published in 1599 as *The Passionate Pilgrim*. Shakespeare's name is on the title page, but only some of the poems are thought to be by him – including today's lead quote, *Number 12*.

Some people never seem to get old; in *Antony and Cleopatra*, Enobarbus praises Cleopatra, saying *Age cannot wither her*. Shakespeare's most famous lines about the golden years are bleak, seeing old age as something of a disaster. They're spoken by Jacques in *As You Like It*:

Last Scene of all,
That ends this strange eventful history,
Is second childishness, and mere oblivion,
Sans teeth, sans eyes, sans taste, sans everything.

*Sans* is the French word for 'without'. Here's to a Cleopatra-type future rather than a Jacques one.

The poet expresses a sentiment often felt by folk who have loved each other for many years – a passionate outcry against the ravages of time.

**There cannot be a pinch in death
More sharp than this is.**

———— ∞ ————

A line for anyone having to say goodbye, whether it be for a short time, a long time, or forever. For those having to watch a loved one disappear into the storms of illness.

And another, from the same play, for any sad sight we might wish to scrub from our eyes:

> I had rather
> Have skipped from sixteen years of age to sixty:
> To have turned my leaping time into a crutch,
> Than have seen this.

Posthumus has left the court at the command of King Cymbeline, and Innogen feels the pain of his departure deeply.

CYMBELINE

When the mind is quickened, out of doubt
The organs, though defunct and dead before,
Break up their drowsy grave and newly move
With casted slough and fresh legerity.

— ⚮ —

The speaker here is certain that, when the mind is *quickened* ('rejuvenated'), the body responds with *casted slough* (metaphorically 'shedding its old skin') and moves with *fresh legerity* ('new nimbleness').

The mind bursts with excitement, and the tired body is dragged along for the ride, refreshed by the new movement. Today people tend to explain a burst of energy rather less poetically: 'It's the adrenaline', or 'It was probably that sixth espresso'.

Hotspur is similarly eager in *Henry 4 Part 1*, as he waits to hear what plans are afoot for rebellion:

> ... the blood more stirs
> To rouse a lion than to start a hare!

The metaphor is from hunting: drawing a lion from its lair and raising a hare from its cover. Bold words: he'd rather fight with a lion than surprise a rabbit.

Many things in the plays quicken the mind. For Tranio, advising Lucentio in *The Taming of the Shrew*, it's the arts: *Music and poesy use to quicken you.* (*Poesy* is an old word for 'poetry'.) For Cleopatra, it's a kiss for the dying Antony: she imagines her lips having the power to make him *quick* ('alive') again, so that she may *quicken with kissing.*

For Ferdinand in *The Tempest*, patiently carrying logs, it's Miranda:

> The mistress which I serve quickens what's dead.

And for Queen Elizabeth in *Richard 3*, looking for ways to curse Richard, it's words. She asks Queen Margaret for help:

> My words are dull. O, quicken them with thine!

It's the night before the Battle of Agincourt, and Henry speaks of how the body may be recharged by the power of the mind ...

No! Time, thou shalt not boast
that I do change ...
I will be true, despite thy scythe and thee.

Time is personified, carrying a scythe like the common image of Death (see October 22nd), and Shakespeare suggests that He is proud of what He does.

In other sonnets, the poet refers to the effects of devouring Time (*Sonnet 19*), and in *Sonnet 65* makes an even stronger affirmation:

> ... rocks impregnable are not so stout,
> Nor gates of steel so strong but Time decays.

The character of Time comes on stage in *The Winter's Tale* to explain the passing of sixteen years in moments, and boasts about His power:

> ... it is in my power
> To o'erthrow law, and in one self-born hour
> To plant and o'erwhelm custom.

*Custom* here means 'usual practice'; *o'erthrow* is the word 'overthrow', and *o'erwhelm* is the word 'overwhelm', each with a syllable removed, so that Shakespeare could measure the spoken rhythm – directing the way he wanted his actors to say the line.

The poet is sure about one thing – he will remain *true* ('faithful'); love won't alter, even despite the passing of time, or death.

TͪᴇSONNETS

Like as the waves make towards
   the pebbled shore,
So do our minutes hasten to their end,
Each changing place with that
   which goes before,
In sequent toil all forwards do contend.

———— ✢ ————

*Sequent* means 'sequential, one after another'; *toil* means 'work'; *all forwards* means 'everything to come'. In other words, 'Everything fighting for its place in the sequence of what's to come.'

*Minutes* receive an especially colourful treatment in the poems and plays. The poet in *The Passionate Pilgrim* uses a celestial image to express his feelings about being away from his love (*post* means 'be over'; *moon* implies a 'month'):

> Were I with her, the night would post too soon,
> But now are minutes added to the hours;
> To spite me now, each minute seems a moon.

The imprisoned ex-King in *Richard 2* meditates on the way time passes for him, turning himself into a clock:

> For now hath time made me his numbering clock.
> My thoughts are minutes, and with sighs they jar
> Their watches on unto mine eyes, the outward watch,
> Whereto my finger, like a dial's point,
> Is pointing still in cleansing them from tears.

THE SONNETS

These are the opening lines of a poem that portrays time as a monster destroying youth and beauty, carrying a scythe that cuts down everything in nature. But the concluding lines affirm that the poet's verses in praise of his love will always be there, regardless of what else time can do.

# Clay and clay differs in dignity, Whose dust is both alike.

— ⚮ —

*Dignity* means 'nobility'; the only difference between us all is that which we impose, our position in society. We come from stardust; we return to stardust. We are all alike.

This idea is echoed in *Julius Caesar* – that social standing is especially reflected in death:

> When beggars die, there are no comets seen;
> The heavens themselves blaze forth the death of princes.

This line comes from Calphurnia, Caesar's wife. Unnerved by the amazing and unnatural atmospheric events seen during the night, she warns her husband not to leave for the Capitol. She believes that such signs accompany the death of great people (and her fears prove justified ...).

For some, comets are thrilling phenomena to marvel at. This is how the King in *Henry 4 Part 1* describes himself before he gained the crown: *like a comet I was wondered at*. And in *Pericles*, Marina tells the man who will turn out to be her lost father that she has been *gazed on like a comet*.

Petruchio in *The Taming of the Shrew* turns up bizarrely dressed for his wedding, and wonders aloud why everyone is staring at him,

> As if they saw some wondrous monument,
> Some comet, or unusual prodigy?

*Prodigy* meant 'omen', but these words suggest a second meaning: long before Shakespeare's time, people thought comets were warnings. In *Henry 6 Part 1*, at the funeral of Henry 5, Bedford explains their role (*importing* meant 'predicting'): *Comets, importing change of times and states*.

CYMBELINE

Arviragus asks the disguised Innogen if they're brothers. She replies that any two men should indeed see themselves so, as they are all made in the same way.

## To what base uses we may return.

———— ⚬∽⚬ ————

*Base* meant 'low', 'unworthy' or 'wretched'. We come from dirt; we will return to dirt. When Claudius asks Hamlet where the body of Polonius is, the young prince rather eloquently reflects on the way worms ultimately rule:

> **Your worm is your only emperor for diet. We fat all creatures else to fat us, and we fat ourselves for maggots.**

The purpose of every creature we raise and fatten is to make ourselves fat; the only creatures we fat ourselves for are the worms (but the worms aren't complaining about their diet).

Hamlet and Horatio have been watching the gravediggers and reflecting on how bodies, turned to dust, can end up being used in a base way. Hamlet goes on to suggest that the dust that was Alexander the Great is probably now being used to make a stopper for a barrel.

**Thou art death's fool,**
**For him thou labour'st by thy flight to shun,**
**And yet runn'st toward him still.**

— ∞ —

Today's lines are for anyone fearing death, or afraid of their own mortality, so hang on tight. The lead quote says it all. We can kick, scream, cry, shout, hide or run away; we can *labour* ('work') to *shun* ('escape') death, but we're still steadily walking towards it.

Or rather, 'him', as death is anthropomorphised in Shakespeare into Death, a character, much as he is in Terry Pratchett's *Discworld* novels. In *Sonnet 18* the poet claims that Death will never brag that he captured the poet's love – because the sonnet captured it first.

But this doesn't mean that when faced with Death we should give up. On the contrary, as *Richard 2* suggests, we must not go gently into that night – we must fight:

> **Fight and die is death destroying death,**
> **Where fearing dying pays death servile breath.**

*Servile* means 'cringing, slavish'. Fear of death is tackled many times by Shakespeare, and courage is often brought along for the ride. Here's a good line from *Julius Caesar*:

> **Cowards die many times before their deaths;**
> **The valiant never taste of death but once.**

It's powerful to reflect that today's lines were all written during a heavily religious time. The salve they yield is pragmatic, grounding and humanist in nature: why fear something you can do nothing about? And the implicit follow-up: better, instead, to celebrate what you have.

MEASURE
FOR MEASURE

The Duke is disguised as a friar, and is counselling the condemned Claudio on how to deal with his imminent death ...

Fates, we will know your pleasures.
That we shall die, we know; 'tis but the time
And drawing days out, that men stand upon.

——— ⧜ ———

*Drawing days out* means 'extending or prolonging each day'. *Man* stands for 'humans'.

*Stand upon* could mean 'make an issue of', 'dwell on', 'waste time with', 'insist on the need for', 'make a stand against', 'fight stoutly or confront boldly', 'depend or rely on', 'resist', 'insist', 'be of importance to', 'maintain', 'defend', 'not be involved' …

What it means to you – that's the question …

Immediately after the assassination of Caesar the situation is understandably tense. There is a rapid discovery of this brutal act, this coup d'état, and the moment becomes full of chaos. Brutus calls up to the Fates …

JULIUS
CAESAR

If it be now, 'tis not to come.
If it be not to come, it will be now.
If it be not now, yet it will come.
The readiness is all. Since no man
knows of aught he leaves, what is't
to leave betimes? Let be.

*Betimes* means 'early'. (As usual, *man* means 'human'.)

Perhaps the most Stoic lines Shakespeare wrote. Ready to be applied to life, and one's relationship to the end of life.

Also, easy to apply to the bus you're waiting for.

Hamlet has told Horatio he has felt his heart flutter in anticipation of a forthcoming duel with Laertes. Horatio suggests they cancel the event, which makes Hamlet respond with these words, almost Zen-like in his pragmatism.

HAMLET

**Men must endure
Their going hence even as their coming hither;
Ripeness is all.**

— ∞ —

*Ripeness* means 'readiness', 'being fully prepared'. (It also means 'to be drunk', which may not be helpful here.) As ever, *men* needs to be read as 'humans'.

The line suggests that we must be as ready to deal with our death as we did our birth. It may be peaceful; it may be full of sound and fury; but prepare yourself for whatever comes next.

*Endure* is an interesting word. It has a sense of 'cope with', and can mean the more negative 'suffer', as well as the more neutral 'undergo'. And it also has the more passive quality of 'let, allow, permit'. A similar notion was expressed by *try*:

**Let the end try the man.**

Let how we face death *try* ('test the goodness of', 'prove') our humanity.

(This last, from *Henry 4 Part 2*.)

Edgar, disguised as Poor Tom, has brought his blinded father to the battlefield. Lear's side has lost, the old King and Cordelia taken prisoner. Edgar thinks he and his father should leave, but Gloucester is too tired, and decides their current position is as good a place to die as any other. Edgar dismisses these negative thoughts with these words.

KING LEAR

## All that lives must die,
## Passing through nature to eternity.

—— ∞ ——

Hamlet has some of the most famous reflections on death. This line is offered at the beginning of the play, and is quite a contrast to Hamlet's musings in his famous *To be, or not to be* ... speech, as he explores what might come after death:

> For in that sleep of death what dreams may come
> When we have shuffled off this mortal coil
> Must give us pause.

And this line from *Timon of Athens* can be read as an alternative to either of the *Hamlet* lines:

> We must all part
> Into this sea of air.

Timon's servants are about to go their separate ways, following Timon's downfall. The Third Servant likens their situation to being on a leaking ship, awaiting the surging sea to take them away and drown them.

But this line also brings the image of a being dissolving into its component particles, like a Hollywood science fiction film, before being carried off into the wind, joining back with the universe in a puff of Pixar sea mist.

Gertrude sees Hamlet still mourning his father's death. She speaks these words to him, and goes on to ask him, 'Why, if this is the case, has he taken the death so much to heart?' Unfortunately for the young prince, he is soon to get a few more reasons to grieve ...

HAMLET

## But to persever
## In obstinate condolement is a course
## Of impious stubbornness.

—— ∞ ——

How long should we grieve after the death of a loved one? At a certain point we need a friend to say, 'Hey, get out of your pyjamas, put the ice cream away, splash some water on your puffy face, you look like you're having an allergic reaction. Perhaps it's time to move on.' As Cleomines says to Leontes in *The Winter's Tale* (after seeing him mourn for 16 years), *You have done enough.*

Less than two months have passed since Hamlet's father's death – and his Uncle Claudius suggests that's enough time for a son's grief. Well-intentioned or not, he's being publicly unkind to his brother's only child.

*Persevering* meant 'persist, keep at', suggesting that Hamlet isn't even grieving authentically, because he has to work at it, being deliberately awkward in lamenting. *Impious* is one of the strongest words for the time. It's literally 'im-pious' – an accusation of lacking reverence towards God.

To have *sympathy* (first recorded in the 1560s, around the time Shakespeare was born) for another's distress is to 'care for another's grief'. To have *empathy* (first recorded in this sense in the early 1900s) is to 'share another's experiences on an emotional level'. We go to the theatre to empathise safely.

*Condolement* (first recorded in 1602, around the time Shakespeare was writing *Hamlet*) comes from *condole*: *con* – 'with', *dole* – 'pain'. So *condole* was to 'feel pain', and later meant 'grieve', 'feel sorrow'. To *mourn* is the oldest word of them all, meaning to 'rest in this place of sorrow'.

King Claudius asks Hamlet why he's still so downcast after his father's death. Claudius speaks to him about the inevitability of death with these words. We'll soon learn, from Hamlet's father's ghost, why Claudius is so unfeeling.

## Death remembered should be like a mirror, Who tells us life's but breath, to trust it error.

———— ∽ ————

Turn the *who* into *which* and these lines might run a little smoother, as we don't expect a mirror to be a 'who' telling us anything, whether or not we can trust it.

OK, Shakespeare, we won't trust the talking mirror. Then there's this line from *All's Well That Ends Well*:

Praising what is lost
Makes the remembrance dear.

Giving praise and lovingly remembering someone or something you miss makes them shine more brightly because you remember them fondly. The memory of them becomes *dear* ('precious', 'heartfelt'). The memory begins to evoke joy, along with a sadness (which hopefully becomes slightly lighter with time, or at least familiar).

*Remembrance* in the plays is often an indication of such a sadness. In *All's Well That Ends Well*, the Countess describes the effect of Helena calling to mind her dead father:

The remembrance of her father never approaches her heart
but the tyranny of her sorrows takes all livelihood from her cheek.

And Sebastian in *Twelfth Night*, thinking Viola is dead, tells Antonio,

She is drowned already, sir, with salt water, though I seem to drown her remembrance again with more.

PERICLES

King Antiochus has shown Pericles the heads of those who have tried and failed to interpret his riddle and discover his terrible secret. Pericles takes the morbid display in his stride, with these words. He heroically tells Antiochus he is prepared, whatever the outcome of his trial will be.

# Hereafter, in a better world than this, I shall desire more love and knowledge of you.

— ∞ —

A difficult situation prompts you to bid farewell. But not to worry – you remember this line from October in *Everyday Shakespeare*, and speak these warm words, which carry a sense of 'Fingers crossed, things will be better next time we meet'.

Leave-taking in the plays is often quite elaborate. Mortimer in *Henry 6 Part 1* bids farewell to Richard with this collection of words:

> ... and fair be all thy hopes,
> And prosperous be thy life in peace and war.

It's pretty grand. Romeo is even grander, anticipating *Star Trek* by a few centuries, when he says goodbye to his servant Balthasar:

> Live, and be prosperous; and farewell.

Not quite Spock's 'Live long, and prosper', but not far off.

Priam in *Troilus and Cressida* wishes Hector well with:

> Farewell; the gods with safety stand about thee.

*Farewell*, and its associated *fare thee/you/ye well*, has a poetic association. It's different from *goodbye* (*God bye*) in the plays, as it often carries a feeling of regret, or a genuine hope for wellbeing, as the *well* implies.

Even more frequent is *I humbly take my leave*, a note of humility in the parting, especially when leaving someone of a higher social rank, as Cornelius says to the Queen in *Cymbeline*, Polonius says to Hamlet, and Montague says to everyone in *Henry 6 Part 3*.

Le Beau has come to warn Orlando that he is no longer safe: Duke Frederick is out to get him. He advises Orlando to leave as soon as possible, and bids him farewell with these kind words.

# I might not this believe
# Without the sensible and true avouch
# Of mine own eyes.

—— ❀ ——

A ghost in front of you. Aliens land in your back garden. Politicians work together. Humans end world hunger. The cat drilling behind the couch.

'I don't believe what I'm seeing', we would say to an incredible or unexpected event.

*Avouch* has the meaning of 'guarantee' or 'assurance'. Usually, it has the general sense of 'declare'. Lysander uses it to make a strong – and public – accusation against Demetrius at the beginning of *A Midsummer Night's Dream*:

> Demetrius – I'll avouch it to his head –
> Made love to Nedar's daughter, Helena.

Nym in *The Merry Wives of Windsor* tells Page of Falstaff's plan: *I avouch 'tis true*. And the sense of 'justify' or 'defend' can be heard in *Macbeth*, as the new King tells two murderers about Banquo:

> I could
> With bare-faced power sweep him from my sight
> And bid my will avouch it.

'I can mentally justify the illegal murder of my best friend,' says the leader of the country, 'with my unrestrained power.'

Horatio has just seen a ghost – the spirit of Hamlet's father. Just a moment before, he had expressed scepticism about ghosts to the sentries on duty at Castle Elsinore … but now his mind is changed.

> 'Tis now the very witching time of night,
> When churchyards yawn, and hell itself
>     breathes out
> Contagion to this world.

———— ∞ ————

Welcome to this year's Samhain, the Gaelic pagan festival! This is Hallowe'en, the eve of All Hallows, the November 1st feast day celebrating all saints in the Christian Church.

The middle of the night can be scary, as Hamlet acknowledges in today's lead quote. A creepy image comes to mind when the 'churchyards yawn': dry ice and shadows (and probably zombies lurking in the darkness) behind the gravestones – and it's all opening up …

*Contagion* meant 'infection', 'poison', 'destruction'. Shakespeare's characters thought the night to be full of misty dampness that could transmit infection – Portia in *Julius Caesar* asks Brutus why he has left his bed *To dare the vile contagion of the night*.

Not everyone sees night in a negative way: the magician Bolingbroke in *Henry 6 Part 2* knows that

> … wizards know their times.
> Deep night, dark night, the silent of the night…
> The time when screech-owls cry and ban-dogs howl,
> And spirits walk, and ghosts break up their graves,
> That time best fits the work we have in hand.

*Screech-owls* are 'barn owls'; *ban-dogs* are 'chained dogs'; *break up* means 'break out of'.

Hamlet has had his suspicions about Claudius confirmed. The King appeared guilty as he watched the murder in a play performed by travelling actors. Then, alone, he reflects on the new sense of determination he feels, and continues with the words *Now could I drink hot blood …*

TE COLD

OF ERRORS

MERCHANT

VENICE

PASSIONATE

PILGRIM

THE RAPE OF

LUCRECE

SONNETS

THE TAMING

OF THE SHREW

TEMPEST

I count myself in nothing else so happy
As in a soul remembering my good friends.

— ∞ —

Henry Bolingbroke has arrived back in England,
returning from banishment, and is travelling with
his ally, the Earl of Northumberland. After meeting
Harry Percy, Northumberland's son, Bolingbroke
reflects on his good fortune.

RICHARD II

I to the world am like a drop of water
That in the ocean seeks another drop,
Who, falling there to find his fellow forth,
Unseen, inquisitive, confounds himself.

—— ⚮ ——

*Confound* means 'destroy'.

Friends and family can suddenly be separated for years. Whether you seek a friend, a lover, or a family member, this quote is for the deep longing some of us feel inside. The unrest that keeps our eyes scanning the crowd, in the hope that we might suddenly find them within reach again.

*As You Like It* has a line for this, which does indeed offer some hope:

It is a hard matter for friends to meet; but mountains
may be removed with earthquakes and so encounter.

And if you find yourself about to be separated from your loved ones, then offer these lines from *Hamlet*:

As the winds give benefit
And convoy is assistant, do not sleep
But let me hear from you.

*Convoy* means a 'method of conveyance', a way to get your message across to me.

Antipholus reflects that contentment is beyond him, as he's unable to find his twin brother.

# We meet like men that had forgot to speak.

— ∞ —

Sometimes it can be hard to know what to say.

Whether the reason is grief, shock, or simply because you're glad to see someone. Some friends are happy to be silent in each other's presence, knowing there are no words that can describe how you feel, or what you want to say.

There are a number of good greetings in Shakespeare. Here's one from *Cymbeline* (the owl is nocturnal, the lark sings in the morning):

> The night to th' owl and morn to th' lark less welcome.

*As You Like It* has a good one too:

> You are very well met. God 'ild you for your last company.

*'ild* was a form of 'yield', and so means 'God reward' – in other words, asking God to reward your friend for their company. *Last* could mean 'previous', but could also mean 'current, latest, present' – so, 'May you be blessed for giving me your company in this moment.'

And a fine, epic way to greet each other from *Pericles*:

> Lysimachus: Hail, reverend sir! The gods preserve you!
> Helicanus: And you, to outlive the age I am, and die as I would do.

Prince John, the Lord Chief Justice, and others have gathered following the death of Henry 4. They still seem to be in a state of shock, judging by John's comment.

## My other self, my counsel's consistory, My oracle, my prophet.

———— ✿ ————

*Consistory* meant 'meeting-place'. Telling a friend that they are 'the meeting place of all good advice' is quite a compliment.

A great friendship is explored in *The Two Noble Kinsmen*, one of Shakespeare's last plays. Palamon celebrates his friendship with Arcite with these words:

> I do not think it possible our friendship
> Should ever leave us.

Friendship is one of Shakespeare's most frequent themes, with over a thousand references to friends. But the theme has a dark side, and friendships can be transient things, as people change. Timon of Athens asks:

> Has friendship such a faint and milky heart
> It turns in less than two nights?

There's another domain where friendship can't be trusted. In *Much Ado About Nothing*, Claudio is succinct:

> Friendship is constant in all other things
> Save in the office and affairs of love.

The sentiment is echoed by Ulysses in *Troilus and Cressida*, although he blames time for the trouble:

> Love, friendship, charity, are subjects all
> To envious and calumniating time.

*Calumniating* means 'slandering, defaming', and is a fun word to say out loud: *cah-LUM-nee-ate-ing*.

And finally for today, Amiens sums up friendship in song, in *As You Like It*:

> Most friendship is feigning, most loving mere folly.

 RICHARD III

Buckingham gives some advice that pleases Richard greatly, and so he praises Buckingham effusively with these words.

Ceremony was but devised at first
To set a gloss on faint deeds,
   hollow welcomes,
Recanting goodness, sorry ere 'tis shown;
But where there is true friendship
   there needs none.

— ∞ —

*Ceremony* first came about to make small accomplishments, sullen greetings or apologies feel better, for all the ostentation that comes with it. It can also mean 'courtesy'. Nothing extra of this sort is needed for true friendship.

And yet, for many occasions, ceremony is both required and respected. In *Hamlet* it's important to Laertes, at Ophelia's graveside; her death was *doubtful* ('disquieting, worrisome, uncertain') and, as a possible suicide, she is not entitled to a full funeral ceremony. Laertes wants a more elaborate service for his sister, and so he asks the priest, *What ceremony else?*

Isabella in *Measure for Measure* also tries to put ceremony in its place (*longs* means 'belongs'):

> No ceremony that to great ones longs,
> Not the king's crown, nor the deputed sword,
> The marshal's truncheon, nor the judge's robe,
> Become them with one half so good a grace
> As mercy does.

None of any of the trappings of greatness gives even half the amount of *grace* ('respect') as compassion, forgiveness – as mercy does.

TIMON ☉ ATHENS

Timon had given Ventidius money to help him avoid going to a debtors' prison, and now Ventidius wishes to repay it, as a courtesy. But Timon refuses, saying that he gave it freely ever, and adds these remarks about ceremony and friendship.

To me, fair friend, you never can be old,
For as you were when first your eye I eyed,
Such seems your beauty still.

— ∞ —

The writer remembers a first meeting with a friend ...

T<sub>H</sub><sub>E</sub> SONNETS

## To keep an adjunct to remember thee
## Were to import forgetfulness in me.

— ∞ —

An *adjunct* is an 'aide-memoire, a written note about something to help the memory'; *import* means 'indicate, represent'.

Today we have diaries and online calendars to remind us to do things, and all kinds of electronic aids to record our slightest thoughts, whether for private reflection or to expound to the whole world.

In Shakespeare's day, the usual assistant was a *table* – a writing tablet or memo pad. Gentlefolk would carry one to jot down their thoughts or observations.

Hamlet has one, and gets it out to reinforce what the ghost of his father has just told him about his murder by Claudius:

> My tables – meet it is I set it down
> That one may smile, and smile, and be a villain.

*Meet* means 'right, appropriate'. Hamlet later uses the word a second time, describing a clown so well known for his jokes that people going to the theatre *quote his jests down in their tables* before they come to the play. The poor comic struggles to get any laughs because everyone knows the punchlines.

Present-day comedians, their routines captured on phones and uploaded to social media platforms, face similar first-world problems.

Rather than use a notebook to record feelings, the poet says he'd rather trust his own imagination. He doesn't need a book, or any other aide-memoire, as his love is never away from his mind ...

THE SONNETS

In companions
That do converse and waste the time together,
Whose souls do bear an equal yoke of love,
There must be needs a like proportion
Of lineaments, of manners, and of spirit.

———— ∞ ————

For friends that talk and *waste* ('spend') time together, if they love each other equally, they're bound to have the *like proportion* ('same balance') of *lineaments* ('personal characteristics'), *manners* ('ways of behaving'), and *spirit* ('temperament').

*Waste* could also mean – as it still does today – 'pass the time uselessly'. We hear it in *As You Like It* when Celia appraises the place where she and Rosalind have found themselves in the Forest of Arden:

I like this place
And willingly could waste my time in it.

If you find yourself with a friendship like this, and with time to waste (either in an actual or a metaphorical garden), then here's a line from *Richard 2*:

What sport shall we devise here in this garden
To drive away the heavy thought of care?

Lastly, another line from *As You Like It* that can be used as a testament to the future of a friendship. How long will we laugh and sing and rhyme together as friends?

I'll rhyme you so eight years together, dinners and suppers and sleeping-hours excepted.

Portia reflects on the close friendship between Antonio and Bassanio with these lines …

# The amity that wisdom knits not, folly may easily untie.

— ∞ —

How are strong *amities* ('friendships') formed? This quote suggests that they're founded on *wisdom* ('good sense and judgement'). In other words, a friendship not built on good judgement can easily be dissolved by foolishness.

This is what Enobarbus predicts, having observed Antony's strategic marriage to Octavia in *Antony and Cleopatra*:

> That which is the strength of their amity shall prove
> the immediate author of their variance.

*Variance* here means 'falling out, arguing'.

The wisdom of the fool is often contrasted with the foolishness of the wise. Maria brings the two together in *Love's Labour's Lost*:

> Folly in fools bears not so strong a note
> As foolery in the wise when wit doth dote.

*Note* means 'reproach'; *wit* here has the sense of 'intelligence'; *dote* means 'behave foolishly'. Viola echoes this idea in *Twelfth Night*, reflecting on Feste the Fool:

> For folly that he wisely shows is fit;
> But wise men, folly-fallen, quite taint their wit.

*Fit* means 'fitting'; *taint* means 'harm'.

Love is often singled out as the source of folly – an insight expressed in *Venus and Adonis* by no less than the goddess of love herself. As Venus says: *love is wise in folly.*

TROILUS & CRESSIDA

Nestor and Ulysses are discussing Thersites, who has stopped being a companion of Ajax and gone into the service of Achilles. Ulysses thinks that it was no surprise, as the friendship was one that a fool could disunite.

# When love begins to sicken and decay,
# It useth an enforced ceremony.

—— ∞ ——

There are no tricks in plain and simple faith.

Have you ever felt this way? That moment when love slips away? Today's quote reminds us of the romantic things people do instinctively at the beginning of a relationship that can sometimes feel artificial later on. *Love ceremonies* or 'rituals' become forced.

*Faith* meant 'constancy, fidelity, loyalty' and 'reliability, dependability, trustworthiness', as well as 'self-confidence'.

Lucilus has reported to Brutus that Cassius received him in a less welcoming way *nor with such free and friendly conference* as used to be the case. Brutus sees Cassius's behaviour as of *a hot friend cooling*. A bitter quarrel is soon to follow …

JULIUS CAESAR

# Give me your hand, and, as we walk,
# To our own selves bend we our needful talk.

— ∞ —

Sometimes, you meet a friend, and all you want to do – all that needs to be done in each other's company – is to walk, talk and, from time to time, take each other's hand. To bond in body, mind, heart and touch.

Perhaps the best part of friendship is hearing each other's stories, *Pericles* tells us. When we learn about the trials a friend is facing, we're freed for a moment from our own worries:

> By relating tales of others' griefs,
> See if 'twill teach us to forget our own.

Some might say the function of a friendship is to hold the *glass* ('mirror') up to each other, to have the things you cannot see yourself shown to you. Cassius in *Julius Caesar* captures the idea well:

> And since you know you cannot see yourself
> So well as by reflection, I, your glass,
> Will modestly discover to yourself
> That of yourself which you yet know not of.

And here's a line for two friends who can say they've 'seen the same films', or travelled to the same places, or stayed up into the early hours together. Whether actual or metaphorical films, stories, places or hours, here's a line you can share with Falstaff and Shallow, from *Henry 4 Part 2*:

> We have heard the chimes at midnight.

Shallow continues:

> Do you remember since we lay all night in the Windmill
> in Saint George's Field?

Who hasn't fallen asleep after drunkenly breaking into a windmill?

TROILUS & CRESSIDA

Troilus and Cressida are walking to where she'll be handed over to the Greeks. He says they have *needful* ('necessary') things to say to each other.

## Speak, breathe, discuss; brief, short, quick, snap!

— ⧓ —

A line for anyone getting impatient with a friend who rather likes to take their time finding their way, or rather, going the long way around, but finally, in the end, getting to the point.

The Host of the inn asks Simple what he wants. Evidently Simple doesn't reply quickly enough, for the Host raps out this series of instructions.

MERRY WIVES OF WINDSOR

# You speak a language that I understand not.

— ∞ —

A line for the argumentative times when you are beyond baffled at someone's rage or accusation, and you're at a full breakdown in communication.

Shakespearean characters often have the same problem. In *Romeo and Juliet*, Capulet tells Lady Capulet *soft* ('be quiet'), and then asks her to explain what she has to say more slowly, so he can follow her:

Soft! Take me with you, take me with you, wife.

'Don't run on ahead and leave me behind', in other words, or, 'Go slowly, so I can follow you.'

More often, one character simply tells another *I understand you/thee not* – usually because someone has been too clever or evasive in getting to a point. Pandarus goes a step further in *Troilus and Cressida*, explaining to a clownish servant:

Friend, we understand not one another: I am too courtly, and thou art too cunning.

*Cunning* meant 'clever'.

The royal court, usually found in the capital city, demanded particular manners, clothing styles, and ways of thinking and speaking. As Corin the shepherd observes in *As You Like It*:

Those that are good manners at the court are as ridiculous in the country as the behaviour of the country is most mockable at the court.

THE WINTER'S TALE

Hermione has been defending herself against Leontes' jealous, tyrannical accusations that she has been unfaithful to him. He refuses to believe anything she says, and doubles down on his accusations. She responds with these simple words.

## An honest tale speeds best
## being plainly told.

— ∞ —

We don't often use the expression *honest tale* these days, but when we do the sense is that the story is 'sincere', coming 'from the heart'. Such stories, this line suggests, *speed* ('are most successful') if told *plainly* ('without rhetorical flourishes'). The implication being that detail and embellishment might suggest deviousness.

*Honest* has a wide range of meanings in Shakespeare, but doesn't usually mean 'truthful'. It can be simply a polite address, as in *A Midsummer Night's Dream* when Bottom asks Peaseblossom: *Your name, honest gentleman?*

Or it can mean 'trustworthy' as well as 'free of deceit', as when Hamlet tells his companions *It is an honest ghost.* But later in the play he harangues Ophelia with the question *Are you honest?*, and there it has the meaning of 'virtuous', 'chaste'.

King Richard is trying to persuade Queen Elizabeth to let him woo her daughter, but she is suspicious and reluctant, and verbally fences with him in a series of one-line exchanges. He asks her to be eloquent with her daughter about his love – and this is one of her evasive replies.

RI<sub>C</sub><sub>H</sub>ARD III

**I am not a day of season,
For thou mayst see a sunshine and a hail
In me at once. But to the brightest beams
Distracted clouds give way.**

— ∞ —

These lines are for any friend with a stormy personality, whose *clouds* ('displeasure') can always be scattered by someone bright and sunny.

Several characters refer to mood using weather as their metaphor. Gonzalo in *The Tempest* tries to cheer up King Alonso, who thinks his son is dead:

**It is foul weather in us all, good sir,
When you are cloudy.**

As ever, replace *sir* with 'madam', 'friend', 'teacher'...

And when Kent asks a gentleman in *King Lear* how Cordelia received the letters informing her of her father's treatment, he describes her as *sunshine and rain at once.*

The King of France has sent for Bertram, whose behaviour had earlier displeased him. But Bertram's prowess in the wars has been impressive, so that any *clouds* ('displeasure') the King has will *give way* ('be hidden') by the 'brightness' of Bertram's success.

ALL'S WELL THAT ENDS WELL

You two never meet but you fall to some
discord. You are both, i'good truth,
as rheumatic as two dry toasts; you cannot
one bear with another's confirmities.

— ⧖ —

A line that will be appropriate for those two friends who always love to
bicker with each other.

The original speaker of this line comically gets some of her words wrong.
She means *choleric* or *lunatic* ('bad tempered, irritable') not *rheumatic*
('suffering from joint pain').

And as for *confirmities*, she means *infirmities* ('physical or mental
weaknesses') – and not *conformities* ('complying with traditions').

Doll has been giving Falstaff a hard time for not
being attentive to her. Mistress Quickly has been
listening, and tells them off.

# I am a kind of burr, I shall stick.

— ∞ —

Whether happily attesting to a newfound friend whom you've decided to spend the day with, or to reinforce many years of togetherness, today's lead quote is for you.

This next line, from *Julius Caesar*, is useful if such stickiness becomes irksome. Brutus and Cassius are having a bitter argument; Cassius speaks this line (*bear* means 'put up with'):

> **A friend should bear his friend's infirmities.**

'We hope friends will put up with each other's deficiencies.' But Brutus responds by telling him *I do not like your faults*. Cassius then rightly says *A friendly eye could never see such faults*. (They make up a few lines later.)

*Infirmity* used to mean a 'defect' or 'weakness'. In the opening lines of *Pericles*, Gower says he has come back to life as a Chorus figure to tell the story of Pericles, *assuming man's infirmities* – 'taking on humanity's weaknesses'.

*Infirmity* usually describes a 'bodily weakness, especially arising from a genetic defect, disease, or old age'. We hear it used in this way in *King Lear* when Regan describes her father's behaviour as *the infirmity of his age*.

And King Lear himself asks Burgundy if he is willing to take Cordelia *with those infirmities she owes* – 'owns'. She isn't ill, but in Lear's upset state of mind, she suddenly has developed 'deficiencies' as a daughter.

Lucio has been irritating the Duke, who is disguised as a friar. The Duke bids him farewell, but Lucio insists on accompanying him on his walk, and admits he's not an easy person to get rid of.

# I love and honour him,
# But must not break my back to heal his finger.

—— ∞ ——

An important aspect of friendship; that you can be there for someone you care about, but it's wise not to get to the point of hurting yourself in the process.

*Henry 8* offers a similar slice of friendship-wisdom:

> **Where you are liberal of your loves and counsels**
> **Be sure you be not loose.**

'Where you are free with your love and advice, make sure you are not ...' *Loose* here could mean 'careless', 'improper', 'casual' or 'flirtatious'.

A senator is owed money by Timon. He asks his servant to go and get it, as he has urgent need of the funds.

TIMON ⓕ
ATHENS

# I rather wish you foes than hollow friends.

— ∞ —

Better to have an enemy, than a *hollow* – 'insincere', 'false' or 'empty' – friendship.

*Hollow* is heard in *Hamlet* when the Player King says to his Queen:

> **And who in want a hollow friend doth try**
> **Directly seasons him his enemy.**

*Enemy* would have rhymed with *try*. Anyone in need, testing the goodness of an insincere friend, is only going to *season* ('strengthen', 'gratify') an enemy, or turn that 'friend' into an enemy. A 'frenemy', we might say.

*Henry 6 Part 1* warns of envy between two friends or factions. Today, envy is less strong than jealousy: to be envious is to want something of someone else's (but to do nothing about it); to be jealous is to want to take that thing away from them.

*Envy* used to have a stronger meaning – of 'malice' and 'enmity'. Here's the Duke of Exeter, reflecting on a quarrel; he thinks the anger *doth presage some ill event* – 'the noise of this upset is a bad omen of terrible things to come' (he's right, for the Wars of the Roses will follow):

> **When envy breeds unkind division,**
> **There comes the ruin, there begins confusion.**

*Unkind division* meant 'unnatural discord'; *confusion* meant 'ruin and destruction'.

HE NRY VI:III

Edward, claiming the English crown, wants to be sure which of the nobles he can rely on. He asks Hastings and Montague if they will support him rather than Warwick. If they don't think they can, he tells them to leave his company straight away, and says this line. They assure him they are friends.

# There is no tongue that moves, none, none i'th' world, So soon as yours could win me.

— ∞ —

There are friends we'll do anything for; hopefully, we each have at least one person who can *win* ('persuade') us to anything.

Polixenes must return home, and so tells this to his childhood friend Leontes. Nothing can dissuade him, he says, not even Leontes. But he does stay when Leontes' wife Hermione asks, which softly sows a seed of jealousy in Leontes' mind …

THE WINTER'S TALE

**What we have we prize not to the worth**
**Whiles we enjoy it, but being lacked and lost,**
**Why, then we rack the value, then we find**
**The virtue that possession would not show us**
**Whiles it was ours.**

— ⚭ —

We never really appreciate what we have until we lose it. *Rack* meant 'increase or exaggerate the value'. It's a term that came into English through the world of textiles, referring to the frame used to stretch cloth. It then developed uses to do with stretching and increasing – most commonly in relation to an instrument of torture.

The merchant Antonio tells Bassanio in *The Merchant of Venice* to go into the city to see how much he can raise for Bassanio's love-suit to Portia: his credit *shall be racked even to the uttermost* – 'stretched even to breaking point'. The motif is still heard in idioms like 'rack my brains'.

The banished Martius makes a similar point to today's lead quote in *Coriolanus*, talking about what will happen after he leaves Rome:

I shall be loved when I am lacked.

A thought we all might hope people have in our absence.

After Claudio shames Hero at their wedding, the Friar devises a plan for the family to announce that the event has caused her death. This, he thinks, will make Claudio wish he had not so accused her, and quench malicious gossip, until they can find out the truth …

MUCH ADO ABT NOTHING

# I must become a borrower of the night
# For a dark hour or twain.

— ∞ —

Need to leave? Have to go? Today's lead quote is a poetic way to make your excuses.

Feel compelled to go, because your host is upset with you, or suddenly isn't speaking to you for some reason? Reach for *The Winter's Tale*:

> Methinks
> My favour here begins to warp.

Not that your *favour* ('friendship') has gone into faster-than-light travel. *Warp* isn't only a unit of measurement in *Star Trek*; in Shakespeare's time it meant 'turn', 'change', 'go wrong' or 'distort'.

Didn't have time to say goodbye properly? Or did you leave without saying goodbye at all (what's called a 'French exit' in the UK, an 'Irish exit' in the US, a 'Polish exit' in Germany, and an 'English exit' in France)? Then reach for *Romeo and Juliet* (as usual, *man* here means 'human'):

> My business was great, and in such a case as mine
> a man may strain courtesy.

Do you have a little time before you have to go? And a particular person you want to spend that time with? Then reach for *Othello*:

> I have but an hour
> Of love, of worldly matters and direction
> To spend with thee. We must obey the time.

*Direction* meant 'arrangements and instructions'.

Banquo tells Macbeth he wants to ride for an hour or *twain* ('two') before the evening banquet. This suits Macbeth very well, as he has murder in mind once more …

**But that a joy past joy calls out on me,**
**It were a grief so brief to part with thee.**

— ∞ —

Today's lead quote may be the most beautiful way to say you'd like to take more time in the moment of leaving someone you love – but you have something joyful to go to, that you're late for, and you must hurry!

To balance, here is a less *brief* ('hurried') leave-taking (and probably the most famous in the plays) – Juliet's to Romeo:

> **Parting is such sweet sorrow**
> **That I shall say goodnight till it be morrow.**

For more goodbyes, head back to May 20th.

Romeo apologises to Friar Lawrence for having to leave him so quickly, but he's on his way to be with Juliet, for their first night together ...

# I must hear from thee every day in the hour, For in a minute there are many days.

— ⨀ —

Time can move very slowly when we're waiting to hear from someone, especially if love is involved.

These words were written in an era when there were few other ways to communicate at a distance other than by slow, horse-drawn means. And if you lived in the country, you'd have to wait for someone to be heading in your general direction. Even in the instant-messaging era – where messages can be received hour by hour, minute by minute, second by second – tiny intervals of time can seem like days if an answer fails to arrive with the hoped-for immediacy.

These varying perceptions of time passing are light-heartedly explored in *As You Like It* when Rosalind, disguised as a man, meets her love Orlando in the forest. She tells him that *Time travels in divers paces with divers persons* (*divers* meant 'various').

Her first example is of Time trotting. Orlando asks her *who Time trots withal* (*withal* meant 'with'), and she explains that Time trots

> ... with a young maid between the contract of her marriage
> and the day it is solemnized.

*Solemnized* meant 'celebrated'. Orlando seems not to have grasped this lesson in time, for he turns up to meet Rosalind again, but he's an hour late, and is thoroughly told off. A real lover, she says, would never *divide a minute into a thousand parts, and break but a part of the thousandth part of a minute in the affairs of love* – let alone a whole hour. Be warned: message often (but not too often), and arrive early.

Romeo is leaving Juliet. He has been banished, and with these words she tells him to write often. He affirms he'll omit no opportunity to be in contact with her.

The leisure and the fearful time
Cuts off the ceremonious vows of love
And ample interchange of sweet discourse
Which so long sundered friends
    should dwell upon.

— ∞ —

*Leisure* here doesn't mean 'free time for pleasurable activities', but 'shortage of time'.

A line for when you and your friends have been *sundered* ('separated') for a long time, and you've a lot to catch up on. If there are restrictions in place around your meeting, you may not be able to have the *sweet discourse* ('pleasant conversation') you'd like, with all the expected *ceremonious vows* ('normal rituals'), because *fearful* ('terrifying') circumstances won't allow it.

*Leisure* in the sense of 'time available' is often heard in the plays. This is how Kate uses it (about Petruchio in *The Taming of the Shrew*) when she refuses to leave her wedding banquet: *he shall stay my leisure* – 'he can wait till I'm ready'.

Lord Derby comes to the battlefield to express support for Richmond, but can't make that support too obvious as Richard is holding Derby's son as a hostage and will execute him if Derby defects. With these words, Derby leaves in haste, apologising for not being able to have a longer conversation.

RI<sup>C</sup><sub>H</sub>ARD III

Make a swift return,
For I would commune with you of such things
That want no ear but yours.

—— ∞ ——

The Duke, disguised as a friar, has learned of
the death of a pirate, Ragozine. The Duke-Friar
tells the Provost to take Ragozine's head to the
Deputy, Angelo, and claim that it is Claudio's
head that has been chopped off. With these
words, the Duke-Friar asks the Provost to come
back as quickly as possible.

MEASURE
FOR MEASURE

## Be Mercury, set feathers to thy heels,
## And fly like thought from them to me again.

— ∞ —

'Come back soon' might sound a little weak, by comparison with today's lead quote.

In Roman mythology, Mercury was the son of Jupiter, and became the messenger of the Roman gods. When characters refer to him, it's often with reference to his speed (the quality people seem to like best with their messages).

On other occasions, it's Mercury's nimbleness and strength that motivate the image. Cleopatra wishes she had Juno's power to lift up the dying Antony into her monument. If she had, she tells him how he would be *fetched up* ('brought') to her:

**The strong-winged Mercury should fetch thee up.**

Several nobles suspect King John of ordering the murder of Prince Arthur, and their anger, along with news of the French invasion, is finally making him reconsider his actions. He believes he has a way of regaining their trust and asks the Bastard to seek them out as quickly as possible, with these words.

# KING JOHN

## Should we be taking leave
## As long a term as yet we have to live,
## The loathness to depart would grow.

— ∞ —

If we were to carry on saying goodbye even as long as we had life left to live, the reluctance to part would only increase.

No you hang up. No you hang up. No you – Oh. They hung up.

Posthumus has to leave the court, at King Cymbeline's command, and is saying farewell to his love, Innogen. He wants to leave without delay, on the grounds that staying would just prolong their pain.

CYMBELINE

## Rogues, hence, avaunt!
### Vanish like hailstones, go!
### Trudge, plod away o'th' hoof, seek shelter, pack!

— ∞ —

If you're keen to send someone away (in seriousness or in jest) here's a good place to start.

A *rogue* was a 'vagabond, vagrant, beggar'; *hence* meant 'away from here'. *Avaunt* is from the French *avant* ('before'), and by the 16th century it had become a fierce dismissal, very often accompanied by an expression showing the speaker's dislike.

*Plod away o'th' hoof* was a reference to being taken away on a slow horse. *Pack* ('take yourself off') was related to 'packhorse', a mule that carried goods and supplies.

*Avaunt* would be used for any unwelcome supernatural being, as when Macbeth tells the ghost of Banquo, *Avaunt, and quit my sight!*

It can be used playfully too. The Princess in *Love's Labour's Lost* is joking around when she uses it to Boyet after listening to his riddling talk: *Avaunt, perplexity!*

*Avaunt, perplexity!* is often used by the elder co-author when the younger co-author presents him with a complicated new piece of technology.

> Pistol and Nym have refused to carry Falstaff's love letters to Mistress Page and Mistress Ford, and the drunken knight is furious. He dismisses them from his service with these words, and they immediately plan revenge …

MERRY WIVES OF WINDSOR

## Good night, sweet Prince,
## And flights of angels sing thee to thy rest!

—— ❧ ——

This line is often used in memoriam of someone who's recently died. King Charles 3 used the second line in 2022, at the end of his global address honouring his late mother, Queen Elizabeth 2.

The quote is also a lovely way to say goodnight to someone, especially if you've been carousing together, and your companion/prince/princess is on their way home to bed.

*Flight* meant 'host, company, multitude' – a whole bunch of winged angels *sing* 'send' you to sleep, or literally, 'chant angelic songs' until you fall asleep.

These are Horatio's words, spoken the moment after Hamlet has died.

## Sleep dwell upon thine eyes,
## peace in thy breast!

Juliet has left her balcony for the final time, wishing Romeo goodnight. This is his response.

IMON OF
THENS  TITU
ANDRONIC
OLUS &
ESSIDA  TWELF
NIGH
TO GENTLEMEN
OF VERONA
TWO NOBLE
KINSMEN
VENUS
& ADONIS

DECEMBER

The west yet glimmers with some
    streaks of day.
Now spurs the lated traveller apace,
To gain the timely inn.

— ∞ —

A group of murderers are awaiting the return of
Banquo and his son to Macbeth's castle. The First
Murderer remarks on the way night is coming on.
Then they hear Banquo approaching … (*Lated*
meant 'belated, overtaken by night'.)

MACBETH

# Each one betake him to his rest;
# Tomorrow all for speeding do their best.

— ∞ —

*Speeding* here means 'success' – the oldest sense of *speed*, out of which developed the modern meanings to do with rapidity and pace. It's never used in that way today, apart from in such utterances as 'we wished them godspeed'.

These words are a wish. It might be offered to your children, as you send them to bed ahead of a big day; to your students at the end of a lesson, in anticipation of an exam in the morning; by a director to actors due to perform a play for the first time. Think of any activity where people have spent time preparing themselves and need a good night's sleep in advance of action.

We also hear *speed* used in Shakespeare to mean 'prosper' or 'flourish'. In *Troilus and Cressida*, Pandarus wonders how the soldiers fared in battle: *I long to hear how they sped today.*

Knights have come to the court of King Simonides for a day of jousting, in competition for his daughter Thaisa's hand in marriage. After the event, they gather together for an evening of entertainment, and at the end of the evening Simonides bids them goodnight with these words.

PERICLES

## The day, my friends, and all things stay for me.

— ∞ —

King Henry 5 offers a fine line for when you have to leave, and you know everyone's waiting for you.

*Stay* is widely used in the sense of 'await'. In *Julius Caesar*, Cassius knows his fellow conspirators are meeting, and he asks not once, but twice, *Am I not stayed for?* – 'Aren't they waiting for me?'

The nervous Master Slender in *The Merry Wives of Windsor* refuses to join the others at dinner, until Master Page calls him in: *We stay for you.* Hear your friends call for you in this way, while you finish reading this book.

The King is spending time alone, praying for success, the night before the Battle of Agincourt. Gloucester comes to find him, and he shakes himself out of his solitude with these words …

HENRY V

# A true-devoted pilgrim is not weary
# To measure kingdoms with his feeble steps.

— ∞ —

How much effort are you prepared to make to achieve a much-desired goal? These lines suggest there is no limit.

The path towards the goal may not be easy, but the tiredness disappears if the traveller has a similar motivation to that of a pilgrim journeying to a spiritual place. The end goal pulls you towards it.

The image in today's quote is one of great geographical distance – passing through entire kingdoms – but of course the lines aren't restricted to literal travel. They can be used for anyone (or anything) that is an object of worship or desire, as they carry logs, shopping, luggage, or as they walk their dog for the umpteenth time in a single night.

We encounter *measure* in this sense of 'traversing' again in *The Merchant of Venice*, when Portia tells Nerissa they have to go on a journey: *we must measure twenty miles today*.

The image of a pilgrim is also used by Shakespeare as Romeo describes his lips as *two blushing pilgrims* when he asks to kiss Juliet. And the poet writing *Sonnet 27* describes his thoughts as making a *zealous pilgrimage* – a devout, passionate journey – to his absent love.

Julia is missing Proteus so much she decides to visit him at the Duke's court. Her maid Lucetta says that the way is wearisome and long, but Julia doesn't care, saying these lines and relying on Love's wings to carry her. The journey's end, however, is not what she wished for …

# Give every man thine ear, but few thy voice. Take each man's censure, but reserve thy judgement.

———— ∞ ————

Be a good listener, but be careful about giving everyone your *voice* ('approval'). Accept the *censure* ('opinion') of others, *but reserve thy judgement* ('express your own opinions judiciously').

(For many of us hooked on social media, this counsel might be much needed and little heeded, as the addictive nature of the platforms fires everyone up.)

It's certainly a good line for anyone you know who's ready to speak but isn't a good listener. Today's quote offers remedial advice in the place of the proverbial 'You never listen to a word I say'.

Shakespeare doesn't use the word *listener*, which was only just coming into use in the early 17th century. He talks instead of *hearers*, as in *King John*, when the news of young Arthur's death is circulating among the people (*gripe* meant 'grip'; *action* meant 'gestures'):

> And when they talk of him they shake their heads
> And whisper one another in the ear;
> And he that speaks doth gripe the hearer's wrist,
> Whilst he that hears makes fearful action.

Laertes is about to leave Castle Elsinore to go back to France, and his father Polonius is giving his son a list of 'do's and don'ts' before he departs. This is one of his many nuggets of advice; most are well put and very quotable ...

# Be checked for silence,
# But never taxed for speech.

— ∞ —

If you don't know whether you should say something or not, today's quote offers the view that it's good to speak up.

That said, if we stay silent, we have to be prepared to be *checked* ('rebuked'). If and when we do speak, it's wise not to say anything that would allow us to be *taxed* ('censured').

It's a difficult balance to achieve, and characters can make the wrong decision – or, at least, a decision that the play then has to sort out. For some, the choice is fraught with danger. Pisanio in *Cymbeline* is told in no uncertain terms by Cloten:

> Speak, or thy silence on the instant is
> Thy condemnation and thy death.

No pressure, then.

Enobarbus makes a decision in *Antony and Cleopatra* to speak out during a conference of the political leaders Lepidus, Pompey, Antony and Octavius Caesar, and is taxed for his pains:

> Antony: Thou art a soldier only. Speak no more.
> Enobarbus: That truth should be silent I had almost forgot.
> Antony: You wrong this presence; therefore speak no more.
> Enobarbus: Go to, then; your considerate stone.

*Go to, then, your considerate stone* can be read: 'OK then, I am your thoughtful, silent, emotionless rock.'

Bertram is leaving home and heading to the French king's court. The Countess, his mother, gives him several words of advice. This is her last piece of advice, before she gives him a blessing and they part.

## The blessed gods
## Purge all infection from our air whilst you
## Do climate here!

— ∞ —

These words might sound especially useful as a greeting to visitors in post-pandemic days. *Climate* meant 'stay, dwell'.

They would have been just as appreciated in Shakespeare's time, when bubonic plague was rife, with London notably affected in 1592–3 (when all theatres were forced to close) and in 1603.

*Infection* meant more than disease; it could be any kind of bad influence. The King in *Henry 6 Part 2* bows to popular opinion about Suffolk, and banishes him:

> He shall not breathe infection in this air
> But three days longer, on the pain of death.

To use *plague* as a curse could be a really forceful expression. We hear it at its strongest from Mercutio, fatally wounded by Tybalt in *Romeo and Juliet*, condemning the *houses* ('households') of the Montagues and the Capulets:

> A plague a'both your houses!

(The *a* in *a'both* was an informal way of writing 'on'.) But for Hotspur in *Henry 4 Part 1*, *plague* is no more than an expression of annoyance when he forgets a place name:

> A plague upon it, it is in Gloucestershire.

Florizel and Perdita have fled from Bohemia and arrived in Sicilia, and are warmly greeted by King Leontes with these words. What they don't know is that Florizel's father King Polixenes is in hot pursuit …

# DECEMBER 7TH

## Not to be abed after midnight, is to be up betimes.

— ⁂ —

A line fit for anyone carousing into the small hours.

Here, *betimes* means 'early'. The quote is from *Twelfth Night*. Toby and Andrew have been out late drinking. Toby offers a Latin phrase too – *diluculo surgere* ('to rise at dawn').

This evidently confuses Andrew, who staggers through a reply of *Nay, I know not; but I know to be up late is to be up late*. Toby doesn't accept that answer, saying it's *a false conclusion*, and then tries to clarify for his friend:

> To be up after midnight and to go to bed then is early; so that to go to bed after midnight is to go to bed betimes.

Then – probably to Andrew's relief – he changes the subject.

Tiredness does funny things to words. In *Romeo and Juliet*, Capulet has been up late talking to Paris, arranging the marriage between him and his daughter Juliet. He then heads to bed, with these lines.

> It is so very late that we
> May call it early by and by.

(As we saw on January 2nd, *by and by* meant 'in due course, soon'.)

And the not-especially-quick-witted Cloten in *Cymbeline* makes a dawn call on Innogen with the words:

> I am glad I was up so late, for that's the reason I was up so early.

TWELFTH NIGHT

Sir Toby and Sir Andrew have just arrived home. By and by, they'll be joined by Feste the Fool, and then the party will really get started …

# Fill our bowls once more,
# Let's mock the midnight bell.

— ∞ —

A sister utterance (to December 7th) available for any group who decide to carry on into the early hours.

These days, *bowls* are for eating or smoking rather than drinking, but not in Shakespeare's time. This line can also be used for anyone wanting some more late-night food.

Brutus in *Julius Caesar* asks Lucius to bring him a bowl of wine. King Simonides has such a vessel on a pedestal when he toasts Pericles: *we drink this standing-bowl of wine to him*. Being much wider than a cup, a *standing-bowl* likely held a lot more wine, perhaps akin to the 17th century's 'yard of ale'.

The *midnight bell* of today's lead quote evidently made a loud and resonant sound. King John talks about it:

> ... with his iron tongue and brazen mouth
> Sound on into the drowsy race of night.

Duke Theseus, in *A Midsummer Night's Dream*, hears it, too:

> The iron tongue of midnight hath told twelve.

And presumably this was the sound Falstaff and Shallow heard when they were younger, as they reminisce about their escapades in London, in *Henry 4 Part 2*: *We have heard the chimes at midnight* (see November 10th).

ANTONY & CLEOPATRA

Antony wants *one other gaudy night* (here, *other* means 'more'; *gaudy* means 'festive, joyful, merry') before he leaves for the battle against Caesar. He asks for all his captains to join him in late-night revelry. This suits Cleopatra very well, as she tells him it is her birthday, and she's pleased to see him so enthused.

# He hath never fed of the dainties that are bred in a book. He hath not eat paper, as it were; he hath not drunk ink.

— ∞ —

*Ink*, an essential medium in Shakespeare's day, was often used as a synonym for 'writing'. *To drink ink* would mean to be educated, having read many books.

Sir Toby in *Twelfth Night* advises Sir Andrew to write a challenge to the disguised Viola: *Taunt him with the licence of ink*, and adds *Let there be gall enough in thy ink*. And Posthumus in *Cymbeline* asks Innogen to write to him in Italy:

> And with mine eyes I'll drink the words you send,
> Though ink be made of gall.

*Gall* has two meanings. It can refer to a secretion produced by the liver, renowned for its bitterness. It can also refer to a growth on trees, especially oaks, caused by insects, used in the manufacture of ink and dyes. The origins are different: the 'tree gall' comes from Latin *galla*, the oak-apple; the liver secretion is Germanic in origin, and is possibly related to *yellow* (skin often turns yellow if jaundiced, when the liver isn't working properly).

By Shakespeare's time, the words 'galla' and 'yellow' looked and sounded similar, so any reference to *gall* carries a nuance of bitterness of spirit. So, Toby is telling Andrew to let his writing be bitter, and Posthumus is telling Innogen he'll devour all her words to him, even if the taste – or the content – is bitter.

LOVE'S LABOR'S LOST

Constable Dull misunderstands a Latin expression used by Holofernes the schoolteacher, who calls him *monster Ignorance*. Nathaniel the curate explains that it's all due to Dull's lack of education.

**That men should put an enemy in their mouths to steal away their brains! That we should with joy, pleasance, revel and applause transform ourselves into beasts!**

— ∞ —

The enemy in question is alcohol. This line is for anyone wishing to berate the factors fostering drunkenness, such as *pleasance* ('pleasure') and the *applause* ('reinforcing shouts') of drinking companions. As ever, read in 'humans' for *men*. Others agree.

Drunkenness is how the goddess in *Venus and Adonis* describes her anxieties:

> ... the proceedings of a drunken brain,
> Full of respects, yet nought at all respecting.

*Respect* meant 'attention'. In other words, a *drunken brain* pays attention to everything, while at the same time, paying attention to nothing.

The Porter in *Macbeth* explains one of the effects of drinking (*desire* here as in 'sexual desire'):

> Drink ... provokes the desire but it takes away the performance.

However, Iago in *Othello* offers that not everything about drinking is bad:

> Good wine is a good familiar creature if it be well used.

In his drunkenness, Cassio gets into a sword fight with Roderigo (pre-arranged by Iago). In the kerfuffle, Cassio wounds Montano, the governor of Cyprus. Othello arrives and dismisses Cassio from his service. As Cassio sobers up, he rebukes alcohol:

> O, thou invisible spirit of wine, if thou hast no name to be known by, let us call thee devil.

# I cannot remember what I did when you made me drunk, yet I am not altogether an ass.

— ∞ —

Not everyone handles alcohol well. In *Othello*, Cassio knows it's bad for him as he gets drunk too quickly. He's also very unusual – the only one in the plays who demurs when offered a drink:

> I have very poor and unhappy brains for drinking. I could well wish courtesy would invent some other custom of entertainment.

Prince Hal in *Henry 4 Part 1* gives us an insight into Elizabethan drinking practices:

> They call drinking deep 'dyeing scarlet', and when you breathe in your watering they cry 'Hem!' and bid you 'Play it off!'

The 21st-century equivalent might be 'Down in one!', 'Down it!', or 'Chugg chugg chugg!'. On the other hand, Falstaff in *Henry 4 Part 2* makes a long speech in favour of drink. The brain is mentioned again, but this time the effect is beneficial:

> A good sherris-sack hath a twofold operation in it. It ascends me into the brain, dries me there all the foolish and dull and crudy vapours which environ it, makes it apprehensive, quick, forgetive, full of nimble, fiery, and delectable shapes, which delivered o'er to the voice, the tongue, which is the birth, becomes excellent wit.

*Crudy* meant 'thick'; *apprehensive* – 'perceptive'; *forgetive* – as in a blacksmith's forge – meant 'creative'; *delectable* – 'delicious'.

And for Lady Macbeth, psyching herself up to murder a king, alcohol gives her confidence, courage, passion:

> That which hath made them drunk hath made me bold;
> What hath quenched them hath given me fire.

MERRY WIVES OF WINDSOR

Slender is accusing Falstaff and his companions of robbing him when he was drunk.

## I had rather fast from all, four days,
## Than drink so much in one.

— ∞ —

A line of regret, for the morning after, or for the moment during.

*Fast* means 'give up', as in 'breaking' your night's 'fast' with your morning meal.

Octavius Caesar, Antony, Lepidus and Pompey have been drinking together – and heavily. Evidently this is not Caesar's usual practice. With these lines, he reluctantly agrees to have another drink, but expresses his disquiet at the same time.

ANTONY &
CLEOPATRA

'Tis ever common
That men are merriest
 when they are from home.

— ∞ —

You can use this line anywhere. With the standard switching of *men* to 'humans' or any gender that you like, you can also read *from home* to mean 'away, abroad' or 'out of their comfort zone'.

Or 'on holiday'. Or generally 'in a different mental or emotional state than normal'. Or … what you will.

King Henry responds to the Dauphin's insulting gift of tennis balls. After these lines he acknowledges his wilder days as Prince Hal, when he devoted himself to barbarous licence. The message he sends back to the Dauphin threatens, boldly …

HENRY V

Therefore are feasts so solemn and so rare,
Since, seldom coming in the long year set,
Like stones of worth they thinly placed are,
Or captain jewels in the carcanet.

———— ∞ ————

Perhaps this will be surprising: *solemn* could have the sense of 'impressive, breath-taking, awe-inspiring'.

*Feasts* can be read to mean 'parties', 'huge celebrations', or any kind of wild adventure that probably wouldn't do you much good to experience too frequently. Special days, such as feasts that we would call 'feast-days' and other public holidays, are rightly *rare* – 'infrequent'.

If holidays were more common (as Prince Hal says on our September 1st) they might become as tedious as workdays. Today's lead quote notes the way holidays stand out in the year, likening them to the *captain* ('principal') stones in a *carcanet* ('jewelled necklace').

Hal's father, King Henry 4, takes up the theme when he contrasts his own behaviour with that of King Richard:

By being seldom seen, I could not stir
But like a comet I was wondered at.

He was seen in public so little that when he did appear people *wondered* ('stopped and stared', 'gazed in wonder') at him.

T<sup>H</sup><sub>E</sub> SONNETS

The poet thinks of himself as a rich man who has a treasure chest, but who doesn't look into it too often because that would spoil his pleasure. In the same way, he appreciates holidays because they're uncommon. He compares all this to the chunks of time that keep him away from his love, so that whenever they meet it's a really special occasion. D'awww ...

They say miracles are past, and we have our philosophical persons to make modern and familiar, things supernatural and causeless.

— ∞ —

Whether you believe in ghosts, fairies, heaven and hell, or the miracles of religion, as Shakespeare's audience did, *philosophy* — our modern sciences — now makes familiar that which was once strange. Indeed, many modern scientific discoveries would have appeared supernatural and causeless in Shakespeare's time.

Lafew, Bertram and Parolles are discussing the amazing recovery of the King after all his physicians had considered him incurable. Lafew opens the conversation with these words.

ALL'S WELL THAT END WELL

That time of year thou mayst in me behold,
When yellow leaves, or none, or few do hang
Upon those boughs which
    shake against the cold,
Bare ruined choirs, where late
    the sweet birds sang.

— ∞ —

*Choirs* here are the branches of the tree, bare of leaves. A *choir* was also a section of a church, with empty pew benches that might remind some of the choir-singers who sang hymns during a service.

Wander (or wonder) along a crisp, wintry lane, along to a park, or if you're lucky, look out of a window – and never see a de-leafed tree in the same way.

The poet is reflecting on old age …

THE SONNETS

**At Christmas I no more desire a rose**
**Than wish a snow in May's new-fangled shows,**
**But like of each thing that in season grows.**

— ∞ —

There are echoes here of proverbs, such as 'a time and a place for everything', or 'everything in its right place', or 'now is not the time for chuckles'.

*Shows* as in 'show of flowers in spring'; *like of* means 'enjoy'; *season* as in 'each season' or 'opportunity'.

In Shakespeare's day, *season* had a wide range of meanings, as it has today. It sometimes referred to all four seasons, as when in *The Winter's Tale* Perdita picks *the fairest flowers o'th'season*. It means 'due time' or 'occasion' in *Hamlet*, when Horatio, anticipating the arrival of the ghost, tells the others that

> It then draws near the season
> Wherein the spirit held his wont to walk.

(*Then*, ironically, meant 'now'; *wont* meant 'accustomed to, in the habit of'.) Ross in Macbeth describes Macduff as someone who *best knows the fits o'th'season* – the conflicts of the age.

And it means 'totes inappropes' in *The Comedy of Errors*, when Antipholus tells Dromio *these jests are out of season*, or, 'now is not the time for chuckles'.

> The King of Navarre and his companions have sworn to study for three years and give up all pleasures. Berowne thinks that the time for study is past, and they should now look to *like of* life as adults, pursuing pleasure as opportunities arise. But in view of the oath he's just made, he reluctantly agrees to sign ...

# LOVE'S LABOUR'S LOST

’Tis mad idolatry
To make the service greater than the god.

‘Do not’, as the saying goes, ‘let the driver be bigger than the car; the bouquet bigger than the vase; nor the bone bigger than the doggie’.

Troilus, Hector and the other nobles are debating whether the war over Helen of Troy is worth the cost. Hector is of the opinion that it is not.

# TROILUS &
# CRESSIDA

**I am not
Against your faith, yet I continue mine.**

— ∞ —

Emilia and her sister Hippolyta have been discussing
the difference in love between men and women,
and agree to disagree with these words.

# I am not of that feather to shake off
# My friend when he must need me.

———— ⚯ ————

A messenger has come to Timon on behalf of a
friend: Ventidius has been imprisoned for debt
and is asking for Timon's help. Timon says he is
not the *feather* ('type') to *shake off* ('abandon')
a friend in need.

TIMON⑪F
ATHENS

## How far that little candle throws his beams! So shines a good deed in a naughty world.

— ∞ —

You're returning home late one winter night, and a light in the window of your house seems to beam out so much brightness it warms your heart.

*Naughty* in Shakespeare's time didn't have the modern sense of 'mischievous' or 'disobedient', as said of children. It had the adult notion of something being 'indecent', 'titillating', 'teasing' or 'just on the decent side of filthy'.

(Best not to think then about Lafew describing Parolles in *All's Well That Ends Well* as a *naughty orator*\*.)

It also has a much stronger meaning – 'wicked' or 'evil'; so, good deeds really stand out in a wicked world. And it was a good, loving, kind deed to light that candle, whoever thought to do so.

---

\* It actually simply means 'bad' or 'horrible' in quality.
Parolles is a bad speaker or storyteller – a liar, in other words.

Portia, on her way home in the darkness, sees a candle shining brightly in the window of her house. Her reflection is a general one, but as she's just performed a good deed by saving Antonio's life, perhaps it applies just as much to her. Although, faced with Antonio's punishment of Shylock, perhaps she also reflects on the horribleness of the world …

THE MERCHANT OF VENICE

**So tedious is this day**
**As is the night before some festival**
**To an impatient child that hath new robes**
**And may not wear them.**

— ∞ —

It would be difficult to find a more striking image of the way time seems to drag while awaiting an eagerly anticipated event.

*Tedious* might seem a somewhat weak word. Then, as now, it carried the sense of 'long and wearisome', but it also had more dramatic meanings, as in *As You Like It*, when Rosalind describes a rich man *knowing no burden of heavy tedious penury*. Here, it means 'painful'.

*Tedious* comes across even more strongly when used to describe days or nights, as the situations are usually tense and emotional. Helena in *A Midsummer Night's Dream* is desperately tired after searching through the forest, and wishes night were over so that she could find her way back to Athens: *O long and tedious night*. A good quote for insomniacs, or those too excited to go to sleep.

Valentine in *The Two Gentlemen of Verona* describes to Proteus the downside of being in love, as time passes *with twenty, watchful, weary, tedious nights*. In *Richard 2* we see Richard taking a final farewell of his wife, and making a suggestion for how to spend winter-time:

**In winter's tedious nights sit by the fire**
**With good old folks, and let them tell thee tales.**

Next time you see your children, parents or grandparents, use this line and change *thee* for 'me'.

Juliet is impatiently awaiting the end of the day, and calling on night to come quickly, when Romeo will visit her for the first time as her husband. The Nurse arrives just after she says these words – but with bad news …

# We'll have flesh for holidays, fish for fasting-days, and moreo'er puddings and flapjacks, and thou shalt be welcome.

— ∞ —

For many cultures there are times of the year when doors are opened and everyone is welcome to join at table. And there are those whose doors are always open to strangers. And yet others who, the less they have, the more willing they are to share it. If you're lucky enough to be able to provide plenty of food during your holiday seasons, then here's a line of invitation for sharing.

*Flesh* as in animal flesh; *moreo'er* is a contraction of 'moreover'. *Welcome* used to be two words, 'You will be well come', as in 'You will be hosted by us very well'.

The shipwrecked Pericles finds himself washed up on a beach. A group of fishermen welcome him, give him some dry clothes, and the First Fisherman invites him home with these words.

PERICLES

# Now good digestion wait on appetite, And health on both!

— ∽ —

*Bon appetit*, or *Enjoy*! – as waiters sometimes say – although the comment is often made that the English language has no great expression for offering good wishes before beginning to eat a meal.

Today's lead quote is perhaps even more sophisticated than the one Cardinal Wolsey uses in *Henry 8*:

> **A good digestion to you all; and once more I shower a welcome on ye – welcome all!**

The welcome before a meal was often accompanied by a toast, or *health*, which people passed on to each other around a table. In *Timon of Athens*, Timon welcomes his guests to his banquet, and toasts a guest sitting next to him:

> **My lord, in heart! And let the health go round.**

*In heart* here means 'in a spirit of fellowship'; and *the health going round* would have been an instruction for everyone around the table to give a 'cheers', drink and refill their glass.

A wish of *health* that never lasted beyond the 17th century was *proface*, from French – pronounced 'proh-FASS' – meaning, 'May it do you good.' It's used in *Henry 4 Part 2*, as someone offers wine to their visitors (*want* meant 'lack'; *meat* meant 'food' in general):

> **Proface! What you want in meat, we'll have in drink.**

King Macbeth has invited his nobles to a banquet, and – after being distracted by a conversation with Banquo's murderer – gives everyone this welcome. They invite him to sit with them at table, but the ghost of Banquo arrives and takes Macbeth's seat …

# Small cheer and great welcome makes a merry feast.

— ∞ —

When *cheer* entered English from French in the early Middle Ages, it referred to the face, or the look of the face, and the mood lying behind it. We hear it in the plays as *Be of good cheer* ('be happy').

*Cheer* is a common wish – *be of good cheer*, or simply *good cheer* – and is close to our 'cheer up', or 'happy day to you'. We don't hear that usage very much these days, apart from in relation to a festive event or time of year, as in 'winter cheer' or 'Christmas cheer'. It's strongly present in Shakespeare when an event is taking place, such as *wedding cheer* in *The Taming of the Shrew* or *royal cheer* in *Timon of Athens*. The association with a good mood or happiness is never far away.

And we hear it again in the common greeting *What cheer?* – equivalent to 'How are you?' or 'How are you doing?'. The word later developed the sense of 'the food and drink provided as part of an occasion', where *small cheer* would mean 'little food'.

But another meaning for *cheer* was 'standard of living'. So, returning to today's lead quote, you don't need expensive furniture for a merry feast. You just need a welcome that is *great* ('full of emotion', 'total, absolute', or 'pre-eminent').

In other words, 'Welcome is the best dish on the table.'

Antipholus of Ephesus has invited the merchant Balthasar to dinner, and hopes his food will cheer him up. They then have a witty exchange in which they debate whether food or welcome is the better offering to make to a guest. Today's quote is Balthasar's view. But neither will get their dinner today, due to the, ahem, comedy of errors that develops around them …

**Lo, as at English feasts, so I regreet
The daintiest last, to make the end
most sweet.**

— ∞ —

Do you hug your favourite person goodbye first or last? Do you eat your favourite part of the meal at the beginning, or save it till the end?

What's the most delicious, most delightful, most daintily pretty part? Do you save the best till last, to *make the end most sweet*?

The co-authors feel about the quotes in this book, as Henry Bolingbroke does about English feasts, that the *daintiest* ('most delicious', 'most delicate') is best left until last (wait for the last quote of the book).

Bolingbroke is about to fight with Mowbray, and is bidding farewell to his family and supporters (in case he dies in the duel). He addresses his father, John of Gaunt, for a second time ...

RI CH ARD II

# Shall we shog?

— ∞ —

'Let's go' would be one modern equivalent.

*Shog* as a verb has been in English since the Middle Ages, but for this sense of 'go away' Shakespeare is the first recorded user. It's only in one play, and only one character says it. Nym uses it twice: as a question and as a command. He threatens to fight Pistol, and tells him: *Will you shog off?*

It sounds really rude; a polite modern equivalent would be 'Be gone!'. *Shog* is probably a variant of *shock*, in its earlier sense of 'move off', and very likely with some influence from *jog* – 'jog on' is still used today. *Shog* also had the meaning 'shake', though that sense doesn't appear to be in Shakespeare's writings.

*Shog* has now largely gone out of use in standard English, but can still be heard in some regional dialects. And the *Oxford English Dictionary* has examples well into the 20th century. Lynne Reid Banks' novel *An End to Running* has one of the characters say, 'I'll just shog off.' That was published in 1962.

And in 2005 the reconstructed Shakespeare's Globe held an improvised celebration for Shakespeare's birthday, curated by actor Ken Campbell. It was called 'Shall we shog' – where it took on a new meaning: 'party'.

So: shall we shog?

Falstaff's friends have been hearing about his dying moments, and are preparing to leave England to go to war in France. Nym tells the others that it's time to get going …

HENRY V

# We are Time's subjects, and Time bids be gone.

— ∞ —

These words will resonate with all clock-watchers, especially when there's some urgency to meet the start time of an event.

This line imagines Time to be personified and in charge. The Bastard in *King John* gives Time a succinct definition: *Old Time the clock-setter.* Political circumstances force Antony to leave Cleopatra, and he eloquently re-frames his departure with these words:

> The strong necessity of time commands
> Our services awhile.

Later in *Antony and Cleopatra*, Lepidus says *Time calls upon's.* (The *'s* is a contraction of 'us'.)

In *Richard 2*, King Richard is taking a last farewell of Queen Isabel. Neither wants the meeting to end. They kiss once, and at Isabel's request they kiss again. Richard then says that their sadness grows (becomes *wanton*):

> We make woe wanton with this fond delay.

*Fond* had a range of strong meanings in Shakespeare's time. It could mean 'foolish' or 'tender' – or both. King Lear admits to Cordelia *I am a very foolish fond old man.*

Lastly for today, this one from *Hamlet*, for a child about to leave home again, for university, or work, or life, who has already had a farewell blessing from their parent, but now they meet again – hence an *occasion* ('opportunity') for a second *blessing* ('benediction', 'prayer of protection'):

> A double blessing is a double grace,
> Occasion smiles upon a second leave.

HENRY IV:II

A group of nobles have met to discuss their likelihood of success in rebelling against the King, and to plan their next steps. They decide to gather their forces together and set on. Lord Hastings ends the scene with these words.

# Time be thine;
# And thy best graces spend it at thy will.

———— ∞ ————

These lines are an elegant way of responding to a request for permission to leave ('Would you mind if I go and ...?'), or a suggestion of departure ('We really must be going').

*Grace* here doesn't have its usual modern meanings of spiritual enrichment or sense of propriety (as in 'he had the grace to apologise'). It is a 'virtue', or 'good quality'.

*Will* had a very wide range of senses in Shakespeare's time, as it still does, but its idiomatic use differs. Whereas today we'd normally ask, 'What do you want?', a common Shakespearean question then was: *What's your will?*

So runs the full title to *Twelfth Night, or What You Will* – 'or whatever you want to call it'. The word can be used in the plural too, as in *Timon of Athens* when Timon asks about the ladies who want to visit his banquet: *What are their wills?*

*Will* could also mean 'desire': *Will you we show our title to the crown?* asks the Duke of York in *Henry 6 Part 3*; he means simply, 'Do you want us to do so?'

*Will* could also refer to someone's last will and testament; a human's sexual organs; and, of course, the first name of the playwright and poet we've been quoting, who liked to play and pun with this word.

> Laertes has asked permission from King Claudius to return to France, having stayed in Castle Elsinore to be present at his coronation. Claudius checks that he has the permission of his father Polonius, and when told so, gives Laertes royal leave to depart, with these words.

HAMLET

**Joy, gentle friends, joy and fresh days of love
Accompany your hearts.**

— ∞ —

An ideal greeting, toast or message for a newly engaged or married couple, a gathering of your nearest and dearest, or a well-wish of joy and kind companionship to a reader you've spent most of the year with.

Duke Theseus warmly greets the four lovers (now happily paired off correctly after all the fairy-induced confusion), and welcomes them to the evening's entertainment at his palace.

A MIDSUMMER NIGHT'S DREAM

**Let all the number of the stars give light
To thy fair way!**

— ∞ —

How to say more than a simple 'goodbye' to someone who is leaving?

Octavia has married Antony, and is about to leave
Rome. Octavius Caesar, her brother, wishes her a
fond goodbye, and Lepidus adds a final farewell
with these words.

ANTONY &
CLEOPATRA

**To thee no star be dark.**

# INDEX OF SOURCES

This index gives all the sources for the quotations used in this book, using the following abbreviations from www.shakespeareswords.com

Below, we show the first words of each quote to help you associate it with
its source.

if you are    Cym 3.4.191


JANUARY
 the air    Ham 1.4.1
1 Jan
 and I have    1H6 2.2.55
2 Jan
 better three    MW 2.2.296
 let us sup    R3 3.1.199
 they shall be    H5 2.2.2
3 Jan
 you come    Ham 1.1.6
4 Jan
 it gives me    Oth 2.1.177
5 Jan
 men's evil    H8 4.2.45
 the evil    JC 3.2.76
6 Jan
 live a little    AYL 2.6.5
7 Jan
 love all    AYL 1.1.62
8 Jan
 enjoy    JC 2.1.230
 for never …    R3 4.1.82
 fresh tears    Tit 3.1.111
 in the heaviness    KL 4.7.21
9 Jan
 infected minds    Mac 5.1.68
 weariness    Cym 3.7.6
 he that sleeps    Cym 5.4.174
10 Jan
 the nature    AC 1.2.96
 jesters …    KL 5.3.72
 this fellow    TN 3.1.58
11 Jan
 for I have    JC 3.2.222
 I speak to thee    H5 5.2.148
12 Jan
 when a world    1H6 2.2.48
 haply a woman's    H5 5.2.93
 full of kindness    TN 2.1.35
13 Jan
 fortune brings    Cym 4.3.46
 fortune's furious    H5 3.6.26

 be fickle    RJ 3.5.62
 smile once    KL 2.2.171
14 Jan
 look he's winding    Tem 2.1.14
 I frown    TN 2.5.58
 since when    TN 5.1.160
15 Jan
 his wit's …    2H4 2.4.235
16 Jan
 'tis not for gravity …    TN 3.4.115
17 Jan
 life is as tedious …    KJ 3.4.108
 life's but a walking    Mac 5.5.24
18 Jan
 O, that a man    JC 5.1.122
19 Jan
 it easeth some    Luc 1581
 sad souls    Luc 1110
 dolour comes    TN 2.1.21
20 Jan
 make not    AC 5.2.185
21 Jan
 for there is    Ham 2.2.248
22 Jan
 'tis with my mind    2H4 2.3.62
 is it not hard    MV 1.2.24
 to be or not    Ham 3.1.56
23 Jan
 be that thou    TN 5.1.147
24 Jan
 to mourn    Oth 1.3.202
 things without    Mac 3.2.11
 care is no    1H6 3.3.3
 mischief    1H6 5.4.90
25 Jan
 cease    TG 3.1.241
 a little time    TG 3.2.15
 O time    TN 2.2.40
26 Jan
 the apparel    Ham 1.3.72
 opinion    Per 2.2.55
 O, what    MW 3.4.32
27 Jan
 there's no art    Mac 1.4.12

for by his face   R3 3.4.53
by his face, a prince   TNK 4.2.77
but heaven   Sonn 93.9
O serpent   RJ 3.2.73
28 Jan
  make not   MM 5.1.51
  our doubts   MM 1.4.77
  steel thy   2H6 3.1.331
29 Jan
  he that will   TC 1.1.14
  you'll lose   TG 2.3.33
30 Jan
  your worship was   MV 1.3.57
  your worship!   2H4 5.3.43
31 Jan
  abide   Cym 2.4.4

FEBRUARY
  I do love   MA 4.1.264
1 Feb
  the sea   Ven 389
  my bounty   RJ 2.2.133
  revenge   Ham 4.7.127
2 Feb
  all days   Sonn 43.13
3 Feb
  as plays   1H6 5.3.62
  for well   Sonn 131.3
4 Feb
  love is not   Sonn 116.2
  still constant   Sonn 105.6
  love goes   RJ 2.2.156
  love alters   Sonn 116.11
5 Feb
  love looks   MND 1.1.234
  but love   MV 2.6.36
  that blind   AYL 4.1.198
6 Feb
  thou art a   2H4 4.4.91
7 Feb
  if I could   Sonn 17.5
  I am ill   Ham 2.2.119
  his words   TG 2.7.75
8 Feb
  his tend'rer   Ven 353
9 Feb
  a lover's   LLL 4.3.310

I am he   AYL 3.2.352
time goes   MA 2.1.330
10 Feb
  the true   TNK 1.3.81
11 Feb
  I had rather   MA 1.1.123
12 Feb
  it is as easy   AYL 3.2.225
13 Feb
  alas, 'tis true   Sonn 110.1
  I wear not   TN 1.5.51
  men's eyes   RJ 3.1.53
14 Feb
  we that are   AYL 2.4.49
  love is   AYL 3.2.383
  it oft falls   MM 2.4.117
15 Feb
  even as   TG 2.4.190
  what a mere   TNK 4.2.52
16 Feb
  is it not   2H4 2.4.255
  all lovers   TC 3.2.82
17 Feb
  I had rather hear   1H4 3.1.125
  I had rather be   MW 3.4.84
  'tis for the dead   Ham 5.1.124
  for there was   MA 5.1.35
18 Feb
  beauty is   MA 2.1.164
  you have   H5 5.2.272
19 Feb
  but jealous   Oth 3.4.155
20 Feb
  O, how   TG 1.3.84
  the April   AC 3.2.43
21 Feb
  our wooing   LLL 5.2.863
  sweet love   R2 3.2.135
  loose now   AYL 3.5.103
22 Feb
  what passion   AYL 1.2.246
  of all base   1H6 5.2.18
  for lovers   Ven 329
23 Feb
  why, what's   MA 5.4.40
  if't be summer   Cym 3.4.12
  what makes   KL 1.4.185

411

24 Feb
  this man's  2H4 1.1.60
  arched  AW 1.1.93
  square  Per 5.1.108
  wears upon  Mac 4.1.87
  see what  Ham 3.4.56
  upon his  RJ 3.2.92
25 Feb
  'tis a cruelty  H8 5.3.76
  some falls  Cym 4.2.403
  there art  RJ 3.3.140
26 Feb
  I think  MW 5.5.34
  I am as  1H4 4.2.56
  do not desire  TN 5.1.4
  this is  TN 5.1.5
  no man's  H8 1.1.52
27 Feb
  I can suck  AYL 2.5.11
  a weasel  1H4 2.3.81
  as quarrelous  Cym 3.4.161
  disgest  JC 4.3.47
28 Feb
  though I  WT 4.4.707
  that's a  AW 2.2.14
29 Feb
  I was adored  TN 2.3.174

**MARCH**
  Grief makes  R2 1.3.261
1 Mar
  in sooth  MV 1.1.1
  the sad  Per 1.2.2
  I hold  MV 1.1.77
2 Mar
  I am amazed, methinks KJ 4.3.140
  I am amazed, and  MND 3.2.344
  O, how full  AYL 1.3.12
  one lost  3H6 3.2.174
3 Mar
  an hour  RJ 1.1.118
  society  Cym 4.2.12
  leave me  H8 5.1.74
  I myself  TN 1.4.37
4 Mar
  what is it  1H4 2.3.42
  how is't  Mac 2.2.58

oft have I  2H4 4.4.1
  degenerate  1H4 3.2.8
5 Mar
  it argues  RJ 2.3.29
6 Mar
  when to  Sonn 30.1
  but if  Sonn 30.13
  all these  RJ 3.5.52
  the worst  KL 4.1.27
7 Mar
  all strange  AC 4.15.3
  'tis double  Luc 1114
  things at  Mac 4.2.24
8 Mar
  melancholy is  TS induction 2.131
  some fit …  Tit 4.1.17
  in a frenzy  KJ 4.2.122
  the melancholy  AYL 2.1.26
9 Mar
  my grief  R2 4.1.294
  O heart  TC 4.4.15
  everyone  MA 3.2.26
10 Mar
  O, full  Mac 3.2.36
  my grief's  KJ 3.1.71
  being that  MA 4.1.247
11 Mar
  if that  KJ 3.3.48
  and that  Luc 1287
  for sorrow  Luc 1493
  though woe  Luc 1574
12 Mar
  sorrow  R3 1.4.76
  so sorrow  MND 3.2.84
  poor  RJ 3.2.57
13 Mar
  when sorrows  Ham 4.5.79
  one woe …  Ham 4.7.163
  one sorrow  Per 1.4.63
14 Mar
  give sorrow  Mac 4.3.209
  sorrow  Tit 2.4.36
  it were not  Oth 3.3.151
  unhappy  KL 1.1.91
  my tongue  TS 4.3.77
15 Mar
  grief  KJ 3.4.93

moderate   AW 1.1.53
some grief   RJ 3.5.72
honest   LLL 5.2.748
16 Mar
  Venus   RJ 4.1.8
  it is no   Cor 5.3.196
  I cannot   3H6 2.1.79
  O, I could   JC 4.3.98
  the spirit   AYL 1.1.20
17 Mar
  mine eyes   AW 5.3.318
  I, an ass   AC 4.2.35
  he has   H8 5.1.156
  I wish   Tem 2.1.194
18 Mar
  'tis pity   AW 1.1.176
  sleep   MND 2.2.70
  I thank   MV 3.4.43
  wishers   AC 4.15.37
19 Mar
  diseases   Ham 4.3.9
  the miserable   MM 3.1.2
  hope is   TG 3.1.246
  true hope   R3 5.2.23
  nor stony   JC 1.3.93
20 Mar
  in Nature   TN 3.4.358
21 Mar
  those wounds   TC 3.3.229
  I had rather   Cor 2.2.67
  I am loath   2H4 1.2.149
  a choking   RJ 1.1.194
22 Mar
  I am   Sonn 121.9
  the raven TC 2.3.209
23 Mar
  'tis in ourselves   Oth 1.3.316
  our sea-walled   R2 3.4.43
  'tis an unweeded   Ham 1.2.135
  our remedies   AW 1.1.212
24 Mar
  good   MM 1.2.106
  a wretched   CE 2.1.34
  I pray   MA 5.1.3
  he will be   TC 2.3.211
25 Mar
  let us not   Tem 5.1.199

full of   2H4 4.5.9
what's gone   WT 3.2.220
things that   AC 1.2.98
when remedies   Oth 1.3.200
26 Mar
  for gnarling   R2 1.3.292
  therefore   2H4 4.2.83
  affliction   LLL 1.1.301
  our content   H8 2.3.22
27 Mar
  your present   Per 5.3.40
  I have   KJ 5.7.108
  I can   TN 3.3.14
  beggar   Ham 2.2.272
28 Mar
  self-love   H5 2.4.74
29 Mar
  thou seest   AYL 2.7.137
  the web   AW 4.3.70
30 Mar
  for this relief   Ham 1.1.8
  give him   Tem 2.2.66
31 Mar
  this above   Ham 1.3.78

APRIL
  wisely   RJ 2.3.90
1 Apr
  a jest's   LLL 5.2.850
2 Apr
  a surfeit   MND 2.2.143
  will the cold   Tim 4.3.226
  surfeit-swelled   2H4 5.5.53
  in time   AC 1.3.12
3 Apr
  a man loves   MA 2.3.231
  that's meat   MW 1.1.274
  cut the egg   KL 1.4.156
  starved   TS 4.3.9
  eat no meat   2H6 4.10.37
4 Apr
  for never   MND 5.1.82
  in her   AW 1.1.42
  your   AYL 2.7.103
  some   AC 2.5.77
5 Apr
  'tis an ill   RJ 4.2.6

413

6 Apr
what need   MA 1.1.295
7 Apr
now is   TN 2.5.83
O, this   TS 1.2.158
we have   AW 4.1.89
why, as   Ham 5.2.300
8 Apr
I can swim   Tem 2.2.125
9 Apr
there is   WT 4.4.702
10 Apr
coward   H5 2.4.69
he goes   MND 3.2.413
something   AYL 3.2.329
11 Apr
suspicion   3H6 5.6.11
I am   Tit 2.3.211
12 Apr
my thoughts   1H6 1.5.19
I am giddy   TC 3.2.16
does the   Cym 5.5.232
13 Apr
the time   RJ 5.3.37
time must   TC 1.2.78
I am a   WT 2.3.153
I know ...   2H4 5.5.50
presume   2H4 5.5.59
14 Apr
the robbed   Oth 1.3.206
15 Apr
my heart   MW 2.2.273
O, that way   KL 3.4.21
O world   Cor 4.4.12
O, for a   Cym 3.2.49
pity me   AC 2.5.118
16 Apr
I have not   R3 5.3.73
I have a   MW 3.5.11
I am weary   Cor 1.9.90
here's the   H8 2.3.1
when the   MA 3.5.33
though I   AYL 2.3.47
I'll play ...   R3 3.2.188
17 Apr
then join   Ven 971
to climb   H8 1.1.131

lion-mettled   Mac 4.1.89
kill thy   KL 1.1.163
18 Apr
between   JC 2.1.63
19 Apr
what ... eschewed   MW 5.5.229
what ... avoided   3H6 5.4.37
thus have   TG 1.3.78
a little   Mac 2.2.67
20 Apr
I know   Mac 2.3.45
I trouble   TC 5.1.64
21 Apr
I cannot   R3 3.7.140
'tis good   AYL 4.1.8
O, when   TC 1.3.101
take but   TC 1.3.109
what is   2H6 5.1.73
you know   Mac 3.4.1
22 Apr
I do not   AC 2.5.50
but yet I   TN 1.5.251
23 Apr
but words   Oth 1.3.216
words are   CE 3.1.75
words of   Ham 3.1.98
for what   R2 3.4.17
you have   TC 3.2.53
24 Apr
I do not   AC 2.2.116
posteriors   LLL 5.1.84
occupy   2H4 2.4.144
his words   MA 2.3.20
here's   KJ 2.1.457
do you   H8 5.4.28
25 Apr
happy are   MA 2.3.223
happy thou   MM 3.1.21
I would   Cor 3.1.281
I beseech   LLL 2.1.183
most   CE 5.1.283
26 Apr
how will   TN 2.2.33
we will have   LLL 5.1.140
we'll dance   TNK 4.1.75
27 Apr
what's the   AYL 1.1.91

414

here comes   AYL 1.2.86
28 Apr
 a night   H5 2.4.145
 'tis a naughty   KL 3.4.106
 no more   Tem 5.1.162
 well, breathe   1H4 2.4.244
29 Apr
 our foster   KL 4.4.12
 O sleep   2H4 3.1.5
 do not omit   Tem 2.1.197
 now leaden   Luc 124
 just lack   Mac 3.4.140
 sleep that   Mac 2.2.37
30 Apr
 the day   KJ 5.5.21
 the moon   Mac 2.1.2
 to business   AC 4.4.20
 we burn   MW 2.1.50
 what a devil   1H4 1.2.6
 more matter   TN 3.4.141

**MAY**
 in Nature   AC 1.2.10
1 May
 O mickle   RJ 2.3.11
2 May
 nature does   H8 3.2.146
3 May
 now would   Tem 1.1.61
4 May
 this earthly   Mac 4.2.75
 some rise   MM 2.1.38
 we must   AW 2.5.47
 there is   H5 4.1.4
 thus may   H5 4.1.11
5 May
 there are   Ham 1.5.166
6 May
 in the night   MND 5.1.21
 wrong   KL 4.6.282
 what devil   MW 3.3.203
 ever-angry   Tem 1.2.289
 from a bear   CE 3.2.162
 pale as   TN 3.4.287
 exit   WT 3.3.57
7 May
 the night comes   KL 2.4.295

here's a   KL 3.2.12
things   KL 3.2.42
the night has   Mac 2.3.51
such a   Per 3.2.5
8 May
 I have been   Tit 2.2.9
 good dawning   KL 2.2.1
 the morn   Ham 1.1.167
 yon grey   JC 2.1.103
 this majestical   Ham 2.2.301
9 May
 the grey-eyed   RJ 2.2.188
 full many   Sonn 33.1
10 May
 it is the bright   JC 2.1.14
 for now   RJ 3.1.4
 this day   KJ 3.2.1
 like one   Ven 878
11 May
 men judge   R2 3.2.194
 either   JC 1.3.11
 this is   KL 1.2.118
12 May
 when clouds   R3 2.3.32
 cloudy brow   2H6 3.1.155
 black   3H6 5.3.4
 cloud in's   AC 3.2.51
 keeps   Ham 4.5.90
13 May
 sometime   AC 4.14.2
 yond same   Tem 2.2.20
 do you see   Ham 3.2.383
14 May
 a thousand businesses   KJ 4.3.158
 perplexed   1H6 5.5.95
 a thousand times   RJ 2.2.154
 that one word   RJ 3.2.113
 with twenty   RJ 3.3.153
 will die   1H4 3.2.158
 thy love   1H4 3.3.134
15 May
 'tis like   WT 3.3.10
 so foul   KJ 4.2.108
 blow   KL 3.2.1
 O, that   KJ 3.4.38
 thy voice   R3 1.4.170

16 May
  like an    R2 3.2.106
  if after    Oth 2.1.179
17 May
  many can    LLL 4.2.33
  I can no    1H4 5.4.73
  the southern    1H4 5.1.3
  all the    Cor 1.4.30
  tyrannous    Cym 1.4.36
  sharp    Tem 1.2.254
  angry    Tit 4.1.103
  rude    TNK 2.1.195
  when    TNK 2.1.192
  fanned    MND 3.2.142
  blew    R2 1.4.7
  here's    Tem 2.2.18
18 May
  such wind    TS 1.2.49
  what wind    2H4 5.3.85
  ill blows    3H6 2.5.55
19 May
  what fates    3H6 4.3.59
  sent him    1H4 3.1.62
20 May
  this world    Per 4.1.19
  every tedious    R2 1.3.268
  this must    R2 1.3.144
  and must    R2 5.1.81
  I have    RJ 3.5.23
  parting    RJ 2.2.184
21 May
  but to stand    2H4 5.5.24
  I know thee    2H4 5.5.50
22 May
  if the dull    Sonn 44.1
  with wings    Ham 1.5.29
  thus with    H5 3.chorus.1
23 May
  when I    AYL 2.4.14
  how heavy    Sonn 50.1
  weary    Sonn 27
24 May
  all places    R2 1.3.275
  come    TS 1.2.57
  why then    MW 2.2.2
  be patient    RJ 3.3.16

25 May
  as full    1H4 4.1.101
26 May
  how many    Tem 5.1.182
  a goodly    MV 1.3.98
27 May
  a good leg    H5 5.2.158
28 May
  wherefore    Tit 2.3.10
  what was he    AC 1.5.50
29 May
  how still    MA 2.3.36
  soft    MV 5.1.56
  in such    MV 5.1.1
  the setting    R2 2.1.12
30 May
  the weary    R3 5.3.19
  I will hope    AC 1.1.61
  the time    AW 4.4.31
  to mow    2H6 3.1.67
31 May
  the dragon    TC 5.8.17
  my fairy    MND 3.2.378
  swift    Cym 2.2.48
  his arms    1H6 1.1.11
  deathlike    Per 1.1.30

JUNE
  thou hast    TC 2.1.42
1 Jun
  as much    Tim 2.2.119
2 Jun
  y'have    Tim 1.2.25
3 Jun
  worse    1H4 4.1.111
4 Jun
  small    TNK 1.2.88
  this is    Cor 3.1.196
  how fondly    R2 4.1.72
  heat not    H8 1.1.140
  he furnaces    Cym 1.7.66
5 Jun
  rumour is    2H4.induction.15
  do you    Ham 4.3.377
  rumour doth    2H4 3.1.93
  upon my    2H4.induction.6

bring   2H4.induction.40
6 Jun
  'tis not   AW 4.2.21
  what shall   RJ 2.2.112
7 Jun
  I learn   AC 2.2.33
8 Jun
  one doth   MA 3.1.85
  these round   Ven 247
  with whom   Per Chorus.1.25
  after your   Ham 2.2.523
9 Jun
  it is   2H4 1.2.122
  a grise   Oth 1.3.198
  couch   Ham 5.1.218
10 Jun
  would   Tim 4.3.361
  a pox   Tem 1.1.40
  break   1H6 5.4.92
  away   2H4 2.1.57
11 Jun
  I understand   Oth 4.2.31
  foul words   MA 5.2.48
  you shall   AC 3.2.60
12 Jun
  thy wit   RJ 3.3.130
13 Jun
  you play   H8 5.3.126
  what have   Ham 3.4.40
14 Jun
  I begin   AW 4.5.54
  he is   1H4 3.1.153
  I do …   AYL 3.2.251
15 Jun
  how now   2H4 4.5.10
  what   R3 1.3.187
  woo't   Ham 5.1.271
  I am   KL 1.4.270
16 Jun
  art thou   Ven 199
  you are   Cor 1.1.170
17 Jun
  like a dull   Cor 5.3.40
18 Jun
  it is not   H5 4.7.40
  patience   Per 5.1.144
  I'll hear   Per 5.1.165

19 Jun
  turning   AYL 1.3.25
  these jests   CE 1.2.68
  'tis no   TS 1.1.273
  what, is it   1H4 5.3.55
20 Jun
  these   Ham 1.5.133
  'tis fit   Cor 3.2.93
21 Jun
  this is   TN 3.4.56
  art thou   Mac 2.1.37
  a hot   AYL 4.1.92
22 Jun
  talkers   R3 1.3.350
  unpack   Ham 2.2.583
  I will   Tem 5.1.70
  for Clarence   R3 1.3.347
23 Jun
  the lady   Ham 3.2.240
  I protest   MA 4.1.275
  do me   MA 5.1.144
  nor earth   Ham 3.2.226
24 Jun
  to wail   LLL 5.2.744
25 Jun
  it were   MW 1.1.50
  we hold   KJ 5.2.161
  this was   JC 4.3.232
26 Jun
  I hold   3H6 4.2.7
  when I   JC 4.3.115
27 Jun
  with all   R2 3.3.125
  tell her   R2 3.1.38
  commend … brother   MM 1.4.88
  commend … wife   Cor 3.2.135
  commends   TC 3.1.65
  with all   Ham 1.5.183
28 Jun
  I will   KL 3.2.37
  a most   H8 2.1.36
  patience   3H6 1.1.62
  upon the   Ham 3.4.124
  she is   TNK 4.3.3
29 Jun
  what, ho   MM 3.1.44
  health   2H4 4.5.225

peace to    H5 5.2.1
hold    TN 2.3.68
30 Jun
but since    2H4 1.2.155

JULY
humanity    KL 4.2.49
1 Jul
the devil    Tim 3.3.28
get thee    KL 4.6.171
2 Jul
my true    Luc 748
I will wear    Oth 1.1.65
to weep    1H4 4.3.81
how    TG 1.2.62
3 Jul
there's    Mac 2.3.137
to show    Mac 2.3.133
look    1H4 5.2.12
I pray    MV 3.5.52
4 Jul
all hoods    H8 3.1.23
cucullus    MM 5.1.261, TN 1.5.50
thieves    MM 2.2.176
in the    Ham 3.3.57
5 Jul
'tis time    Per 1.2.79
O, 'tis    MM 2.2.107
for pity    Tim 3.5.8
tyrants    Per 1.2.84
his foes    2H4 4.1.205
6 Jul
the eagle    Tit 4.2.83
suffered    Tem 1.2.5
if one    TN 3.1.125
7 Jul
I do love    Cor 3.3.111
his promises    Tim 1.2.196
his reasons    MV 1.1.115
8 Jul
runs not    MA 5.1.232
strong    KJ 3.4.182
oftentimes    Mac 1.3.122
if this    TN 3.4.126
9 Jul
the fashion    AYL 2.3.59

10 Jul
and art    Sonn 66.9
11 Jul
say what    MM 2.4.170
12 Jul
nothing    Tim 3.5.3
vice    Per 1.1.97
but mercy    MV 4.1.190
there    Cor 5.4.27
13 Jul
didst    3H6 2.2.45
some    MM 2.1.38
there's    Ham 5.2.10
men that    MV 2.7.18
14 Jul
could    MM 2.2.10
th' abuse    JC 2.1.18
there    Cor 2.2.7
thou    2H4 4.5.98
15 Jul
the King    H5 4.1.99
16 Jul
there's    CE 3.2.88
a skirmish    MA 1.1.58
the more    AYL 1.2.82
brevity    Ham 2.2.90
17 Jul
uneasy    2H4 3.1.31
many    2H4 3.1.4
my crown    3H6 3.1.62
18 Jul
so doth    MV 5.1.93
a beggar's    H8 1.1.122
19 Jul
why    3H6 5.2.27
20 Jul
why    Luc 1478
the selfsame    WT 4.4.441\
what    TN 1.2.33
a long-tongued    Tit 4.2.149
smatter    RJ 3.5.171
21 Jul
they    Cor 1.1.77
22 Jul
distribution    KL 4.1.69
if to do    MV 1.2.12

bounty   Tim 4.2.41
23 Jul
　men   Tim 3.2.88
24 Jul
　think'st   KL 1.1.147
　be not   MW 4.4.10
25 Jul
　wisdom   1H4 1.2.88
　I like   MV 1.3.176
　as slippery   Cym 2.2.34
26 Jul
　as I ,,,   KJ 4.2.143
　let   Cor 3.3.125
27 Jul
　now this   Sonn 140.11
　truth   KL 1.4.110
28 Jul
　'tis the   KL 4.1.46
　madness   Ham 3.1.189
　the man   MV 5.1.83
29 Jul
　the time is   Ham 1.5.188
　the present   KJ 5.1.14
　what physic   1H6 3.1.149
　the time will   KL 5.3.231
30 Jul
　time   Tim 1.1.261
　for   MM 5.1.45
　as there   MM 5.1.223
　the weight   KL 5.3.321
　it is not   MND 5.1.120
31 Jul
　come   Mac 1.3.146

AUGUST
　no evil   CE 4.2.24
1 Aug
　a little   3H6 4.8.7
2 Aug
　the sweets   Luc 867
3 Aug
　the strongest   Tem 4.1.52
　what fool   MM 4.3.70
　celerity   AC 3.7.24
　words   Mac 2.1.61
4 Aug
　no   Luc 853

bribed   Ven 733
　I saw   AC 2.2.233
　my   Sonn 130.1
5 Aug
　guiltiness   Oth 5.1.109
6 Aug
　beauty is   LLL 2.1.15
　beauty itself   Luc 29
　not that   Cor 2.3.18
7 Aug
　beauty   AYL 1.3.108
8 Aug
　to gild   KJ 4 ? 11
　with a   Mac 5.1.18
　lily fingers   Ven 228
　lily lips   MND 5.1.322
　lily hands   Tit 2.4.44
　the lily   Sonn 99.6
　the sweetest   Cym 4.2.201\
9 Aug
　on the   Sonn 96.5
　the jewel of   TS 1.2.117
　the fairest   Sonn 131.4
　the jewel in   Tem 3.1.54
　an empty   KJ 5.1.40
　a jewel   R2 1.1.180
　eternal   Mac 3.1.67
10 Aug
　the crow   MV 5.1.102
　compare   RJ 1.2.85
　light   Mac 3.2.50
11 Aug
　there is   Cor 5.4.11
　painted   MND 3.1.167
　at gilded   KL 5.3.13
　pursuing   Cor 4.6.95
　a gilded   Cor 1.3.61
12 Aug
　there   JC 4.3.216
　thy end   Sonn 14.14
13 Aug
　life's   Mac 5.5.24
　and that   Mac 5.3.24
14 Aug
　manhood   Cor 3.1.245
　baseless   Tem 4.1.151

15 Aug
  when   MM 4.4.31
16 Aug
  nothing will   KL 1.1.90
  nothing that   TN 4.1.8
  but whate'er   R2 5.5.38
  you might   Cor 3.2.19
17 Aug
  in peace   H5 3.1.3
  the gravity   Oth 2.3.185
  who can   Mac 2.3.105
18 Aug
  virtue   MM 3.1.210
  for goodness   H8 3.1.159
  a most   Tim 1.1.10
19 Aug
  I have   R3 4.3.51
  I stand   Cym 5.5.168
  more   Ham 2.2.95
  come   MW 4.2.210
  defer   1H6 3.2.33
  you know   MV 1.1.153
20 Aug
  they whose   Luc 1342
  so full   Ham 4.5.19
21 Aug
  we do   MV 4.1.197
  sweet   Tit 1.1.122
  the Lord   H5 4.1.33
22 Aug
  where   KL 3.5.8
  when   KL 3.4.11
23 Aug
  the apprehension   R2 1.3.300
  thou canst   RJ 3.3.65
  O, who   R2 1.3.294
24 Aug
  the passions   Per 1.2.11
  to worry   R3 4.4.50
  say   R2 3.2.95
25 Aug
  adversity   RJ 3.3.56
  sweet   AYL 2.1.12
  of your   JC 4.3.143
  preach   KJ 3.4.51
26 Aug
  music   MM 4.1.14

why music   TS 3.1.10
  in sweet   H8 3.1.12
  I am never   MV 5.1.69
27 Aug
  he that   KJ 3.4.137
28 Aug
  we turn   TC 2.2.70
  a very   TN 1.3.22
  a bankrupt   MV 3.1.40
29 Aug
  time   Sonn 115.5\
30 Aug
  the words   LLL 5.2.919
  winged   R3 2.1.90
  she-Mercury   MW 2.2.77
  pure   TG 2.7.77
31 Aug
  O Lord   RJ 3.3.159
  O knowledge   AYL 3.3.8

SEPTEMBER
is there   Tem 1.2.242
1 Sep
  a while   R2 3.1.44
  if all   1H4 1.2.202
2 Sep
  'tis no   1H4 1.2.104
  the labour   Mac 2.3.47
  for your   Tem 3.1.67
3 Sep
  the hand   Ham 5.1.69
  I am   AYL 3.2.69
4 Sep
  leave   Mac 3.1.133
  when   KJ 4.2.28
  striving   KL 1.4.343
  why   MV 5.1.263
5 Sep
  like a   Ham 3.3.41
6 Sep
  'tis not   Cym 3.5.26
  if it   Mac 1.7.1
  but yet   R3 1.1.160
  for oft   Ven 1068
  my mind   TC 3.3.308
7 Sep
  frame   KL 1.2.98

420

do what  2H4 2.3.6
my lords  2H6 3.1.195
8 Sep
away  KJ 5.1.54
experience  TG 1.3.22
9 Sep
the task  R2 2.2.144
you may  H5 4.1.194
those  JC 1.3.107
I prize  WT 3.2.109
10 Sep
if you  AYL 1.2.163
checks  TC 1.3.5
11 Sep
what to  Ham 3.2.204
how many  AYL 2.4.26
give me  Ham 3.2.81
12 Sep
now  Tem 5.1.1
everything  Ham 4.3.58
let it go  Tim 5.1.65
13 Sep
why  TNK 1.1.170
14 Sep
if to have  R3 4.3.25
15 Sep
he is  MV 4.1.412
16 Sep
a greater  RJ 5.3.153
the fingers  Cym 5.5.467
O heavenly  Ham 3.1.142
O all you  TNK 5.3.139
17 Sep
one good  WT 1.2.92
with full  H5 1.2.231
tongueless  R3 3.7.42
18 Sep
it is a  MV 1.2.14
furnished  MM 3.2.199
now step  LLL 4.3.149
19 Sep
God give  1H4 1.2.150
better  1H4 5.2.76
the silence  WT 2.2.41
she will  MM 1.2.184
20 Sep
for I know  Oth 3.3.197

21 Sep
I will  AW 4.3.9
'tis in my  Ham 1.3.85
'tis a secret  MM 3.2.128
this secret  H8 2.1.144
had I  2H6 3.2.293
22 Sep
pour  AC 2.5.54
good  R3 4.3.45
such  Mac 4.3.138
speak  Oth 3.3.130
think  Mac 1.3.153
23 Sep
shall  TNK 2.1.165
I must  1H4 3.3.175
thou still  Ham 2.2.42
yet seek  MW 3.4.19
you and  Sonn 76.10
24 Sep
be thou  Ham 2.4.198
it was  H8 5.1.17
I have  MV 3.4.27
speak  MW 4.5.2
thou  R3 4.1.157
25 Sep
the truth  Tem 2.1.39
truth hath  R2 1.3.96
26 Sep
corruption  H8 3.2.444
thy honesty  Oth 2.3.241
honesty  AYL 3.3.27
27 Sep
O, reason  KL 2.4.259
28 Sep
haply  TN 3.3.45
when  TN 5.1.386
I some  AC 5.2.165
show  WT 4.4.797
if money  MW 2.2.164
29 Sep
who  Tim 4.2.31
if thou  MM 3.1.25
I can  2H4 1.2.238
30 Sep
he that  AYL 3.2.23
have  KL 1.4.17
neither  Ham 1.3.75

I commit   MV 3.4.24
there's   Mac 2.1.4

OCTOBER
here   TNK 2.1.132
1 Oct
we are   Tim 1.2.99
2 Oct
thou hast   H8 5.5.64
now all   Tem 5.1.179
he makes   WT 1.2.169
'tis as   H8 5.1.168
3 Oct
I never   MV 4.1.161
thou art   LLL 1.2.29
a gallant   WT 1.1.37
with what   R3 3.1.132
so wise   R3 3.1.79
4 Oct
a decrepit   Sonn 37.1
that some   1H4 1.1.86
5 Oct
is this   Cor 3.3.86
an if I were   R2 5.3.112
6 Oct
I will   AYL 3.2.272
do you   Ham 3.4.107
chide   2H4 4.5.64
I pray ... .   RJ 2.3.81
7 Oct
courage   KJ 2.1.82
he must   AW 1.3.29
a finder   Oth 2.1.235
8 Oct
I have   MM 5.1.532
9 Oct
I am   Oth 3.3.476
10 Oct
hang   Cym 5.5.263
your own   R2 3.3.197
be buried   Per 5.3.44
if, not   WT 4.4.131
11 Oct
my salad   AC 1.5.73
12 Oct
for youth   TN 3.4.3

13 Oct
my age   AYL 2.3.52
let me   TC 4.5.202
14 Oct
thou   KL 1.5.41
I am   2H4 1.2.192
infirmity   TN 1.5.71
15 Oct
crabbed   PP 12.1
last   AYL 2.7.164
16 Oct
there   Cym 1.2.61
I had   Cym 4.2.198
17 Oct
when the   H5 4.1.20
music   TS 1.1.36
quicken   AC 3.15.39
the mistress   Tem 3.1.6
my words   R3 4.4.124
18 Oct
no! time   Sonn 123.1
devouring   Sonn 19.1
rocks   Sonn 65.7
it is   WT 4.1.7
19 Oct
like as   Sonn 60.1
were   PP 14.25
watchful   KJ 4.1.46
for now   R2 5.5.50
20 Oct
clay   Cym 4.2.4
when   JC 2.2.30
like   1H4 3.2.47
gazed   Per 5.1.85
as if   TS 3.2.94
comets 1H6 1.1.2
21 Oct
to what   Ham 5.1.199
your worm   Ham 4.3.21
22 Oct
thou art   MM 3.1.11
fight   R2 3.2.184
cowards   JC 2.2.32
23 Oct
fates   JC 3.1.98
24 Oct
if it   Ham 5.2.215

25 Oct
  men   KL 5.2.9
  let the   2H4 2.2.44
26 Oct
  all that   Ham 1.2.72
  for in   Ham 3.1.66
  we must   Tim 4.2.21
27 Oct
  but to   Ham 1.2.92
  you have   WT 5.1.1
28 Oct
  death   Per 1.1.46
  praising   AW 5.3.19
  the remembrance   AW 1.1.47
  she is   TN 2.1.27
29 Oct
  hereafter   AYL 1.2.273
  and fair   1H6 2.5.113
  live   RJ 5.3.42
  farewell TC 5.3.94
30 Oct
  I might   Ham 1.1.56
  Demetrius   MND 1.1.106
  I avouch   MW 2.1.125
  I could   Mac 3.1.118
31 Oct
  'tis now   Ham 3.2.395
  to dare   JC 2.1.265
  wizards   2H6 1.4.14

NOVEMBER
  I count   R2 2.3.46
1 Nov
  I to   CE 1.2.35
  it is   AYL 3.2.178
  as the   Ham 1.3.2
2 Nov
  we meet   2H4 5.2.22
  the night   Cym 3.7.66
  you are   AYL 3.3.68
  hail   Per 5.1.13
3 Nov
  my other   R3 2.2.151
  I do not   TNK 2.1.168
  has   Tim 3.1.54
  friendship   MA 2.1.160
  love   TC 3.3.173

  most   AYL 2.7.182
4 Nov
  ceremony   Tim 1.2.14
  what   Ham 5.1.219
  no   MM 2.2.59
5 Nov
  to me   Sonn 104.1
6 Nov
  to keep   Sonn 122.13
  my tables   Ham 1.5.107
  quote   Ham 3.2.45
7 Nov
  in   MV 3.4.11
  I like   AYL 2.4.91
  what   R2 3.4.1
8 Nov
  the amity   TC 2.3.101
  that which   AC 2.6.126
  folly   LLL 5.2.75
  for folly   TN 3.1.65
  love   Ven 838
9 Nov
  when   JC 4.2.20
10 Nov
  give me   TC 4.4.137
  by relating   Per 1.4.2
  and since   JC 1.2.67
  we have   2H4 3.2.209
11 Nov
  speak   MW 4.5.2
12 Nov
  you speak   WT 3.2.79
  soft   RJ 3.5.141
  friend   TC 3.1.27
  those   AYL 3.2.43
13 Nov
  an honest   R3 4.4.358
  your name   MND 3.1.179
  it is   Ham 1.5.138
  are you   Ham 3.1.103
14 Nov
  I am   AW 5.3.32
  it is   Tem 2.1.143
  sunshine   KL 4.3.18
15 Nov
  you two   2H4 2.4.54

16 Nov
 I am    MM 4.3.175
 a friend    JC 4.3.85
 assuming    Per Chorus.1.3
 the infirmity    KL 1.1.292
 with those    KL 1.1.202
17 Nov
 I love    Tim 2.1.23
 where    H8 2.1.126
18 Nov
 I rather    3H6 4.1.138
 and who    Ham 3.2.218
 when    1H6 4.1.191
19 Nov
 there is    WT 1.2.20
20 Nov
 what we    MA 4.1.216
 shall be    MV 1.1.181
 I shall    Cor 4.1.15
21 Nov
 I must    Mac 3.1.26
 methinks    WT 1.2.365
 my business    RJ 2.4.49
 I have    Oth 1.3.295
22 Nov
 but that    RJ 3.3.173
 parting    RJ 2.2.184
23 Nov
 I must    RJ 3.5.44
 time    AYL 3.2.299
 divide    AYL 4.1.40
24 Nov
 the leisure    R3 5.3.98
 he shall    TS 3.2.216
25 Nov
 make    MV 4.3.101
26 Nov
 be Mercury    KJ 4.2.174
 the strong    AC 4.15.35
27 Nov
 should    Cym 1.2.37
28 Nov
 rogues    MW 1.3.76
 avaunt, and    Mac 3.4.92
 avaunt, perplexity    LLL 5.2.298
29 Nov
 good    Ham 5.2.353

30 Nov
 sleep    RJ 2.2.186

DECEMBER
 the west    Mac 3.3.5
1 Dec
 each one    Per 2.3.114
 I long    TC 3.1.138
2 Dec
 the day    H5 4.1.301
 am I    JC 1.3.136
 we stay    MW 1.1.191
3 Dec
 a true    TG 2.7.9
 we must    MV 3.4.84
 two    RJ 1.5.95
 a zealous    Sonn 27.6
4 Dec
 give    Ham 1.3.68
 and when    KJ 4.2.188
5 Dec
 be checked    AW 1.1.65
 speak    Cym 3.5.98
 thou    AC 2.2.111
6 Dec
 the blessed    WT 5.1.167
 he shall    3H6 3.2.287
 a plague a    RJ 3.1.106
 a plague upon    1H4 1.3.240
7 Dec
 not to    TN 2.3.1
 it is    RJ 3.4.34
 I am glad    Cym 2.3.31
8 Dec
 fill    AC 2.13.183
 a bowl    JC 4.3.140
 we drink    Per 2.3.65
 with his    KJ 3.3.38
 the iron    MND 5.1.353
 we have    2H4 3.2.209
9 Dec
 he hath    LLL 4.2.24
 taunt    TN 3.2.42
 and with    Cym 1.2.31
10 Dec
 that men    Oth 2.3.281
 like a    TN 1.4.126

424

the proceedings   Ven 910
drink   Mac 2.3.27
good   Oth 2.3.300
O, thou   Oth 2.3.274
11 Dec
I cannot   MW 1.1.158
I have   Oth 2.3.30
they call   1H4 2.4.14
a good   2H4 4.3.95
that which   Mac 2.2.1
12 Dec
I had   AC 2.7.100
13 Dec
'tis ever   H5 1.2.272
14 Dec
therefore   Sonn 52.5
by being   1H4 3.2.46
15 Dec
they say   AW 2.3.1
16 Dec
that time   Sonn 73.1
17 Dec
at Christmas   LLL 1.1.105
the fairest   WT 4.4.81
it then   Ham 1.4.5
best   Mac 4.2.16
these   CE 1.1.68
18 Dec
'tis mad   TC 2.2.57
19 Dec
I am not   TNK 1.3.96
20 Dec
I am not   Tim 1.1.104
21 Dec
how far   MV 5.1.90
a naughty   AW 5.3.253
22 Dec
so tedious   RJ 3.2.28

knowing   AYL 3.2.313
O long   MND 3.2.431
with   TG 1.1.31
in winter   R2 5.1.40
23 Dec
we'll have   Per 2.1.81
24 Dec
now   Mac 3.4.37
a good   H8 1.4.62
my lord   Tim 1.2.52
proface   2H4 5.3.27
25 Dec
small   CE 3.1.26
wedding   TS 3.2.185
royal   Tim 3.6.50
26 Dec
as at   R2 1.3.67
27 Dec
shall   H5 2.3.42
will   H5 2.1.42
28 Dec
we are   2H4 1.3.110
old   KJ 3.1.324
the strong   AC 1.3.42
time   AC 2.2.163
we make   R2 5.1.101
I am   KL 4.7.60
a double   Ham 1.3.53
29 Dec
time   Ham 1.2.62
what   Tim 1.2.116
will we   3H6 1.1.102
30 Dec
joy   MND 5.1.29
31 Dec
let   AC 3.2.65
to thee   TNK 1.4.1

# INDEX OF THEMES

The alphabetical arrangement of this index is letter-by-letter. Month opening quotations have been given the date '0'.

# INDEX OF OPENING WORDS
# OF LEAD QUOTATIONS

The alphabetical arrangement of this index is word-by-word. Month opening quotations have been given the date '0'.

Beauty is a witch   18 Feb
Beauty is bought by judgement of
  the eye   6 Aug
Beauty provoketh thieves sooner
  than gold   7 Aug
Better three hours too soon   2 Jan
Between the acting of a dreadful
  thing   18 Apr
But jealous souls will not be
  answered so   19 Feb
But since all is well, keep it so
  30 Jun
But that a joy past joy calls out on
  me   22 Nov
But to persever / In obstinate
  condolement   27 Oct
But to stand stained with
  travel   21 May
But words are words; I never yet did
  hear   23 Apr
Cease to lament for that thou canst
  not help   25 Jan
Ceremony was but devised at first
  4 Nov
Clay and clay differs in dignity
  20 Oct
Come what come may   31 Jul
Corruption wins not more than
  honesty   26 Sep
Could great men thunder   14 Jul
Courage mounteth with occasion
  7 Oct
Coward dogs / Most spend their
  mouths   10 Apr
Crabbed age and youth cannot live
  together   15 Oct
Death remembered should be like a
  mirror   28 Oct
Didst thou never hear / That things
  ill got   13 Jul
Diseases desperate grown   19 Mar
Distribution should undo excess
  22 Jul
Each one betake him to his rest
  1 Dec
Enjoy the honey-heavy dew of
  slumber   8 Jan

Even as one heat another heat
  expels   15 Feb
Fates, we will know your pleasures
  23 Oct
Fill our bowls once more   8 Dec
For gnarling sorrow hath less power
  to bite   26 Mar
For I have neither wit, nor words, nor
  worth   11 Jan
For I know thou'rt full of love and
  honesty   20 Sep
For never anything can be
  amiss   4 Apr
For there is nothing either good or
  bad   21 Jan
For this relief much thanks   30 Mar
For youth is bought more oft
  12 Oct
Fortune brings in some boats
  13 Jan
Frame the business after your own
  wisdom   7 Sep
Give every man thine ear   4 Dec
Give me your hand   10 Nov
Give sorrow words   14 Mar
God give thee the spirit of
  persuasion   19 Sep
Good counsellors lack no clients
  24 Mar
Good night, sweet Prince
  29 Nov
Grief fills the room up of my absent
  child   15 Mar
Grief makes one hour ten   0 Mar
Guiltiness will speak   5 Aug
Hang there like a fruit, my
  soul   10 Oct
Haply your eye shall light upon
  some toy   28 Sep
Happy are they that hear their
  detractions   25 Apr
He hath never fed of the dainties
  9 Dec
He is well paid that is well satisfied
  15 Sep
He that stands upon a slippery
  place   27 Aug

He that wants money, means, and content   30 Sep

He that will have a cake out of the wheat   29 Jan

Here being thus together   0 Oct

Hereafter, in a better world than this   29 Oct

His tend'rer cheek receives her soft hand   8 Feb

His wit's as thick as Tewkesbury mustard   15 Jan

How far that little candle throws   21 Dec

How many goodly creatures are there here   26 May

How now, rain within doors   15 Jun

How still the evening is   29 May

How will this fadge   26 Apr

Humanity must perforce prey on itself   0 Jul

I am a kind of burr, I shall stick   16 Nov

I am amazed, methinks, and lose my way   2 Mar

I am not / Against your faith   19 Dec

I am not a day of season   14 Nov

I am not of that feather to shake off   20 Dec

I am that I am, and they that level   22 Mar

I am your own for ever   9 Oct

I begin to be aweary of thee   14 Jun

I can suck melancholy out of a song   27 Feb

I can swim like a duck   8 Apr

I cannot remember what I did   11 Dec

I cannot tell if to depart in silence   21 Apr

I count myself in nothing else so happy   0 Nov

I do love / My country's good   7 Jul

I do love nothing in the world   0 Feb

I do not like 'But yet'   22 Apr

I do not much dislike the matter, but   24 Apr

I had rather fast from all   12 Dec

I had rather hear a brazen canstick turned   17 Feb

I had rather hear my dog bark at a crow   11 Feb

I have a motion much imports your good   8 Oct

I have been troubled in my sleep this night   8 May

I have learned that fearful commenting   19 Aug

I have not that alacrity of spirit   16 Apr

I hold it cowardice   26 Jun

I know this is a joyful trouble to you   20 Apr

I learn you take things ill which are not so   7 Jun

I love and honour him   17 Nov

I might not this believe   30 Oct

I must become a borrower of the night   21 Nov

I must hear from thee every day in the hour   23 Nov

I never knew so young a body   3 Oct

I rather wish you foes than hollow friends   18 Nov

I think the devil will not have me damned   26 Feb

I to the world am like a drop of water   1 Nov

I understand a fury in your words   11 Jun

I was adored once, too   29 Feb

I will be the pattern of all patience   28 Jun

I will chide no breather in the world but myself   6 Oct

I will tell you a thing   21 Sep

If I could write the beauty of your eyes   7 Feb

If it be now, 'tis not to come   24 Oct

If that thou couldst see me without
eyes   11 Mar
If the dull substance of my
flesh   22 May
If to have done the thing you gave
in charge   14 Sep
If you are sick at sea   year opener
If you saw yourself with your eyes
10 Sep
In companions / That do converse
7 Nov
In Nature, there's no blemish but the
mind   20 Mar
In Nature's infinite book of secrecy
0 May
In peace there's nothing so becomes
a man   17 Aug
In sooth I know not why I am so sad
1 Mar
In the night, imagining some fear
6 May
Infected minds / To their deaf
pillows   9 Jan
Is it not strange that desire   16 Feb
Is there more toil?   0 Sep
Is this the promise that you made
5 Oct
It argues a distempered head
5 Mar
It easeth some, though none it ever
cured   19 Jan
It gives me wonder great as my
content   4 Jan
It is a good divine that follows
18 Sep
It is as easy to count atomies
12 Feb
It is not well done, mark you now
18 Jun
It is the bright day that brings forth
the adder   10 May
It is the disease of not listening
9 Jun
It were a goot motion if we leave
25 Jun
Joy, gentle friends   30 Dec

Leave no rubs nor botches in the
work   4 Sep
Let all the number of the stars give
light   31 Dec
Let us not burden our
remembrances with   25 Mar
Life is as tedious as a twice-told
tale   17 Jan
Life's but a walking shadow   13 Aug
Like a dull actor now   17 Jun
Like a man to double business
bound   5 Sep
Like an unseasonable stormy day
16 May
Like as the waves make towards
19 Oct
Live a little, comfort a little   6 Jan
Look, he's winding up the watch of
his wit   14 Jan
Love all, trust a few   7 Jan
Love is not love / Which alters
4 Feb
Love looks not with the eyes
5 Feb
Make a swift return   25 Nov
Make not impossible   28 Jan
Make not your thoughts your
prisons   20 Jan
Manhood is called foolery   14 Aug
Many can brook the weather
17 May
Melancholy is the nurse of frenzy
8 Mar
Men judge by the complexion of the
sky   11 May
Men must endure / Their going
hence   25 Oct
Men must learn now with pity to
dispense   23 Jul
Men's evil manners live in brass
5 Jan
Mine eyes smell onions, I shall weep
anon   17 Mar
Music oft hath such a charm
26 Aug
My age is as a lusty winter   13 Oct

My grief lies all within   9 Mar
My heart is ready to crack with
   impatience   15 Apr
My other self, my counsel's
   consistory   3 Nov
My salad days   11 Oct
My thoughts are whirled like a
   potter's wheel   12 Apr
My true eyes have never practised
   how   2 Jul
Nature does require / Her
   times   2 May
No evil lost is wailed when it is
   gone   0 Aug
No perfection is so absolute
   4 Aug
No! Time, thou shalt not boast
   18 Oct
Not to be abed after midnight
   7 Dec
Nothing emboldens sin so much as
   mercy   12 Jul
Nothing will come of nothing
   16 Aug
Now does my project gather to a
   head   12 Sep
Now good digestion wait on
   appetite   24 Dec
Now is the woodcock near the gin
   7 Apr
Now this ill-wresting world is grown
   so bad   27 Jul
Now would I give a thousand
   furlongs of sea   3 May
O Lord, I could have stayed here all
   the night   31 Aug
O mickle is the powerful grace that
   lies   1 May
O, full of scorpions is my mind
   10 Mar
O, how this spring of love
   resembleth   20 Feb
O, reason not the need   27 Sep
O, that a man might know   18 Jan
On the finger of a throned queen
   9 Aug

One doth not know / How much an
   ill word   8 Jun
One good deed dying
   tongueless   17 Sep
Our foster-nurse of nature is repose
   29 Apr
Our wooing doth not end like an old
   play   21 Feb
Pour out the pack of matter to mine
   ear   22 Sep
Rogues, hence, avaunt   28 Nov
Rumour is a pipe   5 Jun
Runs not this speech like iron   8 Jul
Say what you can, my false
   o'erweighs your true   11 Jul
Self-love … is not so vile a sin
   28 Mar
Shall I say more   23 Sep
Shall we shog   27 Dec
Should we be taking leave
   27 Nov
Sleep dwell upon thine eyes
   30 Nov
Small cheer and great welcome
   25 Dec
Small winds shake him   4 Jun
So doth the greater glory dim the
   less   18 Jul
So tedious is this day   22 Dec
Sometime we see a cloud that's
   dragonish   13 May
Sorrow breaks seasons and reposing
   hours   12 Mar
Speak, breathe, discuss   11 Nov
Such wind as scatters young
   men   18 May
Suspicion always haunts the guilty
   mind   11 Apr
Talkers are no good doers   22 Jun
That men should put an
   enemy   10 Dec
That time of year thou mayst in me
   behold   16 Dec
The air bites shrewdly   0 Jan
The amity that wisdom knits not
   8 Nov

The apparel oft proclaims the man
26 Jan

The apprehension of the good
23 Aug

The blessed gods / Purge all
infection   6 Dec

The crow doth sing as sweetly as the
lark   10 Aug

The day shall not be up so soon as
I   30 Apr

The day, my friends, and all things
stay   2 Dec

The devil knew not what he did
1 Jul

The dragon wing of night
o'erspreads   31 May

The eagle suffers little birds to
sing   6 Jul

The fashion of these times   9 Jul

The grey-eyed morn smiles   9 May

The hand of little employment
3 Sep

The King is but a man, as I am
15 Jul

The lady doth protest too much,
methinks   23 Jun

The leisure and the fearful time
24 Nov

The nature of bad news infects the
teller   10 Jan

The night comes on and the bleak
winds   7 May

The passions of the mind   24 Aug

The robbed that smiles steals
something   14 Apr

The sea hath bounds, but deep
desire   1 Feb

The strongest oaths are straw
3 Aug

The sweets we wish for turn to
loathed sours   2 Aug

The task he undertakes   9 Sep

The time and my intents are
savage-wild   13 Apr

The time is out of joint   29 Jul

The true love 'tween maid and
maid   10 Feb

The truth you speak doth lack
25 Sep

The weary sun hath made a golden
set   30 May

The west yet glimmers   0 Dec

The words of Mercury are harsh
30 Aug

Then join they all together   17 Apr

There are more things in heaven and
earth   5 May

There cannot be a pinch in
death   16 Oct

There is a tide in the affairs of
men   12 Aug

There is differency between a grub
and a butterfly   11 Aug

There is no tongue that
moves   19 Nov

There is that in this fardel   9 Apr

There's daggers in men's smiles
3 Jul

There's many a man hath more hair
than wit   16 Jul

There's no art / To find the
mind   27 Jan

Therefore are feasts so
solemn   14 Dec

These are but wild and whirling
words   20 Jun

They ne'er cared for us yet   21 Jul

They say miracles are past   15 Dec

They whose guilt within their
bosoms lie   20 Aug

Think'st thou that duty shall have
dread to speak   24 Jul

This above all: to thine own self be
true   31 Mar

This earthly world, where to do
harm   4 May

This is very midsummer madness
21 Jun

This man's brow, like to a title-
leaf   24 Feb

This world to me is like a lasting
storm   20 May

Those wounds heal ill that men do
give   21 Mar

Thou art a summer bird   6 Feb
Thou art death's fool   22 Oct
Thou hast made me now a man
   2 Oct
Thou hast no more brain than I
   have   0 Jun
Thou seest we are not all alone
   unhappy   29 Mar
Thou shouldst not have been
   old   14 Oct
Though I am not naturally
   honest   28 Feb
Thy wit, that ornament to shape and
   love   12 Jun
Time be thine   29 Dec
Time to be honest   30 Jul
Time, whose millioned
   accidents   29 Aug
'Tis ever common / That men are
   merriest   13 Dec
'Tis no sin for a man to labour in his
   vocation   2 Sep
'Tis the time's plague when madmen
   lead the blind   28 Jul
'Tis a cruelty / To load a fallen
   man   25 Feb
'Tis an ill cook that cannot lick his
   own fingers   5 Apr
'Tis in ourselves that we are thus, or
   thus   23 Mar
'Tis like to be loud weather   15 May
'Tis mad idolatry   18 Dec
'Tis not for gravity to play at
   cherry-pit   16 Jan
'Tis not sleepy business   6 Sep
'Tis not the many oaths that makes
   the truth   6 Jun
'Tis now the very witching time of
   night   31 Oct
'Tis pity … / That wishing well
   18 Mar
'Tis time to fear when tyrants seem
   to kiss   5 Jul
'Tis with my mind / As with the
   tide   22 Jan
To gild refined gold, to paint the
   lily   8 Aug

To keep an adjunct to remember
   thee   6 Nov
To me, fair friend, you never can be
   old   5 Nov
To mourn a mischief that is past and
   gone   24 Jan
To thee no star be dark   year closer
To wail friends lost   24 Jun
To what base uses we may
   return   21 Oct
Turning these jests out of
   service   19 Jun
Uneasy lies the head that wears a
   crown   17 Jul
Venus smiles not in a house of
   tears   16 Mar
Virtue is bold, and goodness never
   fearful   18 Aug
We are born to do benefits   1 Oct
We are Time's subjects   28 Dec
We do pray for mercy   21 Aug
We meet like men that had forgot to
   speak   2 Nov
We that are true lovers   14 Feb
We turn not back the silks upon the
   merchant   28 Aug
We'll have flesh for holidays
   23 Dec
What cannot be eschewed   19 Apr
What fates impose   19 May
What is it that takes from thee
   4 Mar
What need the bridge much
   broader   6 Apr
What passion hangs these
   weights   22 Feb
What to ourselves in passion we
   propose   11 Sep
What we have we prize not to the
   worth   20 Nov
What, ho! Peace here   29 Jun
What's the new news at the new
   court   27 Apr
When a world of men / Could not
   prevail   12 Jan
When clouds are seen, wise men
   12 May

439

When I was at home I was in a better place    23 May
When love begins to sicken and decay    9 Nov
When once our grace we have forgot    15 Aug
When sorrows come    13 Mar
When the mind is quickened    17 Oct
When to the sessions of sweet silent thought    6 Mar
Where the greater malady is fixed    22 Aug
Wherefore look'st thou sad    28 May
Who would not wish to be from wealth exempt    29 Sep
Why good ladies / This is a service    13 Sep
Why should the private pleasure of some one    20 Jul
Why, what is pomp, rule, reign    19 Jul

Why, what's the matter    23 Feb
Wisdom cries out in the streets    25 Jul
Wisely and slow    0 Apr
With all the gracious utterance thou hast    27 Jun
Worse than the sun in March    3 Jun
Would thou wert clean enough to spit upon    10 Jun
Y' have got a humour there    2 Jun
You come most carefully upon your hour    3 Jan
You play the spaniel    13 Jun
You speak a language that I understand not    12 Nov
You two never meet but you fall    15 Nov
Your present kindness / Makes my pain    27 Mar
Your worship was the last man in our mouths    30 Jan

# DOWNLOAD THE *EVERYDAY SHAKESPEARE* AUDIOBOOK

Let the authors read you your daily dose of the Bard. With each quote spoken in both modern and Shakespeare's original pronunciation, this recording is more than just everyday.

Enjoy 50% off on the audiobook edition as soon as it is available by following these instructions:

1. Scan the QR code.
2. Enter BARD50 and select 'Apply'.
3. Check your discount has been applied and proceed through account creation and payment.
4. You will be able to stream online and download the audio to the accompanying app.

Summer 2023, Audiobook ISBN 9781399809368